Edward Abel Smith is a non-fiction author, feature writer, documentary maker and podcaster. He is the author of two previous books: a unique biography of the James Bond creator, *Ian Fleming's Inspiration* (Pen & Sword History, 2020), and *The British Oskar Schindler: The Life and Work of Nicholas Winton* (Pen & Sword History, 2023), a biography of one of Britain's most celebrated humanitarians. A story Abel Smith has been researching for four years about convicted murder Robin Garbutt is being made into a Sky documentary in partnership with Lightbox Entertainment. He is also the co-host and co-creator of the hit podcast *Lucy Letby: Was There Ever A Crime* with veteran investigative journalist John Sweeney. Abel Smith has written about his books for *The Daily Express*, *The Telegraph* and *The Mail on Sunday*. He has appeared on several radio programs including *BBC Radio 4*, *BBC Radio London* and *BBC World Service*, as well as podcasts *A Short History Of...* and *BBC History Extra*. Abel Smith lives near the South Coast of England with his wife, two daughters and their dog, Vesper.

Also by Edward Abel Smith

non-fiction
Ian Fleming's Inspiration
The British Oskar Schindler

Published by Silvertail Books in 2025
www.silvertailbooks.com
Copyright © Edward Abel Smith 2025
978-1-913727-54-3
The right of Edward Abel Smith to be identified as the author of this work has been asserted in accordance with the Copyright, Design and Patents Act 1988 A catalogue record of this book is available from the British Library.
All rights reserved. No part of this publication may be reproduced, transmitted, or stored in a retrieval system, in any form or by any means, without permission in writing from Silvertail Books or the copyright holder.

All characters in this publication other than those clearly in the public domain are fictitious and any resemblance to real persons, living or dead, is purely coincidental.

ANGELS OF PRAGUE

Edward Abel Smith

SILVERTAIL BOOKS ◊ *London*

For my daughters

Contents

Prologue   1

Part One – Liberty
1. The Czech Affair   7
2. Society of Friends   23
3. Labour of Love   33
4. Dire Conditions   45
5. Too Steady   57
6. American Contingent   73
7. Invasion   85

Part Two – Occupation
8. Panic Stations   103
9. Trapped   122
10. Defiance   139
11. The Great Escape   158
12. Enter the Gestapo   174
13. Doreen's Farewell to Prague   192
14. Keeping Going   208

Endnotes
Index

Prologue

Prague, Czechoslovakia
14 April, 1939

Sokolovská Street in the Karlín District was picturesque in the early hours of this chilly spring morning. Sunlight was beginning to dilute the night's darkness, and the only sound in the air was birdsong. It was hard to believe that this quietly beautiful scene lay in the middle of a city that was invaded by the Nazis only weeks earlier.

A black Mercedes-Benz 260D swerved into view, shattering the calm. The new Nazi curfew meant civilians could not drive around until 8 a.m., and that was still two hours away. But the four occupants of this car were not worried about these rules, for they were the ones who imposed and enforced them. The men – dressed in long black overcoats, felt fedora hats and leather gloves – were all members of the Gestapo.

Their car pulled up by Hostel Elf, a grotty boarding house which, in normal circumstances, struggled to attract guests. But since the occupation of Czechoslovakia the previous month, the German invaders had taken over all the decent establishments in the city, leaving everyone else to scramble to find any room they could to escape the bitter late winter weather. As a result, even Hostel Elf was full.

The Gestapo officers left their car running as they marched to the front door. They needed only one knock before the terrified elderly Czech proprietor unbolted it and let them in. They stormed up the creaking wooden staircase and congregated around a door with the number five in fading red paint on the front. It was swiftly kicked in to reveal a tiny cupboard of a room, with barely enough space for the single bed and small chest of drawers within.

In the bed, nestled under a stack of blankets, lay a petite young woman, brown hair still scuffed from a night's sleep. Her eyes had only just started to adjust to the light coming in from her now open door when two of the officers grabbed her roughly by the arms and dragged her from the bed. With her modesty protected by just a nightgown, she was given no opportunity to dress in something more appropriate before being hauled down the stairs, out of the door and into the waiting car, which sped away.

The woman sat in the back between two officers, cold and shaking with terror as one of the men in the front picked up his radio and bellowed with excitement, 'We have got her! We have arrested Doreen Warriner!'

After a few minutes, the car stopped, and the woman was forced out and onto her feet. Her legs were quivering with fear but the woman insisted that she walk unaided into the building she knew was her destination from the moment she woke up – Petschek Palace. Requisitioned by the Gestapo, the former bank was now being used for the interrogation, torture and imprisonment of the people the Nazis deemed to be their fiercest enemies. Its reputation was terrifying.

It is not known how long into the interrogation the Gestapo realised this woman was not Doreen Warriner. She matched Doreen's description perfectly and she was living up to Doreen's stubborn reputation, refusing bluntly to cooperate with her captors. But when her interrogator commented that her voice sounded strange, others were consulted. Eventually it was established this woman was not English. Instead, they now believed she was Canadian.

This time, they were correct. The Gestapo had indeed arrested the wrong person, and the real Doreen Warriner was still at large. This mistake almost certainly saved her life.

*

The occupation of Czechoslovakia on 15 March, 1939, was straightforward for Adolf Hitler's war machine. With almost no resistance whatsoever from the Czechs, 22,000 German troops crossed the border and headed straight for the country's Art Nouveau capital city virtually without firing a shot. Buildings were rapidly requisitioned, giant swastikas hung from what seemed like every lamppost, martial law was implemented, and thousands of arrest warrants were issued for the new regime's enemies.

Had Doreen Warriner not had a British passport, she would probably have been arrested within days – if not hours – of the occupation. She would have then made the 300-kilometre train journey to the Buchenwald Concentration Camp in Germany, where it was likely she would have died.

By the time the Nazis took over the country, she was not only a distinguished academic and lecturer with a degree from Cambridge – exactly the type of person that Hitler wanted to eliminate – but she had already been instrumental in facilitating the escape of over 8,000 of those deemed to be enemies of the Nazis. Some went legally, but many found a way out through the bustling underground network she had established of smugglers, forgers and others who were in a position to help and were willing to accept bribes. Had she not evaded arrest on that morning in 1939, most of the further 7,000 people she saved would likely have perished.

Doreen was not working alone. From the autumn of 1938 she had been joined by many others, who had cancelled anything else they had planned, left their loved ones behind and travelled to Prague to help the hundreds of thousands of refugees who had massed there. As Hitler continued to redraw the map of Europe, absorbing territory into his new empire, millions of men, women and children were put into mortal danger. Most fled their homes, leaving with just the clothes on their backs and anything else they could carry. Believing it to be safe, they looked for sanctuary in the Czech capital, creating one of the worst refugee crises in modern times.

At first Doreen thought she would be able to help by running soup kitchens, sourcing blankets to help keep the bitter Eastern European winter at bay and providing medical supplies. However, she quickly realised that this would do little to help the situation because the scale of the crisis was far greater than she had imagined. She correctly predicted that if the refugee families did not first perish in their thousands from the awful living conditions, it was only a matter of time before the Nazis would invade the country and arrange for their execution.

The only way to help these individuals, therefore, was to get them out of Czechoslovakia altogether, ideally to Britain or even further afield. Her efforts were significantly enhanced in February 1939 by the arrival of an American woman, Martha Sharp, who took the operation to another level at a crucial moment. And so over twelve months, from October 1938 to September 1939, Doreen and Martha worked tirelessly to do exactly that, putting themselves in the gravest danger. They were helped throughout by sixteen others, who were in Prague for the same reason and were equally courageous. They came from different walks of life and different countries, and varied in age, education and political beliefs. But this did not stop them creating an effective and efficient operation. The group included the family of one of England's most successful businessmen, a renowned journalist, a veteran British politician, and a Canadian teacher who would be mistakenly arrested by Gestapo officers hunting for Doreen Warriner; and all were women.

Part One

Liberty

Chapter One

The Czech Affair

Doreen Warriner stepped happily onto Czech soil for the first time in February, 1930. She had been intrigued by the country since it was established in 1918, and now, shortly before her twenty-sixth birthday, she finally had the opportunity to see it for herself. Tall and unconventionally beautiful, with her brown hair worn in her trademark wavy bob, Doreen was an academic who had come to study for her doctorate in the economics of peasant culture. For the duration of her stay, she planned to base herself in Bohemia – the western part of Czechoslovakia which included the capital city of Prague – as it was the economic and political heart of the country. To the east of Bohemia was Moravia, another significant region with a strong industrial base. Slovakia, located to the east of Moravia, was more rural and mountainous. The economic differences between these regions made them ideal for Doreen's research.

Doreen was one of many prominent women drawn to the country for its modern and progressive political climate. Created following the collapse of the Austro-Hungarian Empire, Czechoslovakia was a beacon of hope in post-World War I Europe. This new nation was made up of the historical lands of Bohemia, Moravia, and Slovakia, along with Carpathian Ruthenia, and was intended to be a truly independent and democratic state.

The constitution, adopted in 1920, guaranteed a range of civil liberties. The progressive politician Tomáš Garrigue Masaryk, who became the first President of Czechoslovakia in November

1918, was loved by the people of his country and admired around the world in equal measure. Influenced strongly by his marriage to an American woman, Charlotte Garrigue, he believed adamantly in the equality of men and women and saw marriage as a partnership of equals.

The area of the country which interested Doreen the most was the Sudetenland. This horseshoe of land surrounded three sides of Czechoslovakia, bordering Poland, Austria and Germany. Containing a wide variety of nationalities – mainly Czechs, Germans, Slovaks, Hungarians, Poles and Ruthenians – the 28,000 square kilometres had been confiscated from the Austro-Hungarian Empire as part of the Treaty of Versailles after World War I. The undercurrent of resentment from the three million German nationals in the Sudetenland – who were unhappy that their homes had been used as a bargaining chip to pay retributions for the war – was apparent from the start.

Within a month of living in the country, Doreen had already begun to master the Czech language, which was evident by her attendance in the plush parliament – adorned with chandeliers and wooden panelling – where she would spend hours watching budget debates. Although she was far from fluent, Doreen quickly picked up the gist of what was being said, which was often that the rural areas such as the predominantly German Sudetenland felt they were not being treated fairly. Despite it being an economically significant region, rich in natural resources, heavy in industry and strong in manufacturing, the government appeared to favour other Czech regions for economic development. This was resulting in the neglect of the Sudetenland's infrastructure, public services, and social programs.

Doreen was not a regular attendee at the Czech parliament purely for the debates. Her eye had been caught by a prominent fifty-two-year-old politician. On top of his eloquence, he was always immaculately turned out in well-tailored dark suits, with a neatly groomed moustache and black slicked-back hair. The wire-rimmed glasses, which would often slip down his nose as he was reading something, somehow made him seem more human. This was Milan Hodža, the Minister of Agriculture for Czechoslovakia.

Despite his being twenty-six years her senior, Doreen was quickly infatuated with the politician, who was married. She would ensure she was present whenever he was speaking in parliament, eager to hear him articulate the virtues of agricultural investment across the state. She also started writing to him, using her doctorate in the economics of peasant agriculture as the reason for her contact. His replies – from whenever they started to arrive – have never been seen, however his name appeared in Doreen's diary for the first time in May 1930, simply saying, 'Hodža at 11.'

By October that year, Doreen was regularly having tea with Milan and his wife Emília at their family home. Her relationship with Milan had moved beyond a professional friendship to regular sexual liaisons. He was equally attracted to the tall young Englishwoman who had more energy than anyone he had ever met. The excitement of their physical relationship was never to the detriment of shared political ideologies, and for the next five years, Doreen acted as an unofficial advisor on matters regarding agricultural reform. Her first-class philosophy, politics and economics degree from St Hugh's College in Oxford was being put to good use.

Whenever they planned to meet, the two would arrive separately at a hotel and check into their respective rooms. Doreen would then sneak her way to Milan's room, where they would spend a passionate night together.

The pair had no problem switching back to business after a romantic night, as she wrote matter-of-factly in her diary: 'In the morning we got up and we discussed the paper that he wants to put forward and the idea of concessions. He was dissuaded by me from this.'

By 1935, after five years together, the couple were closer than they had ever been. Hodža's political career was also gaining strength. Jan Malypetr had been serving as Prime Minister since 1932, in which time he had not been able to quash the increasing disquiet from the Czech, Slovak, and German nationalist factions of parliament. Nowhere suffered from unrest by this point more than the Sudetenland, whose populist leaders were demanding change. By November 1935, Malypetr found his position untenable, so offered his resignation to the elderly President, Tomáš Masaryk. His successor was none other than the Agriculture Minister, Milan Hodža. 'Mil to be PM,' Doreen excitedly wrote in her diary when she found out the news.

He became the country's tenth Prime Minister on 5 November, 1935, and according to a reporter for *The Scotsman* who was in Prague, 'received a cordial reception when he arrived here yesterday morning'. It was a time of major political transition for the country. A month later, on 18 December, 1935, fifty-one-year-old Edvard Beneš became the second President of Czechoslovakia, following the resignation of Tomáš Masaryk. Beneš had been a key figure in the Czech independence movement and served as the nation's Foreign Minister from its founding in 1918 until his election as President. He had also long been the assumed successor to Masaryk, and very much respected, but for many he would never be able to fill the mighty shoes of Masaryk, his adored predecessor.

Doreen now had a seat at the very top of Czech politics. Hodža relied heavily on her counsel, far beyond just the topic of farming. As they would sit awake into the early hours of the morning debating the most pressing issues of state, their conversation would always end up back on the Sudetenland. For as soon as he became Prime Minister, Milan had to address the rise of the Sudeten German Party (SdP). Initially founded in 1933 by Konrad Henlein, it presented itself as a legitimate political group advocating for the rights and autonomy of Sudeten Germans within Czechoslovakia. The SdP started as a moderate party, but soon began to adopt radical positions. Henlein and the SdP gradually aligned themselves with Nazi Germany, embracing its ideology, including anti-Semitism, and advocating for the annexation of the Sudetenland by Germany. Small uprisings were instigated regularly in the Sudetenland, conducted by different Nazi supporting factions of the SdP, many of whom had been secretly meeting and training for some years. These included 'Volks-Sport' which, under the guise of a sports' club federation, had been carrying out military training, small arms drills and tactical exercises with its members, all the while stockpiling weapons. By 1935, the SdP had become the dominant political force among Sudeten Germans, winning about sixty percent of the votes in the Czech parliamentary elections that year.

The second largest party, who aligned far more with Milan Hodža's political philosophy of progressive federalism, were the German Social Democratic Workers Party (DSAP). Founded in 1919, they represented the interests of the German-speaking working class in Czechoslovakia. Unlike the SdP, the DSAP was staunchly anti-Nazi and upheld democratic socialist beliefs. In stark contrast, within two years of its founding, the SdP had fully aligned with Nazi Germany, and Henlein had come under the direct influence of Hitler's government, even being funded by the Third Reich. His party 'had made the destruction of this opposition its immediate task' according to a British correspondent reporting the story.

Milan Hodža was delivered demands from Henlein for full autonomy for the Sudeten Germans in 1938, which said, 'In the end, we want nothing less than to be freed from Czechoslovakia.' The SdP claimed that their rights were being suppressed by the government, leading to ethnic German discrimination. In private, Henlein made no secret of what he wanted to achieve. 'We must always demand so much that we can never be satisfied,' he told his advisors. This tactic, used to destabilise Hodža's government, made negotiations impossible and tried to justify external intervention. The stress of the situation in the Sudetenland began to take its toll on Hodža, whose temper became more erratic by the day. Doreen commented in her diary after one encounter that he acted like 'a crawling beast'. After this incident, he sent flowers to her hotel room as an apology.

Hodža was not alone in his anxiety. The growing tension in the Sudetenland was being felt further afield than Czechoslovakia. While Europe was still recovering from the devastation of World War I, British Prime Minister Neville Chamberlain decided that direct British mediation in the Sudetenland might prevent a larger conflict. He therefore set up the Runciman Mission in August 1938, appointing Liberal politician Viscount Walter Runciman to broker a compromise that would address the Sudeten German grievances while preserving Czechoslovakia's territorial integrity.

The mission comprised of eight officials, as well as Walter Runciman's wife Viscountess Runciman – a former Liberal member of parliament – who accompanied her husband in a private capacity. Runciman's right hand man from the start was Robert Stopford, a successful British banker who had extensive experience of international financial negotiations. Arriving in Prague on 2 August, 1938, Viscount Runciman, Stopford and their team had multiple meetings with Czech President Edvard Beneš and his Prime Minister. Stopford wrote to his sister that in their first meeting, the Czech government 'had a tendency to put the worst interpretation on everything the other side says or does'. Hodža recounted these intense sessions differently when talking to Doreen, expressing his frustration that Viscount Runciman was heavily implying that the Czech government should offer concessions to the SdP. He correctly predicted that the same requests were not made of Henlein.

Henlein did not shy away from the fact that he was now working in collaboration with Hitler. He invited Runciman to several grand meetings. Stopford wrote in his diary that, 'Lord R *[sic]* arrived at 5 p.m. for the conference with Henlein. H then drove off standing up in his car saluting, followed by a car full of his stormtroopers, mobbed by supporters.' This meeting, along with the dozens of others, yielded no results whatsoever, only serving to perpetuate the message in the SdP's propaganda that they were trying to cooperate.

After hearing that members of the Runciman Mission had branded Hodža as 'antagonistic', Doreen took it upon herself to step in on the negotiations. Knowing that he had been present with Viscount Runciman in all his meetings, she went to see Robert Stopford directly. 'Called on Stopford,' she wrote in her diary on 19 August, despite being 'very tired in the morning.' Her meeting was informative, but she did not feel able to put forward any of the points she had been discussing with Milan – in no small part because she was absolutely exhausted following so many late night discussions with Hodža – so she wrote to him the following day, laying out her many ideas. 'I would like to ascertain whether you think a solution might be sought along these lines,' she concluded, before asking, 'if I might have an opportunity of seeing you again.'

Unaware of Doreen's relationship with Hodža, Stopford was interested that a British academic's opinions aligned so directly to the Czech government. He was happy to meet with her again, but her intervention did little to influence him nor anyone in the mission. For the next month, Viscount Runciman continued to push the Czech government for concessions, which were always refused. He wrote in one report to the British Government that, 'I have come to the conclusion that it is impossible for the Czech Government, with the best will in the world, to conciliate the Sudeten German leaders to the extent which they demand ... The only practical solution is the transfer of these territories.'

His comments were influenced by the pace of escalation in the Sudetenland. On 12 September, Hitler said in an inflammatory speech, 'God did not create seven million Czechs so they could harass three and a half million Germans.' The next day, buoyed by the Führer's comments, Henlein orchestrated a co-ordinated outbreak of violence, which was described by media as a 'civil war in the Sudetenland', culminating in the Czech Government declaring martial law in the area. Despite this, in a letter to British officials, Runciman reinforced that he 'remained positive that a favourable outcome can be achieved.'

However, those in London did not share his optimism.

When Runciman sent what would be his last report of his progress on 21 September to Neville Chamberlain, he had no idea that the Prime Minister was taking matters into his own hands. He did not know that six days before, on 15 September, Chamberlain had flown to Berchtesgaden in Germany to meet Hitler. Chamberlain later remarked that his goal was to understand Hitler's demands and see if 'reasonable terms' could be reached.

At 2.15 a.m. on 21 September, 1938, the British Minister in Czechoslovakia (an interchangeable title with that of 'Ambassador'), Sir Basil Newton was sent by Chamberlain to Edvard Beneš' quarters at his official residence at Hradcany Castle, where he awoke the Czech President, urging the surrender of the Sudetenland. Beneš was furious, demanding that Sir

Basil leave. Although he took a strong stance, false rumours were spread around Prague that he was going to hand over the Sudetenland to Germany at any moment.

The following evening, as word spread that the Czech government was signalling their agreement to a deal with Hitler, more than 100,000 civilians peacefully marched down to St Wenceslas Square in central Prague in protest. Banners displayed the general mood: 'WE ARE NOT FOR SALE' and 'DOWN WITH THE GOVERNMENT OF SURRENDER.' Their anger was particularly aimed at Beneš who had vowed two years prior at the funeral of his predecessor Tomáš Masaryk on his country's behalf: 'President Liberator, we shall keep faith with the legacy you have passed into our hands.' The Czechs were furious that he appeared to be capitulating.

Despite the demonstrations being mostly peaceful, agents working for the German state did their best to cause disorder. Newspapers in Berlin claimed that peace and order had broken down in Czechoslovakia, resulting in riots and endangering the German population in the country.

On 22 September, during a second meeting in Bad Godesberg, Chamberlain faced Hitler's revised demands, which included the immediate occupation of the Sudetenland by German troops. Although Chamberlain felt uneasy, he was still committed to avoiding conflict, believing that making sacrifices for harmony was a lesser evil than the horrors of war. His viewpoint was influenced by the trauma of World War I, and he stated publicly: 'How horrible, fantastic, incredible it is that we should be digging trenches and trying on gas masks here [in Britain] because of a quarrel in a faraway country between people of whom we know nothing.'

Milan Hodža and his cabinet resigned in protest that day, dissolving the government after nearly three years of rule. Panic was rife across the country, and at 10 p.m. on the evening of 22

September, orders for reserve soldiers to mobilise were broadcast, flashing up on cinema screens and announced by loudspeakers on vans driving down the streets of Prague. The country was preparing for war.

In London, just before 3 p.m. on 28 September, 1938, Chamberlain rose from his seat in parliament and said, 'I have now been informed by Herr Hitler that he invites me to meet him at Munich tomorrow morning.' The announcement was met with rapturous approval from his parliamentary colleagues.

At this meeting, the Munich Agreement was signed on 30 September, 1938, allowing Hitler to peacefully take control of the Sudetenland in return for assurances that there would be no wider European conflict. Chamberlain believed he had secured stability with Germany, famously returning to Britain with the declaration that he had achieved 'peace for our time.'[1] For Chamberlain, this was a diplomatic triumph that averted imminent war. Later that same day, as celebrations ensued around the country, Chamberlain appeared with King George VI on the balcony of Buckingham Palace in front of cheering crowds.

Not everyone in the country was supportive. Just days after the agreement was signed, Winston Churchill delivered a devastating speech in the House of Commons where he condemned the decision. 'You were given the choice between war and dishonour. You chose dishonour, and you will have war.'

Those who knew the implications of handing Hitler the keys to the Sudetenland were equally as scathing. Czech President Edvard Beneš fumed that, 'Munich will not save peace but will make the war more inevitable and more general.' And he was right. Fighting on an unimaginable scale would quickly follow.

*

Doreen Warriner was ashamed of her country. 'The Munich Agreement left us not only with a terrible sense of betrayal of the Czechs', she wrote, 'but also with a sense of shame that the West had abandoned its moral and humanitarian principles.' She was also bitterly disappointed that her lover was no longer in the position of power he had once been. After he stepped down as Prime Minister, her relationship with Hodža quickly petered out. Not because Doreen was only interested in him due to his position – he was, after all, her first great love – but rather they found they now had very little to talk about. Hodža felt bitter and scapegoated, something he never really recovered from. But he continued to hold Doreen in high regard after their relationship ended, to the extent that he quoted her in his memoir in 1942: 'Doreen Warriner took up the task of advocating an organic connection of both the Two Europes *[sic]*, saying ...' It surprised many that an unknown academic was quoted in the account of a world leader.

Edvard Beneš resigned as President of Czechoslovakia on 5 October, 1938, under immense pressure following the signing of the Munich Agreement. Despite having fervently objected to it, he was held ultimately responsible. He was succeeded by Emil Hácha on 30 November, an elderly lawyer, judge, and former President of the Czech Supreme Administrative Court, chosen for his reputation as a neutral and non-partisan figure. He was thought to be a safe pair of unthreatening hands.

*

'We had driven as far as the town's main square,' said Herbert Lowit, the teenage son of a senior Social Democrat who lived in the Sudetenland and was forced to flee. 'Through the open window we heard the news bulletin that the Czech government had agreed [to] cede to Germany the Sudetenland.'

As the broadcasts filtered through the wirelesses, for many of those in the Sudetenland the Munich Agreement spelled complete disaster. 'With these words the world as I had known it for fifteen years of my life collapsed' Herbert continued sadly. From the moment it was signed, Henlein's party now had ultimate power. 'SdP banners and quite a few swastika flags were already fluttering from apartment blocs and villas in our neighbourhood' Herbert noticed. Henlein's men wasted no time in focusing their hatred on anyone who had dared oppose them over the years, taking particular pleasure in terrorising members and supporters of the anti-Nazi DSAP. A memo written about conditions in the district of Kaaden within the Sudetenland, reported that 'there were about sixty-four arrests in the first few days (with a population of 2,500 inhabitants) ... each prisoner was bound to a bench and beaten so mercilessly with heavy belts and straps that they received terrible wounds'. The SdP also started to act on their commitment to support Hitler's obsession with the obliteration of all European Jews.

The 1930 census showed that more than 325,000 people in Czechoslovakia identified themselves as Jewish by religion, and many of those were German Jews living in the Sudetenland. At the end of September, fearing for their safety, thousands of men, women and children began escaping across the Sudetenland border to seek refuge from the violence in what was left of Czechoslovakia. By 10 October it was estimated that between 150,000 and 200,000 people had left their homes and headed to Prague. It was a bizarre time for the residents of the Czech capital. They were now dealing with a refugee crisis at the same time as they were preparing for war. The streets were already full of local residents queuing to be issued a gasmask or donate blood in makeshift centres, often formerly Red Cross offices. Air raid wardens appeared suddenly, banging on doors at night telling people to extinguish any lingering light, no matter how dim. The mass of displaced people flocking in only added to the overwhelming and chaotic atmosphere.

Franziska Mykura was one of those who had to escape. She wrote: 'The last days of September 1938, we, the Anti-Nazis, had to leave the Sudetenland and had to go into the heart of the Czech speaking part of Czechoslovakia, to find there refuge for a time ... So we hurriedly packed suitcases, a roll of blankets and set off.' She only had a matter of hours to take in the fact she may never return to her home again. 'So that was goodbye to our town' she remembered, and 'goodbye to the life we lived, to our small house and garden.'

Franziska and the thousands of other new arrivals in Prague presented a serious dilemma for the capital's residents and the surrounding area. As many of those who fled were German speaking Jews, they were seen by the Czechs as symbolic of the enemy and were not only treated with suspicion, but in most cases as outcasts. A British official who was present in Prague watching the situation unfold in front of his eyes, believed there was an 'unwillingness of the Government to retain within its shrunken borders men of German race [with] anti-Nazi opinions who are likely to be the cause of friction with the German Government.' Logistically as well, there was simply a lack of space to house everyone permanently, meaning that already over 20,000 people were having to make do with being accommodated in refugee camps which were being erected around Prague.

The three largest camps were Světlá Castle, Dolná Krupá Castle and Nížkov village school. These makeshift shelters were incredibly overcrowded and quickly conditions became uninhabitable, with no heating and a scarcity of food. As winter encroached, the refugees who now called this home had to struggle on without basic amenities such as coal, straw or blankets to keep warm. Some charities from Britain were quick to pick up on the issue, with a handful of aid workers setting up operations in Prague. Doreen Warriner was already in the Czech capital, and on impulse decided to remain there indefinitely. In September she flew back to Britain for a few weeks to tie up some loose ends before returning to Prague on 13 October where she would remain for the foreseeable future. Her trip home was also to accept an official position. As *The Scotsman* reported, 'Working in co-operation with the Lord Mayor's Fund for Czech refugees is the Save the Children Fund, which has appointed a woman, Miss Doreen Warriner, B.A., Ph.D.(Oxon), as its honorary commissioner in Czechoslovakia.' She had been given £150 by these organisations in order to set up a temporary soup kitchen. Along with this, Doreen had also been able to collect £300 from sources which were unrecorded, though she recalled it was probably 'from friends and colleagues.' She would use all of that £450 to buy some immediate relief.

But she needed far more. Writing from Prague, several newspapers reported her appeal. The *Nottingham Evening Post* wrote: 'The Save the Children Fund has today received from its honorary representative in Czechoslovakia, Miss Doreen Warriner, who flew to Prague on Thursday, the following cable: "Situation demands utmost possible effort on part of Save the Children Fund. Impossible to estimate numbers at present. Majority in country around Prague in grave need of immediate help. Czech authorities faced with overwhelming task. Imperative that Save the Children Fund secure generous help to safeguard future of the children. This welcomed by all concerned".' Trying anything she could to raise more money, a picture of Doreen also appeared in the *Daily Mail* with the caption 'Cash for Czechs.'

The Czech government were genuinely trying to help with the situation, but the number of refugees pouring into Prague was unsustainable. It was becoming too much for the authorities to handle, leading to troubling scenes of Jewish refugees being sent back to the Sudetenland in trains, coerced aboard by the sharp point of Czech soldiers' bayonets, only to be attacked by pro-Nazis upon their return. Back in their homeland, many of these people 'were arrested on arrival', an official remembered sadly. A government spokesman commented that they were concerned that sheltering German-speaking anti-Nazi people could 'serve as an excuse for further intervention and territorial demands from Berlin.'

After just two months, pictures and videos from Prague of families who had not been forced to return to the Sudetenland and were now living in appalling and deteriorating conditions started to appear regularly in Britain's newspapers and on newsreels.

Pressure intensified on Neville Chamberlain's administration to try and assist the refugee calamity, with critics of the government accusing them of causing the crisis, a condemnation which remains associated with him to this day. Feeling the burden to act, in October 1938 the British government allocated £4 million (worth £337 million in 2025) to aid those in danger from the Nazi Sudetenland takeover, with a further £10 million (worth £843 million in 2025) being loaned to the Czech government. In his statement, Chamberlain announced that, 'the Chancellor of the Exchequer of the Government has addressed a letter to the Bank of England requesting the Bank provide the necessary credit ... and when the House resumes its sittings in November, Parliament will be asked to pass the necessary legislation.'

The British Government needed someone who they could trust to ensure that this money was distributed appropriately. Ideally, they wanted a businessman who also had intimate knowledge of the political situation in Czechoslovakia. Fortunately, they had just the person. Re-enter Robert Stopford. As the Runciman Mission had now ultimately failed, he found himself at a loose end, so was delighted to be asked to become the de facto British *chargé d'affaires* in Prague, responsible for spending the £4 million fittingly. His appointment was announced in the Houses of Parliament in London on 9 October.

As he made Prague his temporary home from 6 November, he soon started to receive regular visits from Doreen. Over their meetings, she began to lay out an ambitious scheme which she thought could save not just hundreds, but thousands of the refugees.

Chapter Two

Society of Friends

Wenzel Jaksch never thought of himself as brave. Perhaps hardy, but certainly not brave. His upbringing in Austria-Hungary's region of Langstrobnitz, within Bohemia, was tough. Born on 25 September 1896 into a rural working-class family, he witnessed first-hand the economic hardships faced by fellow farmers. It was the cultural tensions between German and Czech communities he saw throughout his childhood that moulded his lifelong obsession with social justice.

Wenzel would most likely have moved straight into politics when he outgrew adolescence. However, during World War I, at the age of eighteen he was conscripted into the Austro-Hungarian army. Despite his youth, he quickly earned a reputation for courage under fire. While serving on the Italian Front, he was shot in the abdomen, an injury which he had no right to survive. But he did, spending the rest of the conflict in and out of hospital.

It was his experience during the war that led Wenzel to a life dedicated to trying to establish peaceful coexistence for everyone in his now new country, Czechoslovakia. Determined to address the inequalities he witnessed growing up, he was an early member of the DSAP, passionately championing the rights of the German-speaking working class.

His natural leadership abilities, which had been well tested in battle, propelled him through the party ranks, culminating in his appointment as chairman in 1938. His arch nemesis was the now-powerful puppet of Adolf Hitler, Konrad Henlein.

Leading the DSAP was the honour of Wenzel's life, but it came with huge responsibility. By the winter of 1938 he had more than 60,000 party members who were in unspeakable danger from Henlein's populist pro-Nazi party, who in turn were being encouraged to act violently towards those they disagreed with. The DSAP members – many of whom were Jewish given it was the only mainstream party to opposed Hitler – looked to their leader for a solution. Although he was fanatically anti-Nazi, his political style was that of a moderate. 'Let us not be persuaded that one nation consists only of devils and the other only of angels,' he told his followers, when asked about his views of the German state. 'The forms of an honourable, peaceful coexistence of the nations must be found,' he concluded.

As soon as the Munich Agreement was signed, in an extraordinary move, Wenzel encouraged his members, as well as the many others who feared retaliation from the Nazis, to flee their homes, head across the border and meet in the Czech capital. He believed that over one million people would likely heed to his warnings.

Meanwhile, he made a trip to England to beg for help. 'In London Herr Jaksch intends to discuss the situation with his British friends,' the *Belfast Telegraph* reported of his visit. Terming the British as friends would most probably not have been first in Wenzel's vocabulary, as Chamberlain's orchestration of an agreement with Hitler spelled disaster for his people. But there was no time for reflection, his only priority in London was to appeal to those he thought would be sympathetic the DSAP. And the first place that he started was his political brethren, the British Labour Party.

He met with some of the most prominent players in Britain's left-wing political circle, asking the same simple question to each of them: 'Why must your government try to strengthen the position of Herr Henlein?' He had meetings with the leader of the British Labour Party, Clement Attlee, who would later become Prime Minister 1945. He also spent many hours with Hugh Dalton, who in turn would serve as Attlee's Chancellor of the Exchequer, as well as Labour MPs William Wedgwood Benn and Philip Noel-Baker. From Wenzel's perspective, these meetings were generally positive, recalling that those he met 'understand that any attempt to Nazify Sudeten Germany means war'. The positive morning was overshadowed by his next meeting with a diplomat from the Runciman Mission – an assignment he blamed in large part for the situation he now found himself. But as he sat with Robert Stopford in a chilly Westminster room, he was immediately captivated. 'This was the beginning of a close friendship with this remarkable man,' Stopford recalled. Responsible for distributing the money earmarked for aid, Stopford seemed to really grasp the problem and sympathise with the DSAP. Wenzel was starting to think that there could be hope for his people after all.

Another consequential encounter was with a person Wenzel assumed would have the least influence. Thought to be a 'has-been' in politics, by 1938, Philip Noel-Baker was a Labour MP for Derby and an ardent advocate for disarmament, a stance reflected in his close work with the League of Nations. A staunch pacifist, he was a leading critic in Chamberlain's appeasement policies with Hitler, as he believed this would only result in more European conflict. Described as 'the greatest authority on armaments in the country', his dogged belief in disarmament was not purely political, as he was strongly influenced by his Quaker upbringing. He told Wenzel in their meeting that not only would he support the Sudeten Germans and Jews who were now fleeing to Prague in any way that he could, but he would come to the Czech capital to see the situation for himself. He was the only member of parliament who had made such a promise to Wenzel. He did not, however, believe for one minute that Noel-

Baker would ever follow through. They were all politicians, after all.

His surprise was evident when a few days later, upon his return to Prague, Wenzel was visited by Noel-Baker. The British man wrote to Robert Stopford after his first day, saying, 'I have seen lots of people of different parties and want to give you my impressions,' going on to say that he believed that 'Wenzel Jaksch's manifesto is at an impasse'. The Sudetenland was now perpetually under Nazi rule and that was something which he did not believe could be reversed.

He was not one to give up though. Seeing the unfolding refugee crisis in Prague directly helped motivate Noel-Baker to do what he could to help. But he was even more troubled by the evident preparations for war. His staunch pacifist beliefs meant that his main priority was to avoid conflict, stating to a group of Czech politicians before he left: 'Is disarmament so difficult a matter that it must remain a distant dream?' He hoped so strongly a peaceful solution could be sought. For now, he needed to focus on easing the refugee crisis, which might just prevent more conflict in Europe. Overwhelmed by the scale of the task ahead, he returned home, where he went straight to visit his sister for advice.

Having a brother of Philip Noel-Baker's stature was sometimes tiresome for Mary. Seven years his senior, she watched from the sidelines as her famous brother went from strength to strength. 'I doubt if any other man before or after him would achieve as much,' remarked a family friend in a gushing tribute to Philip. As well as being a British representative at the Treaty of Versailles, which was apparently not enough of an achievement for him, he took part in the 1920 Antwerp Olympics where he captained the British track team, following his runner-up place in the 1,500 metre race at the 1912 Stockholm Olympics. Mary was a very proud sister as her brother carried the Union Jack in the opening ceremony in Belgium and was awarded a silver medal, one of the fifteen won by the country. As with all things in his life, Philip returned as a hero but was modest in his personal achievement and gracious towards the country's rival in the games, the victorious United States. He wrote in the *Dundee Evening Telegraph* that the sporting bond between the two nations was still very strong: 'The fact that U.S.A. beat us makes no difference. There has never been warmer friendship and understanding between the athletes of the English-speaking races than there is now'.

As a 56-year-old woman, it was very hard for Mary to make a mark for herself in 1930s Britain, let alone when all her acquaintances referred to her as 'Philip's sister'. Born in Highbury, London, on 31 August 1883, Mary, along with Philip and their siblings, were brought up with strong Quaker beliefs, inherited from their father, who worked in the confectionary industry with several other prominent Quaker businessmen.

By 1911, twenty-one-year-old Philip was still living with his parents, but studying at King's College, Cambridge where he was president of the Cambridge Union Society. As the youngest, he was the last of the children yet to leave home, apart from Mary, who at the age of twenty-eight was listed as unemployed and still lived with her parents, not sure what to do with her life.

Her younger sister Elizabeth had met and married the twenty-seven-year-old Frank Garfield Penman in Middlesex. Penman was a successful solicitor who was accepted by the Baker parents as a suitable addition to the family. Upon Elizabeth's death in 1920, Mary moved into their family home to help Frank look after his two children. Mary and Frank quickly built up a strong bond, before eventually marrying and themselves having two children. The relationship caused rifts in the family, with several of Mary's siblings feeling she had committed the ultimate betrayal to the deceased Elizabeth. But Philip, in his constant conquest for peace, refused to take sides, never falling out with Mary. The two were always close so it was unsurprising that he went to see her after his return from Prague to share his grave concerns.

Over dinner, Philip talked through what he had seen: thousands of people wandering aimlessly around the streets of the beautiful city, desperate to find somewhere to live. He described the refugee camp he had visited, which having only been set up for a matter of weeks, was already overcrowded and under-resourced. And most troubling, the fact that after the Nazis took control of the Sudetenland, the Czechs were preparing for an invasion of the rest of the country.

At the time, Adolf Hitler was addressing his Generals in Berlin, making his intentions clear. 'Have the armed forces ready to march,' he told them. 'The Czechs may squeal, but we will have our hands on their throats before they can shout. And anyway,' he concluded with a chuckle, 'who will come to help them?'

Mary had never really found her calling in life. She had not left home, remaining to care for her parents. She then immediately moved in with Frank, where she had since played the part of aunt, stepmother, mother and wife all at the same time. But with Philip's description of Prague, she felt this could be something for her to dedicate her life to. With the children now having grown up and left home, she decided this was her moment. She would go to Prague.

*

The description given by her brother did not prepare Mary for what greeted her as her twenty-seater airplane touched down on the runway of the brand new Ruzyne Airport in Prague just after midday. Arriving at the end of September meant that the weather in Eastern Europe was starting to plummet. Whereas it was a mild seventeen degrees centigrade in London as she left, a bitter five degrees greeted her that afternoon.

As Mary's taxi made its way into central Prague, the city which she had heard so much about, with its mystical blend of Gothic, Baroque, and Art Nouveau structures, appeared more like a horror story. Through the smudged window of the car, as the city centre neared, she started to see refugee families. They were unmistakeable with their dirtied clothes and few possessions, and usually in some sort of makeshift cart. Often with small children in tow, what really stood out to Mary was how slowly they walked, with nowhere to go, but unable to stay where they were. She was soon passing schools, guesthouses, and even old factory buildings that were being turned into temporary shelters. Although some parts were still running as normal, shops, restaurants and businesses were starting to shut down, leaving some parts of the city completely abandoned.

Before leaving, Mary had spoken to her fellow Quaker leaders, who were happy to sponsor her aid work. When she telephoned Emma Cadbury – representative for the American Quakers in London – from the empty Prague apartment she had rented, her shaky description of the scale of the problem prompted fear in London. Mary on her own would not be able to do much. She needed help.

Luckily, Emma had just finished speaking to her friend's daughter, Tessa Rowntree, who was looking to get involved in further charity work having spent the last month in Vienna helping displaced Jews. Thanks to her position and experience, Emma knew a good aid worker when she saw one, and Tessa was certainly that. Hanging up the phone, she called Tessa back. 'They wanted some help in Prague, so Emma asked if I would like to go, so I said yes sure,' Tessa remembered.

Central to Quaker belief is the Peace Testimony, which opposes all forms of violence. This commitment to peace meant direct action was required to alleviate the suffering caused by conflict. Tessa grew up being taught that her 'Inner Light' – the divine presence within every individual – made each person as equally valuable and deserving of compassion and support. Thus, an event such as the refugee crisis in Europe was everybody's responsibility.

Born in York, Tessa was the second child and eldest daughter of Arnold and Katharine Rowntree. She was the great-great granddaughter of John Rowntree who had founded the confectionery business Rowntree and Co., of which Arnold was a director, while also being a member of the leadership team for two newspapers and a Liberal member of parliament for York. Tessa was raised knowing the meaning of hard work. She attended The Mount School, York, a Quaker establishment, and later graduated from the London School of Economics (LSE).

In February 1938 she and her friend Bridget – a fellow LSE student – were in Germany on a canoeing holiday down the Danube. This quickly evolved into aid work in Vienna, where refugees fleeing from Hitler were ending up. The Friends' Centre in the Austrian city was swamped with displaced people, many worried about family and friends they had left behind. Tessa and Bridget volunteered to join a contingent of foreigners – who still had the freedom to travel unhindered –checking in on those who had stubbornly stayed behind. 'I went out to the countryside for a few weeks trying to find people and see if they were okay. One of the people was the writer of Bambi, who I was sent to look for.' She found author Felix Salten safe and well, passing the news back to his relieved relatives.

After a month, Tessa received the call from Emma Cadbury asking her to go to Prague.

By the time she arrived, Robert Stopford had got a grasp of

the magnitude of the problem. He was able to report that the number of refugees registered was a staggering 91,000 dispersed throughout the city, including 5,000 in the camps. But these were only the registered refugees, as those who had friends or family in and around Prague had moved in unofficially. There was a fear that if people registered themselves as refugees, then they could be forced to return to the dreaded Sudetenland.

Of the displaced, the vast majority – more than 70,000 – were Czechs, while just over 15,000 were German and/or Jewish. It was this smaller group who were in the most immediate danger, and most were now calling the squalid camps their home. The danger posed was not only that their living conditions were so poor that the weaker of the inhabitants, mostly the elderly or unwell, were unlikely to survive the winter conditions, but also the threat of being summoned by the Germans. The Czech government were simply not strong enough to be able to refuse such demands from their neighbours. Stopford explained to Tessa that, in his mind, there was only one option for this group which was they 'would have to emigrate.'

Tessa fully grasped the significance of this, dashing off a telegram to someone she knew she could rely on. 'Tessa sent for me, and I went out,' her cousin, Jean Rowntree reminisced. The women had been at school together in York, before Jean went on to study history at Somerville College in Oxford. She had been pondering what to do during her sabbatical from teaching at the prestigious girls' boarding school Downe House in Newbury, when she was contacted by her cousin. 'I think I went partly to work off the guilt by [helping] the people who would suffer from the agreement that let us out of war'. The cousins moved into Mary Penman's flat, which doubled as the Quaker's Prague office.

They hosted several meetings in those early days, of which the most consequential was between Tessa, Jean, Mary and Doreen. Between them, the women had a deep and intimate understanding of the European political situation. Mary's brother was a leading political figure in Britain. Doreen had been cosily plugged in with Czech politics – and although her relationship with Hodža was over, she kept herself well informed on the geopolitical situation in Europe. Jean was encyclopaedic with her knowledge and comprehension of the recent history that had caused this situation. Tessa brought a whole additional perspective. While in Vienna, she had been to one of Hitler's rallies and understood in some way the appeal he had to his followers. 'I have to tell you, I was at the far end of the square, I could feel his personal magnetism ... I could understand why a lot of people were swayed by him,' she confessed to the others. Given the immense suffering since the start of the century, it was perhaps no surprise that he had such a following. Tessa was also unsure about the allure of other members of his inner team. After the rally, she was walking down a busy street when suddenly a surge of people pushed her to one side. A car appeared with Joseph Goebbels, the Reich Minister of Propaganda, inside. Everyone was trying to reach out and touch him, but Tessa had no interest in doing so. 'We were much closer to him than Hitler, but I remember Goebbels being gruesome.'

The women's combined expertise was admirable. But, Doreen reflected, they were not writing a book about European politics. They needed to act. She recalled, 'I went to see Mrs Penman, representing the Society of Friends; but they had not as yet begun any relief work.'

Sensing her disappointment, Mary mentioned that they had hosted Wenzel Jaksch the previous day. Perhaps Doreen should visit him next.

Chapter Three

Labour of Love

Doreen was taken aback to find Wenzel was a middle-aged man, weak in stature and on crutches due to a recent car accident. From hearing one of his impassioned speeches on the radio, she had imagined an older, taller, broader man. But aged just thirty-eight, the stress he had been under since becoming the leader of his party had not aged him at all well. Even so, Doreen was instantly attracted to him. After fleeing with his people from the Sudetenland, Wenzel was now living alone in a flat that belonged to one of his supporters. This was partly out of respect to his party's leader, but also as a safety precaution for Wenzel, who was now one of the most wanted men by the dreaded German secret police, the Gestapo.

For several months Nazi agents had been operating freely in the city and were now grabbing people at will. Back in 1936, 2,900 suspects 'allegedly acting for the German state' were arrested by Czech police. By 1938, the situation was even worse. The government was not powerful enough to put a stop to the ever-increasing number of agents now embedded in Czechoslovakia and it was compelled to turn a blind eye. It was even believed that if anyone was called for by Hitler, the Czech administration would have no choice but to hand them over to avoid tensions.

Wenzel was only too aware that he would be summoned soon. It was because of this that he made the decision that he would remain in hiding until further notice. His hideout was not perfect, after all Mary had known his address to pass it on to

Doreen, and Robert Stopford had it scribbled in the address book he always carried with him.

Over a cup of tea that afternoon, Wenzel described the predicament of his party to Doreen. He was impressed by how knowledgeable she was about Czechoslovakia, in particular the inner workings of the government. He saw in her a person who could be incredibly useful to helping his people.

As the afternoon turned to evening, Wenzel staggered to his feet with the help of his crutches and asked if Doreen would accompany him the next day to meet with two Labour Party politicians, both of whom had answered his cry for help.

It took place on the morning of 14 October in the Steiner Hotel, a short walk from Wenzel's apartment. The meeting was with David Grenfell and William Gillies from the British Labour Party. Grenfell was a formidable character, his brown hair cut too short, his moustache too thick. He came from a poor Welsh family and had joined his father in the coal mines at the age of twelve, before they were forced to go to Canada to find work. It was this experience that drove his desire to be elected to represent the Gower constituency in South Wales. Having sat as a delegation member for the London Trade Council, his peer Philip Noel-Baker had suggested he see the situation in Prague for himself.

His colleague William Gillies was a larger-than-life rotund individual, who gave Grenfell a run for his money with his own moustache, which ran across his top lip and down past his mouth to both sides of his chin. As International Secretary for the British Labour Party, he was feared by all in the British Houses of Parliament.

Doreen wrote in her diary that both politicians were 'horribly rude and very difficult to get on with', particularly as they were immediately dismissive of meeting with a woman. But with limited help coming from elsewhere, neither Gillies nor Grenfell were in a position to turn their moustache framed noses up at Doreen. The Labour Party had agreed that their delegation of two should select 100 endangered members of the Sudeten Democratic Party. The politicians needed all the help they could get.

Wenzel was disappointed on hearing that it was only one hundred people they were planning to help. He now had many thousands of people who needed to be evacuated out of the reach of the Nazis. Discussions soon became heated, as he tried to explain to the politicians that they needed a more radical solution. Gillies shot back that it was simply not possible to secure the funds, transports or visas for anything larger at this point. The offer was to help 100 people, and that was it. Wenzel quickly backed down.

To calm the situation, a disguised Wenzel took them on a trip around the city, where they stopped off at the British Legation to try to find out more about visa applications. They met with Passport Control Officer Harold Gibson. Known to his superiors as Gibby, he was described by a colleague as 'a small, slight figure with a moustache in proportion.' Doreen reflected many decades later 'that Mr Gibson was always fully informed, his word would always be trusted.' Unbeknown to her, Mr Gibson's exhaustive knowledge of events came from his work as an agent of British Secret Intelligence Service (SIS), commonly known as MI6.

That evening, Doreen returned to Wenzel's apartment with Gillies and Grenfell, where they sat round the kitchen table, Wenzel with a ream of blank paper and a pen. Joined by several of his deputies who trickled into the room through the course of the evening, he started to write out a list of the most endangered Social Democrats they knew of. Despite several suggestions that he put his own name on there, Wenzel flatly refused. Like the captain of a ship, he would only leave once everyone else had got out safely, or he would not leave at all.

Doreen remembered the distant sound of the bell of St. Vitus Cathedral in the centre of Prague chiming midnight, by which time the group believed it had identified in excess of 2,000 people who were classed as endangered. As the bell rang, silence fell around the crowded room, the air thick with smoke from the constant cigarettes being puffed on as the group tried to ease the tension.

The quiet was broken by a woman with a heavy German accent. 'There are too many to save,' she said.

This was Marie Schmolka, a stern Jewish Social Democrat, who had the enviable ability to always look elegant no matter the effort she made. Having been the sole Czech representative on the League of Nations Committee for Refugees, she was a well-known figure around Europe. She was a powerful presence and held a room whether it contained hundreds of people or, as in this case, only a handful.

Although no one answered, everyone knew she was right. The British politicians had come with an agenda of getting 100 people out. Not two thousand. The list needed to be shortened. And significantly.

So where should they start? Where does anyone start when thousands need you but only a handful can be helped? How can you decide someone is in more danger than others? Or someone is more deserving of help?

They knew they had to begin somewhere and so Doreen reluctantly picked up a pen and began the grim task of crossing names out. The group were all painfully aware that when they agreed to cross a name off the list, as inevitably they would have to do, they could well have been signing their death warrant. The mood was bleak as they debated whether one person writing an anti-Nazi column in the newspaper two years ago could be deemed as more dangerous than a party treasurer. Is an elderly man with a weak heart more worthy than a younger amputee? Ultimately, by this point, they were just guessing. Doreen grudgingly agreed with the majority that women and children should all be crossed off. After all, it was the men who were in danger. The Nazis would not target the family members, they thought. While tempers were high in the room, through all the discussions, Marie Schmolka remained unfazed.

By 6.30 a.m., as the apartment started to fill with that dim pre-sunrise light, there were just 250 names left on the list. With a sense of hollow achievement, they had reached the lowest possible number.

There was no fanfare or sense of triumph as the room emptied of exhausted figures, most heading back to one of the refugee camps which they now called home. Doreen returned to her hotel room where she managed a few hours sleep, before reuniting with Gillies and Grenfell for lunch.

The following day, with the finalised list in hand, the two British politicians flew back to London. They knew the task in hand was to now get as many visas as possible. The first visit upon their arrival in England was to see Lord Halifax, Foreign Secretary under Chamberlain's Conservative Government. He had been instrumental in the negotiations of the Munich Agreement and was an ardent supporter of the appeasement strategy. Prepared for some tough negotiations, Gillies and Grenfell were pleasantly surprised when Halifax approved their visa request for 250 individuals without hesitation or protest. Credit for this act has been given to Lord Halifax's humanitarianism, but should also be attributed to Gillies' fearsome reputation in Westminster. Associates were known to do anything he asked, just to get him out of the building without a shouting match.

For a refugee to come to England, they required a £50 guarantee (about £5,000 in 2025) to fund their return when it was safe to do so at some point in the future. Although they had initially only agreed to 100 people, the Labour Party was happy to guarantee all 250 men.

Back in Prague, Doreen had been left in charge of organising a mode of transport to take these men back to Britain. She had several options, travelling by air being the easiest and most direct, without the need to pass through other countries. However, the cost and limited capacity of air transport ruled out that possibility. Travelling through Poland to its north coast by train before embarking on a boat to England was the next best choice.

Along with the Rowntree cousins and Mary Penman, the women used the dining room table in Mary's apartment to work through the list. Each man needed to provide them with their passport, which the women in turn would take to Harold Gibson at the British Legation where it would be cross-referenced with the approved names by Lord Halifax's staff in London. Each passport needed ratifying and stamping one by one – a time-consuming and arduous task. They then needed to be taken to the Polish Legation, whose disobliging, painfully slow and disorganised staff would hopefully issue a travel visa.

It was a painstaking process, but within two days of Grenfell and Gillies returning to London, all 250 men on the list were approved to travel. This was a remarkable achievement by these four women, none of whom had any previous experience in these types of logistics.

On 19 October, Grenfell returned to Prague, as he was to act as the leader of an advanced party of fifty men to ensure the route was safe. The remaining 200 would follow soon after. Poland continued to be a free country, but as in Czechoslovakia, there were now thousands of agents swarming around, recruiting officials who were sympathetic to the Nazi cause. Doreen believed that one of the women should act as the leader, after all they had planned the journey and knew the area far better than Grenfell, even after such a short amount of time. Yet, it was decided from London that this would not be a task suitable for a woman. This time they should watch from afar.

*

It was the night of 23 October, 1938, and Prague was in complete darkness when Grenfell set off following a route which had only roughly been sketched out. Arriving at Wilson Station late that evening, Doreen, Mary and the Rowntree cousins stood with the wives and children of the fifty men, all saying their goodbyes. Emotions ranged from sadness, uncertainty and fear, through to hope and relief. Most of the men who were lucky enough to be escaping did genuinely believe that by leaving they were helping to protect their loved ones who would remain in Czechoslovakia.

Punctually at 11 p.m., the train pulled slowly out of the station. The women and children who had crowded the platform dispersed into the darkness of the night, unsure if they would ever see these men again.

The next day was agonising for Doreen, as she waited in their makeshift office for news of the success – or otherwise – of the voyage. It was not until late that evening that the phone rang, with Grenfell bearing news. Travelling by slow night train, it had taken twenty hours for them to cross the 300 miles to Poland, but the group had arrived safely, albeit exhausted, in Krakow. From there, they were waiting for a fast train to the seaport of Gdynia, where they would head by ferry to England.

This fast train did not leave for another two days, and during the call Grenfell told Doreen he had been told there were still spaces available on the ferry.

'Book them,' she said.

Before he could protest, she had already hung up the telephone.

There were just under two hours until the same train was due to leave that evening, and, with no time to lose, Doreen scanned through the list and picked twenty men who she knew were most in need of escaping. The women dashed from the flat, with Mary driving Jean to Světlá Castle camp, while Tessa and Doreen tried to hail a taxi to a local hostel which was housing several of the men.

Miraculously, in one hour and with time to spare, all twenty men were queuing up at Wilson Station. Similar to the scene from the night before, a group of trembling women and children formed a solemn line along the platform, watching the men of their households disappear into the darkness behind a sea of steam.

Despite having caught the flu, Doreen sat cheerfully among the men as the train sped away from the city. Some of them wept, others quietly fixed their gaze on the ground, while a few sat reading a newspaper as if they were on their daily commute.

It was a long and tedious journey, heading through the depths of Slovakia by steam train, before changing to a motor train to pass through the ruins of Orava Castle in Oravský Podzámok, up into the Slovakian mountains. They arrived in the northern village of Suchá Hora, where there was a tiny frontier post at the border with Poland. Disembarking from the motor train, Doreen wrote, 'We had to wait the whole day in this poor Slovak village, where they could give us only eggs at their inn.' But despite winter drawing in, 'We sat in the sun and my flu was cured.' It was not until night fell on 26 October that their connecting train reached the Polish side of the border. The men did not comprehend why Doreen appeared so nervous; they were nearly out of Czechoslovakia. But she worried that they only had a short length of time to make it across Poland to the ferry which was due to leave later that day.

Now the train had arrived, they could cross the border – after the endless questioning, passport checking and bag searching – before they boarded their carriage and were slowly rattling towards the southern Polish town of Nowy Targ, which would be invaded by the Nazi war machine under a year later and then become a major Jewish ghetto.

Once in Nowy Targ, having missed their connecting train due to the border delays earlier that day, 'Frozen and tired, we drank vodka in the waiting room,' Doreen recollected. With no way of getting a communication to Grenfell in Krakow, Doreen managed to book a seat on the Luxtorpeda train which took her at 120 km/h to Krakow, linking up with Grenfell within four hours, where she passed on the message that the men were catching the Midnight Express to Krakow.

Grenfell's response to Doreen was less than gentlemanly. 'He pushed me on to the express for Warsaw, gave me a plane ticked back to Prague and said, "Go and get some more".' He hoped that she would be able to get back to Prague in time to bring the rest of the group to catch the same ferry, as it only sailed fortnightly.

Early on 27 October, Doreen was back on a train, hurtling towards Warsaw, where she just managed to catch the 7 a.m. plane to Prague. Two days after first leaving, five trains, two border crossings and very little sleep, she arrived back in Prague only to do the same again.

While she was enduring her gruelling journey back to Czechoslovakia, Grenfell discovered there would not be time to get another group there in time. He got word to Doreen's hotel that he was taking both groups – now consisting of seventy men – to the boat in Gdynia. From there the seventy persecuted men who had been earmarked for arrest by Hitler went onto the safety of Britain where they would be able to seek asylum.

Doreen was relieved to have a note from Grenfell telling her the next voyage was be postponed. Without having a chance to undress or wash, she collapsed onto her bed and fell into a deep sleep.

*

'She looks like a tough girl!'

Grenfell was sitting at the kitchen table in Mary's apartment a week later, having journeyed back to Prague, triumphant from the first mass transport he had initiated. He had returned to the Czech capital to try to appoint an official courier to take his place in escorting the rest of the listed men through Poland and on to Britain. It was not something he intended to do again.

His instinct – and indeed his intention – was to find a man. But now he found himself quarrelling with Doreen, who had taken umbrage at the idea. She was now part of an established team and one of them should be taking on that role. It just happened that her team was made up of four women.

While Grenfell argued that this was not a job suitable for a woman, Tessa Rowntree walked in. At which point Grenfell looked up and commented that she actually looked quite tough. And he was right. She was indeed sturdy, resilient and very brave. And so it was settled. Tessa would take the next group on the same route as the past two journeys through Czechoslovakia, into Poland and up to the north coast where she would wave the men off to Britain.

Karl Lowit was among the men who left his family behind to make the journey. He recalled: 'Accompanied by Miss Tessa Rowntree, we left Prague on 2 November, 1938, and travelled via Brno to Žilina. Using a variety of local trains we eventually crossed the Polish border at Nowi Targ. We then had to hire a bus to take us to Krakow where we boarded the express train to Gdynia. The Polish freighter Warszawa took us to Harwich where we disembarked on 8 November.'

For the courier, having a British or American passport was indispensable. There was a sense that Nazi collaborators and sympathizers would be happy to arrest anyone from Central or Eastern Europe under the auspice of being an enemy of the Third Reich but for the British and Americans, that was a step too far. Tessa remembered being told by Doreen that, along with seeming hardy, it was one of the reasons for her selection: 'My British passport was supposed to be good, and it was, it helped!' When entering Poland, she was the first of her group to show her passport to the guard, who was impressed at the sight of the dark blue booklet with the King's crest on the front. He thumbed through the document until her got to the photo page.

'Name?' he asked.

'Tessa Rowntree' she replied.

The guard's face screwed up as he re-examined the passport, before calling over his superior. She was asked to wait at the side. Poor Tessa had no idea what was going on, but she was receiving more scrutiny than the refugees she was meant to be responsible for, who were all passing through without trouble. She had no idea why they had stopped her.

Born Elisabeth, 'She was always and only known as Tessa by everyone inside and outside the family,' her daughter Alison later explained. Up to that point, 'The only time she was ever addressed as Elisabeth that I am aware of was by a doctor in a hospital who read it off her chart, and she didn't immediately recognise that he was addressing her!'

A simple mistake, but one which could be costly. The Polish guards did not understand the nuances of the name Elisabeth being shortened to Tessa. It was one of the refugees she was escorting who came to her aid, and explained the situation to the Polish soldiers. Eventually she was allowed through. 'It was touch and go,' she reminisced.

By 9 November, just seventeen days after the first voyage

began, all 250 men from that infamous list were out of Czechoslovakia and in the safety of Britain. 'It was a fine effort and showed what could be done by determined people,' Stopford wrote in a report to London. An achievement indeed, but only the beginning of what Doreen Warriner was planning.

Chapter Four

Dire Conditions

Světlá nad Sázavou Castle is a glorious sight: a 15,000 square foot fusion of Gothic, Renaissance and Baroque styles framed by impeccably manicured gardens. Thanks to the generosity of its owners, the Salms family, by November 1938 the castle housed thousands of Sudeten refugees.

Doreen was impressed by those inhabiting it. 'The men were running the camps themselves with an impressive semi-military discipline.' She saw some even wearing the Socialist Party uniform with its finely ironed blue shirt, red tie and high black boots. These were proud people, trying to uphold and honour what they stood for and where they came from, even when they had no home. To Doreen, it seemed that all the residents at Světlá nad Sázavou Castle were exceedingly respectful of the building, seeing it as somewhere they needed to leave in the same state they found it while also appreciating they had it better than many others.

After driving two hours in Mary's car to the castle, Doreen, Wenzel, Mary and the Rowntree cousins then went on to a converted school building at Nížkov, a further thirty miles from Prague. Here, conditions were worse, but as Doreen consoled herself: 'The winter cold had not begun which was as well because they had no blankets.'

Nothing prepared the women for the horror that greeted them when they reached their next stop, what had been an abandoned seventeenth-century castle in the town of Dolní Krupá. 'It was in a filthy state before the refugees arrived,' Doreen reflected. 'The walls were covered with fungus, floors and walls cracking, windows broken.' A two-tier system was in place for the refugee community. The hostels in Prague and Světlá nad Sázavou Castle were far nicer than the school in Nížkov or this castle. Yet everyone they met was remarkably accepting of the situation.

Lit only by a dim oil lamp, Wenzel perched himself at the top of the grand staircase in the castle where he spoke passionately to his followers. 'We will make no recriminations,' he shouted. 'We have lost our sight and we are beaten. But we have not lost the important thing: we have been true to our socialist faith, and perhaps our tragedy has a meaning.' Met with rapturous applause, he finished with his voice cracking through emotion: 'We will find a way, and we will clear the forest in Bolivia rather than live without liberty. And we will remain together.' As the four English women watched in awe, Doreen felt something strange when looking up at Wenzel. How extraordinary, she thought. She had not had this feeling since she had first started getting to know her former lover, Milan Hodža. Was she now falling for Wenzel?

Robert Stopford had attended a similar meeting a few weeks before and although his thoughts were platonic, he was equally impressed. 'I went with him to visit one or two of the refugee camps and was very much struck by the great welcome [Wenzel] received from his people there.'

As Mary drove back to Prague in the cold dark night, the women sat in silence, Doreen and the Rowntree cousins squished into the back and Wenzel sitting like a dignitary in the passenger seat. The families they met could have sworn their allegiance to Henlein's party and remained in the safety of their homes in the Sudetenland. Yet, their belief was so strong in opposition to Hitler, they had given up everything. They were now homeless.

With winter drawing in, Doreen would be fighting a battle on two fronts. She needed to try to get as many of these families out of harm's way and onto trains and boats as they had for the first 250 men. But this, she recognised, would take time. In the interim, they needed to keep these people alive.

'Mrs Penman, with funds from the Friends, had already got blankets to them before the real winter came,' Doreen remarked. But they needed to go much further with their assistance and with just four of them, they couldn't do enough. They needed to build alliances, which they started most prominently with the Czech Red Cross, who were already deeply entrenched in providing aid to the camps. The organisation was able to get things done that would be impossible for others, thanks to the influence of its leader. Daughter of the first President of Czechoslovakia, Alice Masaryk was brought up in a household where it was continually reinforced that men and women are equal. After studying in Prague and Berlin in 1903, her parents encouraged Alice to spend a year in the United States, where she completed a post-graduate course on social care. This was her first foray into what would become a life cause for her, the support of refugees. She set up an organisation in America which would help settle Czech immigrants who were starting a new life in the country.

Upon returning to her home country, Alice had irons in various fires. But, by 1919, she decided to dedicate herself to the Red Cross. 'After the Great War, when conditions here were very difficult, the idea came to me,' she reminisced. By 1938, it had grown in prominence so significantly, with Alice at its helm, chairing the organisation through what would now be some of its most essential work. Her mantra would always be: 'The peace of the Red Cross has been proclaimed. Let the peace of the Red Cross be maintained.'

Alice was a great believer in collaboration, in particular with like-minded women. It was for this reason that the Red Cross partnered with the Czechoslovakian Women's National Council, spearheaded by Františka Plamínková, the Jewish daughter of a cobbler. Despite their different upbringings, the two women got on famously. Františka had become an ardent suffragette prior to World War I after she was forbidden to marry because she was a teacher. Between 1870 and 1918 enforced policies known as 'teacher celibacy' mandated that female teachers remain unmarried, for the reason that married women were obligated to their domestic responsibilities, including child-rearing, supporting their husband and household management.

The election of Alice's father in 1919 eliminated class, gender, and religious barriers, and gave women political, social and cultural parity with men. In the first parliamentary elections for the newly formed state in 1920, fifty-four percent of the voters were women, with Františka being elected to the Prague City Council as a member of the Czech Socialist Party. Her pride in the nation and admiration for Alice's family was absolute. In a speech in 1937 to an American audience, she explained: 'After the war, the Czech nation immediately gave its women equal rights with men ... There are women judges, women teachers and public officials, all sharing executive power, advancement and remuneration on a basis equal with men.'

As Hitler's terror continued to spread across Europe in 1938, Alice and Františka did not hold back in their condemnation of the man who wanted to remove the rights they had so passionately fought for in Czechoslovakia. In an act of defiance, Františka wrote an open letter to Hitler, calling him out as a liar. 'As an honest democrat I consider it my duty to write to you, Mr. Chancellor,' she opened her letter, 'because I am firmly convinced that truth will prevail even against military rule.' Following the occupation of the Sudetenland, such outspoken critics of Hitler were in more danger than they had ever been.

The Quakers, Red Cross and Czechoslovakian Women's National Council joined together with shared responsibility for the refugee camps. Though their work was varied, it would mainly consist of the provision of food and clothing distribution, medical assistance, advocacy of their plight and the housing of orphaned children.

Every day was different for the women of these organisations. Alice would be giving a speech in the Czech parliament, while Františka was in Switzerland lecturing, Doreen was looking for a more efficient route for people to travel to England, and the Rowntree cousins were shopping. 'I've just purchased a thousand men's undergarments. Now, not many girls can say that, can they!' Tessa wrote in her diary after a day of distributing the essential supplies. The cousins would drive with Mary to the camps each day, where they would deliver huge crates of provisions, funded and sourced by them.

*

Back in Britain, very few people took notice of the plight of the Czech people. To raise awareness, David Grenfell had joined forces with fellow British politicians Arthur Salter and Victor Cazalet, creating a cross-party Parliamentary Committee on Refugees. The men were happy to include a formidable independent politician, Eleanor Rathbone, who became Honorary Secretary. They described the Parliamentary Committee on Refugees as being 'concerned not with individual refugees, whose cases are dealt with by the appropriate voluntary organisations, but with the general problems of the refugee question as a whole.' With the reputation as being the 'MP for refugees', Eleanor was a pioneer, not only because she was one of just nine female Members of Parliament, making the male representation still just under ninety-nine percent, but for her work championing causes such as equal opportunities, a family allowance and the plight of refugees. She had been a vocal opposer to the appeasement of Hitler, recently attending Trafalgar Square for a rally in support of the Czech people. Following her rousing speech, she led a march to the Czechoslovakian Legation in London to deliver a resolution.

Eleanor was sixty-six years old, but her age did not reflect any decrease in energy and determination. She was patron of the Youth Relief and Refugee Council and a member of the Friendly Aliens Protection Committee, the Council on Aliens, the Committee for Development of Refugee Industries, the Central Committee on Refugees, the Advisory Committee of the Czech Refugee Trust and now Honorary Secretary of the Parliamentary Committee on Refugees.

Amazingly, she still had plenty of time to make a nuisance of herself in Parliament. Eleanor was a thorn in the side of her fellow politicians in Government, who she fervently held to account on every possible occasion. 'He detested her,' reflected an advisor of Neville Chamberlain, when asked what the Prime Minister thought about Eleanor. This was because she was like a dog with a bone. If she was passionate about a cause, she would not stop fighting for it. Eleanor was proud to have been one of the first politicians in Europe to speak out about the threat Hitler posed, in no uncertain terms: 'He and his colleagues have let the world see plainly their feelings which cherish about questions of blood and race.' She watched on in disgust as the German Führer grew in prominence, with leaders – notably Neville Chamberlain – bowing down to him.

The thin end of the wedge for her was the Runciman Mission. She publicly called out its failings on 3 August, the day that Viscount Runciman and his delegation first arrived in Czechoslovakia. 'Neither he nor anybody else has the slightest belief that it will be efficacious,' she said in a speech. And she was of course absolutely correct.

After the Munich Agreement, Eleanor was clear that, along

with everyone in Britain, she had a duty to help. Robert Stopford attended a meeting about the refugee crisis during one of his visits to London, where Eleanor was present. Around the crowded table of dignitaries, politicians and officials in a Downing Street office, she cut off Sir John Simon, Chancellor of the Exchequer, as he suggested the plight of the refugees might not be as bad as was being reported. She asked, 'Which would you rather be, Sir John, a rat in a trap about to be drowned in a bucket of water or a free man living in a free country.' Stopford never forgot the look of distaste on Sir John's face at such insubordination. No one had ever spoken to him like that, especially not in front of his peers. There was no one better to fight for your cause than Eleanor Rathbone. And the Czech refugees had her in their corner.

At the first official meeting of the Parliamentary Committee on Refugees, Eleanor proposed that they should combine efforts into one organisation in Czechoslovakia to take forward, in a co-ordinated fashion, all refugee aid. With the committee approving the motion on the spot, Eleanor then turned the agenda onto who should run this new organisation. The men all looked in her direction, silently nominating her, while absolving themselves from such a task. She would be damned if she was going to take this on, along with all her commitments. But she had someone in mind.

Sir Walter Layton was a prominent British figure who had until recently served as editor of *The Economist*. He had left his post so he could stand as a Liberal Party candidate but had failed on serval occasions. With time on his hands – during which he co-authored an anti-Nazi book titled *Germany, the Last Four Years* to warn about its growing threat – Eleanor thought him ideal to head their organisation.

A tall, austere man, with a long nose, Sir Walter was always impeccably well dressed; never being caught without a finely tailored three-piece suit and gold pocket watch. His style was at odds with Eleanor, who notoriously never made any effort towards fashion. 'She never dressed, she just covered herself', one colleague mused.

Following the Munich Agreement, Sir Walter had been rapid in his response, setting up the Czech Refugee Fund in the *News Chronicle* on 3 October, 1938, asking the public for donations. The response was incredibly generous – perhaps reflecting the country's opinion of the agreement – with £7,200 being sent in on the first day alone and a total of £44,000 (nearly £1 million pounds in 2025) by the end of the month. He had been in close contact with Eleanor throughout, encouraging her to speak up in Parliament, which she did. On 1 November she stood up in the House of Commons to ask ministers what they intended to do about 'the meagreness of British help to Czechoslovakia'. Then two days later, she was back on the offensive, pushing the Czech agenda further. She did not stop that year until 24 December, when Parliament was put into Christmas Recess.

Sir Walter held Eleanor in high esteem, so was delighted to accept the position leading the newly formed British Committee for Refugees from Czechoslovakia, known simply as the BCRC. The mission statement for this organisation was to 'use the funds collected from both the British public ... to assist Sudeten Germans, Reich Germans and Austrians to leave Czech territory and reach Britain.' As his first act in role, Sir Walter travelled to Prague on 4 December. He had been there on several occasions that year, including one visit to Prague in May where he had a lengthy discussion with President Beneš before his resignation and 'acquired a detailed first-hand knowledge of Czech thinking and plans', one observer recalled.

Accompanying him that November was his eldest daughter, Margaret. Having just returned from America, where she was the editor of a magazine focused on the social work of the

Labour movement in England, the *Edinburgh Evening News* reported that 'her return coincided with the September crisis [and] within a few days she had plunged into Czech relief work'.

Born in 1911, Margaret was the apple of her father's eye. He adored her. As someone who was difficult to read – he was renowned for 'long silences in conversation, which worried his staff until they got used to them', a subordinate commented – he made no attempts to publicly suppress his love for Margaret. He recalled after her birth, 'standing round the fire ... Margaret holding mother's hand', as one of his fondest memories. Margaret would soon have six siblings to keep her company.

But her early life was not easy. Aged five, she fell ill with a tubercular leg, and had to spend the whole of 1916 in Leysin, Switzerland, to be cured. A year spent abroad did wonders for her tubercular leg, but she returned home as a fluent French speaking six-year-old who could not understand her parents' mother tongue anymore, though she soon re-learned English.

Sir Walter pined for his daughter every day she was gone. As is so often the case, temporary separation brought them closer together.

Along with her mother's feminist inspiration, she was influenced by her father's views on religion. 'You do not need a higher being to guide your morals,' he said. 'You will always know when you are doing right – your conscience will tell you.' It was in part because of this that Sir Walter asked her to accompany him to Prague. He wanted her advice. A close family friend, David Hubback, commented that 'Margaret was beginning to prove that she had inherited much of Walter's ability,' something which her father recognised. As if her intelligence and aptitude were not enough, Margaret was exceptionally beautiful, with Hubback recalling from an early age 'there were many young [men] who fell in love with Margaret' and she was not shy of their advances. Sir Walter wanted to keep Margaret busy, so to avoid her getting caught up with too many male admirers.

'Sir Walter Layton came to Prague and went round the camps with Jaksch,' Doreen wrote in her diary. She immediately got along well with Sir Walter, but in particular with his extraordinary daughter. Along with Tessa, Jean and Mary, they hosted Margaret for tea at their makeshift office in Mary's flat. The feeling of admiration was mutual. She was so impressed with Doreen, that as soon as she returned to her father, Margaret was emphatic with her praise. She was particularly liked how Doreen spoke her mind. Her father felt the same.

'Sir Walter asked me to act as their representative in Prague,' Doreen wrote excitedly the next day. He had offered her the position of heading up the Prague section of the BCRC and, although he would be the figurehead, he was handing over day to day operations from London to Margaret. Like Doreen, she was equally delighted to accept the position and happy to work in collaboration with the Quakers.

Along with Mary, Tessa and Jean in Prague, Margaret's counterpart in London would also be a woman. Bertha Bracey was born in 1893 in Birmingham, where her father worked in Cadbury's chocolate factory. According to her great-niece, 'Bertha, who worked hard and did well at school, persuaded her father that she wanted to go to Birmingham University instead of working in the factory.' He allowed it, and by 1919, Bertha lived in Vienna working at the local Quaker Centre, helping to set up clubs for young people. For the next ten years, she conducted aid work between Vienna, Nuremburg and Berlin, before taking the lead on all management of the Quaker's operations around Europe. Managing fifty-five workers – forty-eight were female, including Tessa, Joan and Mary – her remit was far more varied than Margaret, having multiple countries to look after.

Bertha agreed that her team of women in Prague would work under Doreen, in their shared desire to streamline operations. Not only did Doreen now have an official position and a team, she also had funding from Sir Walter. 'He did me the honour of giving me the *News Chronicle* fund to look after.' The pot of £44,000 already raised was growing. Although there was also government financial support, this was to primarily be a non-sectarian organisation comprised of and funded by three key areas: the Labour Party, the *News Chronicle* and the Society of Friends.

The money also allowed the BCRC to move out from working in Mary Penman's kitchen to some new offices on Voriliska Street, which they shared with the Sudeten German leadership. Doreen was now also in the same building as Wenzel each day, and she could not stop thinking about him. As soon as they begun working in such close proximity, they started a passionate love affair, spurred on by the married man's personal jeopardy. With his wife now with family in England, Doreen was able to spend most of her evenings with Wenzel in the privacy of his apartment.

At the office, Doreen now had enough budget to employ an assistant, picking a Sudeten refugee Hilde Patz, whose husband had gone to England with David Grenfell on that first transport. Recommended by Wenzel, she was a twenty-two-year-old bombshell, who worked exceptionally hard. Now comprising of Doreen, Tessa, Jean, Mary and Hilde, the team in Prague started to compile all the names of those they wanted to help, which within a matter of weeks, totalled 4,000. Their details were sent to Margaret in London, who – assisted by Bertha – started to sort through them. The list included about twenty orphaned children who were either lost, abandoned or their parents had died. Doreen provided money to the Young Women's Christian Association (YWCA) in Prague to set up a small orphanage to look after them.

It was not just the *News Chronicle* fund that the BCRC could rely on. Dozens of ad hoc ad committees all over Britain started to raise urgent funds. Other money started to come in from the Council for German Jewry who raised more than half a million pounds by 1938. The Lord Mayor's Fund raised a similar amount. The women instantly had the ability to apply for funds from multiple places to pay for transports and the welfare of the refugees. The BCRC now had an influential team behind them, not least the senior well-regarded Labour Party figure, Ewart Gladstone Culpin, who assumed the role of chairman. Culpin was a seasoned politician, who had spent nearly fifteen years as an alderman for the London County Council.

Along with his leadership team in London, the Culpin started to contact as many organisations around Prague, with the ambition of further collaboration. The response to members of the English political elite writing to offer help was received badly by many in Czechoslovakia, the sense of betrayal by the British still bubbling at the surface.

When Eleanor wrote to Alice Masaryk and Františka Plamínková, she received a very frosty and curt reply.

Dear Miss Rathborne [sic],
You ask me how you could help my country! Now it is the turn of other countries to show that they are aware of the responsibility of their international decisions.
Františka

Chapter Five

Too Steady

The women in Prague were more successful at harvesting support than their counterparts in London. With funding now available, Doreen was able to organise for further transports to start, taking more men, along with some women and children out of Czechoslovakia, through Poland and then on to England. At the end of 1938, large groups left on a weekly basis.

Now the experienced courier for the BCRC, Tessa had got her job down to a fine art. But every journey had its own challenges and the one on 14 December – where she had 100 men, women and children on the platform at 8.30 p.m. ready to leave – was no exception.

The group was all hushed as they waited patiently, scared of what lay ahead. Needing not to raise her voice, Tessa told the group, 'The train should leave for Ostrava at nine. At times we will travel close to territory controlled by Germany so please do not draw attention to yourselves.'

She had spoken too soon. As she finished, it was announced that the train was delayed by four hours, not leaving until after midnight. The passengers had to sit and wait. 'I believe two carriages had been reserved for our group which unbeknown included my future wife and her mother,' recalled fifteen-year-old Herbert Lowit, who was travelling with his mother Johanna.

When the train did finally depart, Tessa could not get the heating to work. 'By God, it was bitter,' another traveller commented. Herbert reminisced that, 'As the train steamed out of the station clenched fists appeared at every window ... accompanied by defiant anti-Nazi slogans and the unanimous chanting "we shall return".' So much for not drawing attention to themselves, Tessa thought.

The occupation of the Sudetenland meant the line between Prague and Ostrava now crossed into German-controlled territory on several occasions. What should have been a four hour journey was now greatly increased, as the train needed to divert onto regional lines rarely used by such enormous locomotives.

About an hour from Ostrava, the train entered enemy territory. Panic ensued on the carriage as one refugee saw men in German uniform ahead next to the railway line. 'Behave calmly and quietly!' Tessa hissed when a man started shouting. 'Ignore them! We are crossing occupied territory.'

It took over half an hour to get back in Czech territory, after endless rural stations and level crossings, all of which were manned by German soldiers. Finally, a passenger named Josef, about whom nothing else is known, spotted a red, white and blue flag. They were back in Czechoslovakia. 'We were safe. The most perilous forty minutes of our lives were over,' he wrote.

Tessa walked up the carriage to make another announcement. 'Soon we'll arrive in Ostrava, ... Everything will be alright, the Polish Government knows about us. But let's not ruffle any feathers,' she said, thinking about to her experience as they drew out of Prague. 'Let's keep ourselves to ourselves. They probably won't take us off the train, but if they do, just keep silent, direct any questions to me.'

An official climbed into the carriage upon arrival, saying with a smile, 'You are now in Poland,' and then jumped back down. The train growled on along the river valley, surrounded by silver-birch trees and beautiful Polish countryside. At 7 p.m. they arrived at the city of Katowice, where an elderly couple clambered into the carriage laden with an urn of hot cocoa, biscuits and cakes. Without a word, they started handing around cups of the steaming chocolate drink. 'Quakers!' Tessa said when quizzical eyes darted towards her. 'They are friends of mine, in every sense,' she joked, although it went over most people's heads, everyone too busy enjoying their first hot drink in more than twenty-four hours.

The following morning, the train headed through the Polish corridor, the sliver of land which separated Germany from East Prussia. Panic again began to fill the train. Were they really heading through Gdansk – also known as Danzig – the 'free-city' under the protection of the League of Nations, which was now predominantly Nazi?

'Gentlemen, ladies, do not worry,' Tessa tried to reassure them. 'I've already made this journey several times and passed through without interference.'

She was right. They were soon back into Poland, arriving in Gdynia where two coaches were waiting to take them to their guesthouse. The Corniche Hotel was nothing to write home about, but this was the first bed many of the group had slept in for a month. No one was able to sleep, as their peace was literally shattered by the rocks being thrown at the windows. Tessa peered out to see a small group of men chucking debris at the hotel, knowing they were within. This had not happened before, but the presence of so many refugees was conspicuous. The feeling of antisemitism was not absent in Poland.

Tessa called a meeting the following day at noon in the hotel's empty ballroom.

'You are all asking what's happening, where will you be going, how you will travel,' she summarised. 'I have some answers,' she said to great excitement.

The previous journeys from Gdynia on to England went through the German-controlled Kiel Canal. But this was now thought to be too dangerous. The last boat was interfered with by German police but was able to continue. Margaret and Tessa had been conferring all morning on the telephone and had come up with a solution.

'You will travel on a trans-Atlantic Polish liner to Copenhagen,' Tessa told her audience. Everyone's breath was now being held in. 'Then by train to Denmark's west coast, and ferry to the English port of Harwich.' Her words were followed by applause.

While speaking with Margaret, Tessa expressed her concerns for their safety in the Corniche Hotel. Their ship did not leave until the next day. The women agreed that the group should be moved to the Riviera Hotel, a larger and more expensive establishment, but the hotel of choice for the British Consul, who was currently in residency. If the yobs tried to attack them there, the police would be far more willing to step in.

The move was a success and after a restful night with no violence, at 6 p.m. the refugees were on the stunning Polsudski Liner, on its way to New York, but stopping at Copenhagen. 'We were waving "goodbye" from the deck to Miss Rowntree who returned to Prague to arrange other transports,' a passengers recollected. They were in awe of the beauty of the boat and the politeness of the staff. 'Imagine it, being addressed as human beings once again!' another passenger wrote back to his family in Prague.

Successful transports such as this were greeted with exaltation by the committee in London. But in Prague, Doreen could not supress her disappointment. *Why did it take so long for the visas to arrive?* There were thousands of people in desperate need, but she did not see any urgency towards the task.

Only 100 were leaving each week. Why not double that? Or triple? Doreen tried to plead with the London committee, writing several letters to Sir Walter Layton, including one where she said, 'You ask what Prague is like today ... it is one of the most beautiful cities I know, but two worlds. Our work with the refugees and in the other, the bands are playing. Suicides in the midst of opera and good restaurants.' But it appeared her appeals were falling on deaf ears.

Next, she took it upon herself to write a strongly worded letter to all the BCRC's honorary presidents. The great and good of British high society, including Archbishop of Canterbury the Most Reverend and Right Honourable Cosmo Lang, The Earl of Lytton and Chief Rabbi Dr. Joseph Herman Hertz. With no reply, Doreen pondered how she could get their attention, before coming up with an idea. If they would not listen to her in private, perhaps they would do so in public. Updating it slightly, she sent the letter on to newspapers.

Daily Telegraph, 14 December, 1938
Sir – I want to call the attention of your readers to the urgency of the refugee situation here in Czechoslovakia.

The real tragedy is the position of the Sudeten German Social Democrats numbering about 4,000. They have had eight weeks of semi-starvation and neglect, and despair of any improvement. Since the option decision they cannot hope for employment here.

No Sudeten German remains in the camps except those who cannot return to Germany without risking their lives. But they begin to ask whether it would not be better to return even so.

Arrangements for direct relief to the camps through the Lord Mayor's Fund have been carried through with the maximum of inefficiency and delay.

Everywhere the situation is the same. All the camps I have seen are appallingly overcrowded, few have any coal and in a certain number the people are suffering from starvation, through the action of the local authorities who are economizing on the food allowance.

The only way of helping these people is to find wider collective possibilities of emigration. Any other way is a palliative for one's own conscience only. In the last few days I have received several offers of cigarettes and chocolates for Christmas, including one from the Peace Pledge Union, which indicates that there is some confusion in Great Britain about the real state of affairs.

These men fought a losing fight against Nazi-ism for five years; in the crisis, in conditions of great danger, they remained true to their principles; and for the last two months they have endured organised neglect, persecutions and complete lack of hope in the future.

Thus, as refugees they are in a special category, and the arrangements for emigration must be reconsidered.

First, it is essential to abolish the present visa scandal. The people who came to me to ask for visas are all relatively well-to-do middle-class folk who think that by exerting influence they can get to England, and in fact this is perfectly true. In several cases English people with the best intentions have assisted fraudulent attempts.

But the men in the camps do not know these methods and have no connections with England. The only just and practical way for organising emigration is to grant block visas for a definite number, and then to send representatives of the Dominions to select the most suitable people for definite jobs. Organisation through charities inevitably leads to abuses of the present kind.

Secondly funds to assist overseas settlement are needed. There are only about 2,000 families to consider, and from the financial standpoint the problem is not a large one.

Once the right organisation is found, and sufficient financial resources are available, the problem can be

easily solved. From the standpoint of the labour market these men are invaluable, and the Dominion's representatives are well aware of their quality. But unless a decision can soon be made, the opportunity will be lost.
Yours,
Doreen Warriner
Prague Representative, British Committee for Refugees from Czechoslovakia.

The next morning BCRC chairman Ewart Culpin was flicking through the newspapers in his plush breakfast room when he read Doreen's letter. Coffee spluttered from his mouth. His committee was reliant on the goodwill of the public to provide donations and the Government for their visa allocation. A letter publicly attacking these groups so viciously could shut the entire organisation down. And how dare this woman leak a private letter to the press. What side did she think she was on? He called an urgent meeting of the BCRC in London and then dashed off a telegram to Prague:

LETTER IN DAILY TELEGRAPH HAS MADE GREAT DIFFICULTIES STOP YOU MUST REFRAIN FROM ANY SUCH PRONOUNCEMENTS STOP CULPIN

After agreeing damage limitation with the committee – which included a plan to take the Lord Mayor of London Major Sir Frank Henry Bowater out for an expensive lunch – Culpin moved on to what to do with their Prague representative. Minutes from the subsequent meeting show serious consideration was given to the sacking of Doreen, who had only just been officially appointed, and replacing her with Tessa. But two factors put a stop to this. One was that Tessa was not seen to have the same leadership abilities as Doreen, and secondly,

Eleanor jumped to her defence. And no one dared argue with that. It is not known why she stuck up for Doreen in the way she did, but it helped no end.

Margaret wrote to Doreen after the emergency meeting: 'Your letter did put the cat among the pigeons! In one way it was very needed. But unfortunately, [our] chairman, Culpin thinks that our representative doesn't know her place.' She suggested she come to England urgently to talk through her concerns with the committee directly.

Just before Christmas 1938, Doreen was back in London. Her evening flight was followed by a meeting with the BCRC chairman. She wrote in her diary: 'Evening ticked off by Layton and Culpin.' But despite her dressing down, she had hung onto her job, returning to Prague on Christmas Eve.

*

It is easy to underestimate the importance of momentum. Sometimes, the smallest of things can create impetus. And as the world welcomed the start of 1939, Doreen and her team felt an almighty shift in momentum in Prague. An optimism, an energy that she had not felt before. There were three causes for this sudden improved feeling. Firstly, the BCRC was up and running, they had an effective team of women and most importantly, people were being taken out of Czechoslovakia to safety.

Secondly, the arrival of two men – Nicholas Winton and Martin Blake – had added a new section to their structure. That sick feeling that Doreen had at the pit of her stomach every night as she got ready for bed with Wenzel, worrying about the abandoned children who she was now funding their care with the YWCA was starting to ease, albeit slightly. 'Winton is doing splendid work for the children!' she happily reported back to Margaret on 12 January.

Under Doreen's leadership, Winton was able to take advantage of a movement sweeping across Europe, which was closely connected to several of the women in the BCRC. While leading the Quaker's relief, Bertha Bracey had met Wilfrid Israel, a homosexual businessman described in his obituary in *The Times* as having 'a prominent position among the Jews of Berlin, who had devoted [himself] to the plight of Jewish children from Nazi hands'. On 21 November, 1938, Bertha and many dignitaries met with British Home Secretary Samuel Hoare to discuss a possible scheme. According to the minutes from the gathering, the delegation asked for 'facilitated entry for all children whose maintenance could be guaranteed either through their own funds or by other individuals'.

Along with Bertha in the delegation was Eleanor Rathbone, whose tireless campaigning had enabled the deputation to lobby Hoare in the first place. She pleaded with him to 'consider very substantially increasing the number of [visas] to enable more of the estimated several thousands of children in danger [to] come to Britain'. The meeting proved successful, and off the back of this the British Government gave their approval for Kindertransport. Hoare stated that following a discussion, 'I believe that we could find homes in this country for a large number [of children] without any harm to our own population.'

As soon as this announcement was made, Bertha, dashed off urgent letters to the 'Inter-Aid Committee' and the 'Movement for the Care of Children from Germany and Austria' to understand whether they would be able to support the BCRC. The response was positive and she wrote to Doreen on 17 December, 1938 that these committees had 'agreed to take over German and Austrian children from Czechoslovakia'. Doreen gave Nicholas Winton responsibility for looking after the operation. He was joined by Trevor Chadwick who took over running the children's section in Prague, while Winton carried on from London.

Thirdly and very significantly, the shift in momentum was due to a change in the British government's attitude towards the plight of those trapped in Prague. 'The refugees ceased to be objects of charity and became emigrants,' Doreen explained. This change in opinion was in no small part due to the British offer that 5,000 Sudeten and Jewish refugees could receive £200 each, with the loose condition that the money was 'to cover the cost of transport and settlement'. This was different to the British loan, which was primarily used for resettlement within the Czech borders.

As if out of nowhere, there was an immediate desire from all corners of Britain to start accepting these displaced people. The need for money against dire economic backdrop made the prospect rather appealing.

Yet, despite the positivity this news was received with in Prague, weeks went by and still no word came from London as to the mechanics of how the BCRC could use this money. Margaret Layton was on the receiving end of Doreen's wrath, as she complained bitterly and aggressively about the delay. The lack of progress was only partly the reason for her frustration.

Doreen's feeling of lust towards Wenzel – which started from that visit to the camps – and was now being reciprocated, caused her no end of hassle. She longed for more than just an affair, she wanted to marry him. But with his wife in England, he made no suggestion that was a possibility.

'We would have a child and I would remain to bring it up. We'd go back to the Sudetenland together,' she wrote wistfully. This was never going to become a reality. She was in love with a married man. And this married man was in such danger, she could do nothing but worry about him.

So, her irritation towards poor Margaret was amplified by her complicated love life.

When Eleanor got wind of Doreen's complaining, she was

furious. She had defended the Prague representative so vehemently – saving her job, in fact – and here she was grumbling again. Eleanor flew straight to Prague on 14 January to speak with her directly. Doreen described the politician arriving 'with that splendid energy and determination to get to the truth'. Having made the journey to put Doreen back in her place, Eleanor quickly found herself agreeing entirely. 'Miss Warriner is extremely competent, and indefatigable worker,' she wrote to Margaret after her first day in Czechoslovakia. She provided some mitigating context to Doreen's attitude, adding, 'She is though very overtired.' The constant bureaucracy in Britain was costing lives. Doreen said, 'Unlike so many who came out to Prague, [Eleanor] did realise that there was no hope for the refugees if they remain.' For the first time, Doreen felt listened to.

Eleanor wanted to see the true condition in Prague, so over her six days stay, she visited ten refugee camps, requesting nothing be hidden from her. Various relief workers would escort her, including Nicholas Winton who was responsible for showing her Dolní Krupá. He was given specific instructions by Margaret Layton to watch over the politician carefully as she was notoriously forgetful and would often misplace her belongings wherever she went. This was evident in a recent trip she had made to Bucharest where she lost her coat and umbrella within minutes of arriving in the city, according to a colleague who accompanied her. Margaret was often sweeping up Eleanor's left-behind belongings from their committee meetings in London.

Winton's visit to the camp did not go particularly well. After only a few minutes, he had been so focused on Eleanor, he almost immediately lost the other man he was also showing around. He continued the tour with Eleanor alone and not until an hour later did they find the missing dignitary sitting alone, head in hands, crying like a baby. Despite being a very typically British stiff-upper-lipped gentleman of the time, who had witnessed his fair share of atrocities during World War I, the suffering in the camp was too much for him. Winton decided that they had seen their fair share, so suggested they withdraw. He quickly had to return to retrieve Eleanor's handbag, which had strayed from her grasp, before retreating for a second time.

Eleanor was shaken by the state of all the camps she saw, but in particular Dolní Krupá – the camp where the previous year Doreen had watched in awe as Wenzel had given an impassioned speech – which she found unbearable. The insanitary and rat-ridden castle had claimed the lives of four children, who died of diphtheria before Christmas.

'It is a living grave,' a doctor told her.

Following her visit, Eleanor returned to London with a simple message. There were no more than six weeks left until the refugees would start to perish in vast numbers due to the conditions of the camps.

The absolute maximum she believed the BCRC could get out per week was 200, but that would be double what they had achieved up to that point. Nowhere close to enough. So she wrote to the Prime Minister, fellow members of parliament and officials from the Home and Foreign Offices asking to secure 2,000 visas with immediate effect. She did not mince her words:

> *Remember what we owe these refugees. They are the greatest sufferers from the Agreement which Mr Chamberlain made with Herr Hitler at Munich. They are not the ordinary type of destitute alien, but men and women whose only offence is that they have been leaders in their own districts in standing up against Nazi doc-*

trines. There is reason to believe that unless they are got out quickly, perhaps within the next fortnight or so, it may be too late.

Despite being someone who could usually get her way, Eleanor saw another week slip by with no action, which to her meant 200 lives might have been lost because of another delay. Why were the Government not issuing more visas? The truth was that the mechanisms of the authorities were not designed for speed.

At last, on 24 January, Doreen received the call she had been longing for. 'A large move-out will be made soon,' Margaret told her over the phone.

Smaller transports could start from the following day. Finally, thought Doreen.

The BCRC office in Prague had not been sitting idly while the time slipped away. They had hundreds of refugees on standby to leave at a minute's notice. The next day, the first group of twenty refugees left on a KLM plane, flying straight to Britain. Three more planes followed in the same number of days, taking the total people evacuated to 500. An incredible achievement in many people's eyes, but not for Doreen.

She felt it was all too small. How did people not understand the urgency? 'In Prague we lived on tenterhooks,' she moaned. 'But London were detached and calm ... it was impossible to get through the cotton wool which prevented them from hearing.'

It was understandable that those in England were struggling to grasp the situation around Europe given all the false optimism they were being fed. By the start of February, Neville Chamberlain felt 'a general sense of greater brightness in the atmosphere ... all the information I get seems to point in the direction of peace'. It was astonishing that a world leader with the amount of intelligence he was privy to was so misled by the situation. Little wonder that so many believed Europe to be in a better state than it actually was. Robert Stopford's view was that, 'In spite of Miss Warriner's and my efforts, London seemed unable to realise the imminence of the danger [so] no new permits were coming through.'

Doreen was fed up. So, she took matters into her own hands. 'I decided that I would go to London and try to hurry up the visas,' she recorded in her diary. She dashed off a telegram to Margaret in London:

> RETURNING SUNDAY STOP ESSENTIAL DISCUSS NEW DEVELOPMENTS STOP PLEASE RESERVE PLANE TICKET STOP

On 29 January, she flew back to Britain, to be received with some chagrin from her colleagues, particularly Margaret who was distinctly put out at her impromptu visit. Attending her first committee meeting, Doreen was shocked by 'how little of the true danger they had grasped'. She had asked Eleanor to provide some reflections on her recent visit to Czechoslovakia. 'No one I saw in Prague,' the veteran MP told the committee, 'shares the optimistic views that I hear expressed in London.' Despite being an unwanted entity around the table, Doreen's presence had the desired effect, for unexpectedly, the following day, the Home Office approved the first mass list of 600 visas. Upon hearing of her success, Robert Stopford was impressed with Doreen's persuasion skills. 'She argued valiantly to make the plight of the refugees known in England,' he wrote.

With that task complete, Doreen spent the next couple of days in London going around the offices of the different departments the BCRC were reliant on. She was determined to streamline the process as best as she could. Time at the Home Office bred a new system whereby all documents would be sent to Prague by air, to avoid the inevitable delay of standard post. It meant that the BCRC would be able to get visas approved in a couple of days, rather than several weeks.

On 2 February, Doreen flew back to Czechoslovakia, having accomplished all she had set out to. She had a new process arranged and crucially, the visas agreed for 600 people. The moment she arrived back to her office that evening, she announced to Hilde, Tessa, Jean and Mary, 'Now let's start work,' and they did.

With 600 visas approved, Doreen wanted them all to travel together, at one time, on the same train. This would hopefully reduce the amount of administration, but more importantly, work as a trial for a much larger operation. She wanted to evacuate thousands, not hundreds. Doreen earmarked the train leaving at 11 p.m. on 15 February. They had under two weeks and the clock had already started to tick. Working from 8 a.m. each day until the early hours of the following morning, the women laboured tirelessly. Visas would arrive from London by the plane load, which would be assigned to passports, taken to the various Legations for stamps and finally reunited with their owners.

By 10 p.m. on 15 February, Tessa boarded their train at Wilson Station, along with the 500 men, women and children. They had not been able to secure the places for the remaining 100 visas, but these families would follow in a few weeks. Unbeknown to Tessa, several of her passengers were travelling on forged documents, hidden among the genuine ones, thanks to Doreen.

As had become tradition, Doreen, Hilde, Jean and Margaret stood on the platform with family and friends not lucky enough to have been on that train, waving these people to safety. 'February was wonderful,' Doreen remarked happily. Robert Stopford had been invited to witness the event and was so impressed that he scribbled a note as soon as he got back to his hotel to the BCRC in London, saying that, 'Doreen Warriner has laboured valiantly to achieve this.'

Chapter Six

American Contingent

Back in London, Margaret Layton was still struggling to keep the enthusiasm for the mass emigrations to continue. The general opinion, she felt, was that the situation in Europe which she knew to be desperate and escalating was actually improving. Fortunately, the train of 500 had already left Prague when, from Downing Street, Neville Chamberlain briefed news reporters that, 'The foreign situation is less anxious and gives me less concern for possible unpleasant developments than it has done for some time.' An unbelievably guileless statement to make given the situation around Europe, particularly in Czechoslovakia.

The 1,000 people who had been evacuated from Prague by the BCRC and the tens of thousands all desperately trying to escape would take another view. This included a second group of 100 refugees who departed from Prague on the evening of 24 February, taking the total who had left to 1,100. Tessa could not help but notice as she was boarding the train that on the opposite platform a group of well-dressed men, all wearing suits, smart overcoats and hats had assembled. Their casual demeanour quickly turned formal when an approaching train made its presence known. Standing now as if to attention, Tessa saw the men fall silent as the train – the luxurious Orient Express – drew to a halt. Out of the first-class carriage emerged a well-attired handsome tall man, with neatly combed blonde hair and incredibly broad shoulders. He was holding the hand of a small woman, equally as elegantly dressed, who Tessa assumed was his wife. One member of the welcome party leapt forward with a large bouquet of red, white and blue flowers, presenting them to the grateful woman with an exaggerated bow.

The colours were picked deliberately, for these two dignitaries were thirty-seven-year-old Waitstill and thirty-three-year-old Martha Sharp, who had travelled to Prague from America. Waitstill recalled that, as he stepped from the platform and noticed the contrast between the magnificent sleeper he had been on and Tessa's train on the other platform, 'The air was full of sorrow, disillusion and foreboding.' As a Minister in the Unitarian Church, Waitstill had been chosen to lead the religious organisation's relief efforts to the refugee crisis in Czechoslovakia. Named the Commission for Service in Czechoslovakia of the American Unitarian Association, their mission was to provide assistance with $13,000 ($300,000 in 2025) of their funds. Learning of their journey, Waitstill had been asked to also represent the American Committee for Relief in Czechoslovakia, known as Amrelczech, who gave him an additional $30,000 ($700,000 in 2025) to also spend. As Waitstill was being accompanied by his wife, they had left their eight-year-old and three-year-old children in America under the care of Martha's Aunt Edna.

The Unitarian Church had sent their director of the Department of Social Relations Robert Dexter to assess the impact of the Munich Agreement in November 1938. 'The situation in Czechoslovakia was critical,' he reported on 16 November upon his return. He estimated that, 'A quarter-million refugees from Germany, Austria and the Sudeten region had already poured into what was left of the country.'

The church decided they would take action. The funds were allocated, but who to send to carry out the task of coordinating the aid? It fell to Everett Baker, vice president of the church, to decide. 'We had deliberated at length over whom [to] send to Czechoslovakia,' Baker reflected. This was a task for missionaries, and tradition was that a husband and wife would take on the role.

There were many candidates for the job. And Baker saw all of them, in order of preference. But each turned it down, until they got to the final names on the list, Waitstill and Martha Sharp. He told them as such when they met to discuss the assignment.

'Do I understand from you that I am the eighteenth choice?' Waitstill asked, as they sat in Baker's living room after dinner with a glass of port. He was understandably slightly miffed at falling so low on the pecking order.

'Yes,' replied Baker, without any hesitation or explanation.

Waitstill and Martha shared a look. 'Why did they turn you down?' he asked, referring to the seventeen who had presumably sat in the same room before him.

'They didn't want to break up their families,' he replied, before adding matter-of-factly, 'They also think a war is definitely coming and don't want to be in danger.'

As he waved the Sharps off, who had had promised to think about it, Baker was certain they would be added to the list rejecting the assignment.

Waitstill seemed more enthusiastic than his wife. Martha had their two young children to think about. And this was not just leaving them for short a period of time. She was heading into a potential war zone for at least six months. But her mind kept creeping back to the report Robert Dexter had submitted. 'Refugees in the Sudetenland had been murdered; people were being imprisoned and hurt,' it read. 'I was torn between my love and duty,' she said. After much deliberation, the couple decided they would go. The choice was met with much criticism locally.

'A lot of people thought Martha was out of hand and irresponsible not to stay home and take care of her children,' one of their contemporaries said. Martha worried that she would receive the same reaction in Prague, especially as she assumed that everyone involved in the aid work would be white middle-aged men, who believed a woman's place was at home.

*

Along with their secretary, Virginia Waistcoat, the American contingent was shepherded out of Wilson Station into a waiting black car, where another welcome party stood.

'Brother Sharp, Mrs Sharp,' one of the men said. 'You've come to a nation in crisis. We are very glad and relieved to see you here.'

'Thank you,' replied Waitstill, then asked, 'What is the meaning of that very unusual train two platforms over? Who were all those people?'

The group looked at each other, hoping someone might have the answer.

'They were Social Democrats, fleeing the Sudetenland,' another man said, proud to have realised Waitstill was referring to the Tessa's transport.

'Where are they going?'

'London, if they can get through ... And somebody is taking it upon themselves to convoy them,' he added. Whistles blew, and the train started to pull away from the station.

The Sharps were driven in the opposite direction to the four-story Hotel Atlantic on Na Porici Street. Their large consignment of luggage followed behind in a small truck. Not sure what to bring, Martha had overpacked with all types of items, including hot water bottles, thick knitted jumpers, woollen underwear and a huge American flag which had once been raised over a battlefield during World War I.

Their hotel was not quite to same standard as the Alcron Hotel, in which Doreen was now living. Martha was frustrated by 'woefully inadequate single rooms', in which they needed to try and unpack everything that had travelled with them. Virginia ended up with a stack of trunks against the wall in her even smaller room.

For their first evening, they were treated to a banquet in the hotel restaurant, hosted by the many dignitaries who had met them at the station. Martha was seated next to Jaroslav Podhajsky Czech Commissioner for Refugees. A man of huge influence and possibly the trickiest job in Prague, he had become distracted in the last month, having fallen head over heels in love with Doreen. Not knowing that she was involved in a secret relationship with Wenzel, who she was besotted with, much of Jaroslav's time was spent in the BCRC offices. Officially his job was to ease the refugee crisis with the help of the BCRC, but he devoted much of his time to attempts at courting its leader.

Jaroslav shocked and impressed Martha in equal measures. He would start with a depressing prognostication, such as: 'The situation is worsening by the day. There will soon be concentration camps for refugees and others,' Then he would follow it with an expression of optimism inspired by the successes of the BCRC's evacuations to date. This went on all through dinner.

Czech cuisine came as a surprise to the Sharps. America had not felt the impact on supply chains in the same way many countries in Europe were experiencing. Imported or luxury goods such as chocolate and tropical fruits were among the foodstuffs that were becoming increasing scarce in Prague. But in particular, spices were no longer being imported and stocks were running low. This led the chefs across the city needing to be more inventive when flavouring their meals. 'We were surprised by caraway seeds on the bread, in the soup, the meat and gravy, the dumplings, and the desert,' Martha reflected bemusedly.

The foreign meal was a sudden reminder of how far she was from America. 'The surroundings intensified my feeling of home,' she wrote in her diary that evening. 'I tried [to] picture what the children were doing.'

Sitting on their bed in the hotel room after dinner, Martha broke down in tears.

'Tired? Homesick?' Waitstill asked, coming in from the bathroom. 'It will all be over before you know it,' he said.

'I miss the children so much,' she sobbed.

Sitting next to her on the bed, he put his arm around her. She snuggled into him.

'That's natural,' he told her. 'But we can't dwell on it. Come, let's go to bed. We'll have to be up early.'

And they were. Their first full day was spent being shown around Prague, being introduced to the many influential people in the city, all wanting their support. One of their first meetings was with Robert Stopford. A man who knew the political situation better than most, he was ideal in providing a holistic and unbiased opinion.

Waitstill fired questions at him, as if he were interviewing the man.

'What was the makeup of the camps?'

'Most of the German refugees had been anti-Nazi,' Stopford replied.

He scribbled intensely in his notebook, before posing the next question. 'Who was the most vulnerable?'

'The Jews in Czechoslovakia itself appeared to be in greatest danger.'

'How many Jews are there?'

'The census figure for racial Jews in the remaining territory was about 150,000, but Jewish sources tell me that the number was really nearer 250,000,' he answered.

And the questioning went on.

Thanks to their nationality and status, the Sharps were immediately able to infiltrate a Czech social circle which had previously been closed to the likes of Doreen. That morning, the couple were invited to join the official government's coordinating committee which met each Monday in the office of Dr Kotek, the official in charge of emigration at the Ministry of Social Welfare. They had a seat at the top table of power within only a few hours in Prague. Waitstill carried within his jacket pocket an array of letters from influential people, most prominently a signed memo from US Secretary of State, Cordell Hull, asking for anyone who read it to offer their utmost to support to the Sharps.

This worked well. Whereas the BCRC had only just managed to secure official office space, having worked out of Mary's apartment, the Sharps were offered a suite of rooms in the Ministry of Health Building. Martha now had a desk, while her husband occupied a private room within the office. Behind his desk, Martha hung the American flag she had brought next to the Czech one.

Virigina Waistcoat typed a sign for the front door, with the title of American Relief. It had the schedule any visitor should expect; apart from an hour for lunch, they were open for business from 8 a.m. to 6 p.m., with reduced hours on the weekend.

As the leader, Waitstill planned to focus their efforts on the living conditions of the refugees with a new radical approach. His intention was to find work for displaced people, for on that first day alone, he discovered a need for 200 iron workers and fifty seamstresses in Prague during their tour. Employing refugees would be an ideal solution for the shortage of skills in and around the capital, while providing much needed money to those who had fled from the Sudetenland. He even planned to hire from among them carpenters, plasterers, plumbers and painters to work on renovating old buildings into homes for the refugees.

He would use funds he had brought from America to pay for

this, along with hiring from the refugees' numbers administrators, doctors, nurses, teachers, cooks and gardeners to the new communities. With other representatives of the Czech government, they 'hoped to be able to absorb 100,000 skilled workers,' Martha recalled. This was a bold number by anyone's standard but their first day flew past with so much achieved in a remarkably short time that it felt possible.

However it would not all be plain sailing. 'This was the end of the honeymoon,' Waitstill wrote that evening.

On their second day, Martha was invited to meet with the BCRC. Despite only having been in their new headquarters for a matter of weeks, Doreen's private office already had papers spread across every conceivable surface, while the walls were covered top to bottom in bookshelves, all lined with thick, dark red leatherbound books. Gesturing to a chair facing her desk, Martha needed to move the stack of papers covering the seat before making enough room to be able to uncomfortably perch among the chaos.

She was completely taken by Doreen's argument that the only way to save people was to allow them to leave. On top of this, the BCRC had large transports leaving each week and Waitstill's solution would only prove effective if Czechoslovakia was never invaded, and that she was told was an inevitability. 'People would have to be helped to emigrate,' she concluded.

Doreen had been equally impressed with Martha. The American appeared to instantly grasp the situation, something she felt her colleagues in London were still unable to do. Martha had asked all the burning question that were eating up Doreen.

As she walked out of the BCRC offices onto the street just before noon, Martha noticed a man in a coat and hat reading a magazine leaning on the lamppost. She realised with a shudder that the same man had been in the same spot in the same position when she arrived three hours earlier. This, she later discovered, was part of a large surveillance operation carried out by the Nazis. From that moment, like Doreen, she was followed constantly.

Later that week, Waitstill and Martha were driven around the countryside in an official car flying the flags of the National Czech Church and the Republic on each side of the bonnet. They spent time with Alice Masaryk, whose brother Jan was a friend of the Sharps. Martha had not met Alice before, but she was instantly impressed by her, saying, 'She was a self-effacing, pious, kind and devoted daughter.' Having been sentenced to death in Austria for treason, Alice had been imprisoned for nine months before being released. This had severely impacted her health, but as Martha witnessed, she approached the task of running the Red Cross with admirable energy. She was a high priority for the Nazis, who were threatened by the devotion the Czech people had for her. They had launched a propaganda campaign against her, accusing her of stealing funds intended for the Red Cross, but this had done little to dent her popularity.

Alice was now constantly being tailed by German agents, who knew enough to send a report back to Berlin linking Masaryk with the Sharps and the BCRC. This only intensified their intelligence operation.

Over the next week, Martha started to notice that Prague was increasingly full of Gestapo agents. Noticeable from their poor disguise of a leather shiny jacket, back gloves and hat pulled down in front of their eyes, they could often be found lingering in the hotel reception pretending to read the same out-of-date newspaper all day. It got to the point when the Sharp's hotel room was, without warning, redecorated one morning. They returned to find everything out of place, papers re-ordered after reading, books fanned for secret documents and most upsetting, both of their diaries had been opened. Infuriatingly, the chemical smell of fresh paint made it nauseating to be in the room and it was too cold outside to keep the windows open.

From that day, Martha was savvier with her work in Prague. Doreen put her in touch with a Czech woman who would help her adapt. She asked Martha: 'Do you know how to keep notes so that if found by hostile persons they cannot be understood?'

'No,' she replied. 'I have never heard of it!'

'Would you like a few pointers?' the woman asked, before giving her several memo-taking techniques that mean the notes cannot be deciphered.

Her new skills worked so well that when Waitstill wanted to find the contact details of one Czech official they had met to include in his first report to send back to America, he thought Martha was writing in a different language. She was able to translate for him and he sent a sobering account of their first week in Czechoslovakia:

> *The situation is serious here both for the Jews and the life of the state ... [people] are coming to us, begging for help in escaping to America. They will starve or commit suicide if some large-scale plan of emigration is not worked out.*

After several more meetings together, Doreen and Martha had built a strong working relationship. The American suggested that both their organisations should join forces, helping people leave Prague for England, and then potentially onwards from there. Martha wrote to Margaret Layton in London, who agreed to come to the Prague for the first few days of March to discuss.

A true unsung hero of the operation, Margaret spent most of her time glued to a desk in London, putting out metaphorical fires from her team in Czechoslovakia, government officials, families lobbying her for their loved ones to be prioritised, while always being answerable to the mostly male committee leaders. All the time, she was supposed to be planning her imminent nuptials. She needed no additional motivation, but what she saw in Prague was sobering. Trying to imagine the extent of suffering without witnessing it first hand was impossible. She now knew why Eleanor fought so passionately in their meetings. Most of all, Margaret witnessed the feeling of utter despair from the city's residents at not knowing what was happening around Europe. They knew not how much time was left before the inevitable Nazi invasion.

The official news coming from Slovakia was so contradictory that not only could it not be trusted, but it was impossible to follow. When Doreen, Martha and Margaret compared notes from their respective sources, everything was confused. Some reports said it had been occupied by the Nazis, others that it remained free. To try to gander more information, Tessa agreed that she would travel to Slovakia's capital, Bratislava to find out more.

Margaret therefore took responsibility as courier for the next group of 120 refugees, guiding them safely through Poland and on to England. Meanwhile, Tessa made her way to Bratislava. Arriving on the evening of Friday 10 March, she found it in what she assumed was an unusual state. She had expected to see Nazi soldiers parading through the centre, with swastikas flying from every corner. Instead, the streets were relatively deserted, but it looked as if a tornado had crossed the city, but only affecting certain buildings. Next to a perfectly normal looking shop would be one with its windows smashed, everything inside ransacked and graffiti across the walls. Then the next shop along would be completely untouched. This, she soon learned, was the aftermath of a targeted attack on Jewish businesses, properties and people.

As the evening turned to night, the noise outside her hotel started to intensify. Peering through her window she could see a mob of men whose protests were becoming more passionate.

'I'm in a strange hotel, in a strange place, hearing strange noises,' she said to Doreen on the telephone, before having to dive onto the floor as a flurry of rocks smashed through her window, thrown from the rioters below. 'My impression of Bratislava reminds me of my visit to Vienna,' she told Doreen as she heard giddy laughter from the mob outside. 'The few happy folk could not possibly make up for all the suffering ones,' she concluded, before hanging up. Having crawled into the bathroom, she clambered into the bath and sheltered for the whole night, scared, uncomfortable and freezing cold. She did not dare emerge until it was light the next morning, on Saturday 11 March.

Chapter Seven

Invasion

Monday 13 March, 1939
8 a.m. Berlin – 46 hours until the German invasion of Czechoslovakia
The official black car sped through the chilly spring streets of Berlin, the impatient young soldier at the wheel unconcerned about the plump priest being thrown around on the back seat. The passenger wore the usual attire of a man in his position: black shirt and trousers, white clerical collar and a thick double-breasted overcoat. But this priest was not on his way to carry out Holy Orders. This was Father Jozef Gašpar Tiso, Prime Minister of Slovakia, a country now under the ultimate control of the Czech government, an arrangement Tiso wanted to end. Since the Munich Agreement, he had taken advantage of the annexation of the Sudetenland by attempting to make Slovakia its own independent state. He was now on his way to meet with the only man he felt could make his vision a reality – the leader of the Third Reich – and to ask for his assistance.

For Hitler, Slovakia was strategically key to the expansion of his empire as it underpinned both Poland and Czechoslovakia, so was only too happy to assist.

9 a.m. Hotel Alcron, Prague – 45 hours until the invasion
News of Tiso's upcoming secret meeting with Hitler filtered to Doreen from MI6 operative Harold Gibson. Precise information about intentions and outcomes was lacking, but there were rumours that the Slovakians would make a deal with

Hitler to avoid military aggression. This scenario would mean Czechoslovakia was surrounded by the Nazis from all sides, except to the north where it bordered Poland.

Doreen was beside herself with worry. 'Situation very uncertain. Committee should prepare emergency plan,' she dashed off by telegram to London as soon as she heard the news.

Her primary concern was for the wives and children of the hundreds of men she had sent to Britain in those first transports. Unwittingly, Doreen had put their already vulnerable families in unimaginable danger. It was assumed that once controlled by the Third Reich, no residents would be allowed to leave. Doreen was right to panic – she was now in a race against time to get them out.

The Prague morning was bitterly cold and the rumour mill was turning non-stop, with stories of the Nazis arriving any minute rattling around everyone's households, even though the newspapers and wirelesses had ceased reporting it. Robert Stopford described the atmosphere as 'tense and sultry, like the ominous pause just before a thunderstorm'. Many people believed it was normal for the Germans to cease their propaganda in the immediate lead up to an invasion, and that was now happening in Czechoslovakia.

12 p.m. Café Slavia, Prague – 42 hours before the invasion
Doreen Warriner's lunch appointment with Robert Stopford had taken on new importance, as Doreen felt a man as well informed as he was would only improve her understanding of the situation.

Over their meal, she told him the news she had received from Tessa in Bratislava, while Stopford explained what he was hearing from the government in London. The pair discussed the possibility of arranging another mass evacuation, this time for all the remaining women and children who had been left behind after the men had departed.

Doreen asked if all 700 could go at once.

Stopford looked sheepishly at the floor, before dropping a hushed bombshell. 'It may be impossible to get all the women and children away,' he said apologetically.

His worry stemmed from the widely held belief that when the Polish Government found out about the escalating situation in Slovakia, they would quickly and completely shut their borders in anticipation of the takeover of their neighbour, Czechoslovakia. A key escape route would thus be blocked.

Doreen was stunned. Placing her knife and fork down on the table, she got up from their meal and rushed out of the restaurant without another word, leaving Stopford to pick up the bill.

2 p.m. Polish Legation, Prague – 40 hours before the invasion
Doreen hurried straight to the Polish Legation, for she felt they *must* be able to provide a mass permit for the 700 to just travel through Poland. Trying to organise them one by one, as had been done with the first groups, would take a matter of weeks, time they simply did not have.

As soon as she arrived, heated conversations erupted between Doreen and the officials at the Legation. After initially refusing outright to her request, they eventually agreed to a compromise. The Polish Government would give a single stamp of approval to cover all 700, but only once they had physically seen that the British had issued all the visas individually.

3 p.m. British Legation, Prague – 39 hours prior to the invasion
Next for Doreen was a meeting with Harold Gibson, which Robert Stopford also attended. It was a success. Gibson was happy to approve a collective British visa, as long as he got word from London.

Wasting no time, she immediately telephoned the BCRC in London but got no answer. *Had they not seen her telegram?*

Subsequently, she tried William Gillies, who picked up straight away and listened intently.

'Put all the women and children on a train at once,' he instructed, saying to pass the phone over to Gibson. Doreen and Stopford eavesdropped in silence as Gibson listened to the politician's confirmation that he should approve a mass visa as soon as Gillies telegrammed confirmation from London. Gillies told Gibson not to worry, he would get it sorted in time.

Handing the phone back to Doreen, she suggested a departure date of Wednesday 15 March, just two days away.

'No, tomorrow!' Gillies barked down the phone, before hanging up.

6 p.m. BCRC Offices, Prague – 36 hours until the invasion
Doreen rang Hilde Patz and asked her to come to the office urgently. Despite the time, she needed as much help from her secretary as possible to arrange the train for the following day. The women were desperately sending out telegrams to the various refugee camps. Some of these temporary homes were over ten hours from Prague by train, meaning they would have a very tight window to take what seemed likely to be their last chance of escape.

Tuesday 14 March, 1939
6 a.m. BCRC Offices, Prague – 24 hours until the invasion
A few hours earlier, Doreen had insisted that Hilde return to her hostel for some rest. But Doreen herself had stayed all night, and was now sitting at her desk alone, watching out of the window as the city around her started to emerge from darkness. Her desk was covered with papers, empty coffee cups and brimming ashtrays. The stress she felt was immense. 'The strain of waiting for news of the approval from home on that day I shall never forget,' she later remembered.

7 a.m. Ruzyně Airport, Prague – 23 hours until the invasion
Exhausted, but having at least had some sleep the previous night, Martha was starting the bus journey from the airport back to the city. She had had the pleasure of seeing off Trevor Chadwick – the man who had taken over running the children's section of the BCRC in Prague when Nicholas Winton returned to London – in a small plane, along with twenty unaccompanied children, as they made their way to Britain.

The plane had been cancelled the day before because of the terrible weather. That morning was only slightly better, but the pilot agreed to fly them, although it would be a bumpy ride. 'The children were all cheerfully sick,' Trevor remembered as the plane took off.

Just before he boarded, Martha had been standing with a throng of sobbing parents who were watching their children leave, perhaps never to see them again. Lost in the scene, she started to weep herself. As a parent away from her own children, she was sharing in their sadness, when suddenly Trevor Chadwick was besides her, his arm on her back in comfort. He pulled her in for a hug, which was unusual behaviour on his part. She quickly realised he was passing her a message. 'Chadwick secretly pointed out a woman Gestapo agent he recognised and told me to watch out.'

To her horror, after the plane left and the bereft families slowly shuffled onto the bus, so did the Gestapo agent. She was following them.

10 a.m. BCRC Offices, Prague – 20 hours until the invasion
The office was now a hive of activity, with Doreen, Jean, Tessa, Mary and Hilde assembled. The noise was extraordinary. 'All day the phones rang as people reported that [parts of Czechoslovakia] were already occupied,' Doreen remembered. Then another report would come in that in fact no occupation had happened.

Such was the confusion and hysteria in the building that none of the women heard the banging on the door. It was only in a rare moment of quiet that Mary noticed the sound. A deathly silence fell on them. Typewriters stopped tapping, phone receivers were put down, the kettle was taken off the boil. The women looked around each other. *Who could this be?* They were all there.

Doreen opened the door a crack and peered into the hallway. She paused, then breathed a sigh of relief, before letting the door open fully. Right along the corridor, down the five flights of stairs and into the street, queued almost 100 women and children. Those they had summoned had started to arrive.

Over the next three hours, a total of 300 people appeared at the offices. They were all sent to Wilson Station, to await their paperwork.

1 p.m. British Legation, Prague – 17 hours before the invasion
In increasing desperation, Doreen drove backwards and forward between the office and the Legation, but still nothing had come from home, no visas or instructions.

There were now more than 300 women and children at the station, who had been told they were leaving for safety. But as things stood, that was not true. Harold Gibson would only be able to issue visas once he received authorisation.

Doreen was sickened by the sight of the elation on the faces of the families, reassuring their children, mothers saying, 'We are going to be united with Daddy very soon,' and, 'We are safe now.' They had no idea that at present they were trapped.

4 p.m. Czech Special Train, Dresden – 14 hours before the invasion
In a true sign of his power, Adolf Hitler summoned the elderly Czech President Emil Hácha to meet with him immediately.

President Hácha and his Foreign Minister, František Chvalkovský, dropped everything to travel to Berlin.

Hácha had been looking forward to the performance of a Dvořák opera that evening, where he was due to be accompanied by Alice Masaryk. The sixty-six-year-old President was instead travelling by special train to Berlin, as his serious heart condition meant flying was out of the question on health grounds.

6 p.m. National Theatre, Prague – 12 hours until the invasion
In a somewhat unusual display of stubbornness, despite the rumours of an occupation, Martha had insisted that she and Waitstill return to their hotel after work, wash and change into evening attire before going to watch the opera.

Had Hácha gone, Alice would have been accompanied by hundreds of guards who protected the President. But given he was now on his way to Berlin, there would be no security for Alice and so she had asked that the Sharps go instead.

She knew they loved the opera, and it was a hidden sign of solidarity. The chatter from the stalls and circle as to why the presidential box was occupied by two unknown faces rather than their leader was soon hushed by the rousing performance of *Rusalka* which went down so well subsequent reports said, 'Prague's Orchestra's rendition of Smetana's patriotic suite, Ma Vlast (My Country) was followed by a wild ovation which lasted a full quarter of an hour.'

7 p.m. BCRC Offices, Prague – 11 hours until the invasion
Everyone in the room stopped what they were doing and froze as the telephone started to ring. They had been so desperate for news, keeping the line clear for the last two hours and standing by for an update, and now it appeared something might be happening.

Doreen snatched up the receiver and without saying a word, listened intently. She then hung the phone up, and turning to her colleagues said calmly, 'The Passport Control Officer has had his instructions ...' The noise of a pin dropping could have been heard at that point as everyone collectively held their breath ... 'He has put his seal of approval on the entire list!'

The room erupted with excitement. Finally, the visas were approved.

Doreen rushed down the stairs, almost tumbling the final two stories, and out onto the street. Snow was starting to drop. Despite the horror of what was happening, there was a magical feeling in the air that evening.

Doreen raced to the British Legation, skidding along the roads at breakneck speed. She was shocked by the billowing smoke coming from makeshift furnaces along the streets. Expecting occupation any minute, people were desperately burning all the records they kept, no matter how innocent, in fear that something might be deemed incriminating.

She was met at the doors of the Legation by Harold Gibson holding a box of passports, on the top of which was a collective visa for seven hundred people to leave the country that evening. Doreen barely stopped the car, as Harold literally threw the box onto the back seats, and she sped off, heading for the Polish Legation.

8 p.m. Social Democrat Office, Prague – 10 hours before the invasion
Racing across the city, Doreen had left Wenzel busy inside his office where he had accumulated thousands and thousands of pages of essential information about DSAP members. This included personal papers, records and reports. But there was no time to sort through them. He knew everything must be destroyed. 'My office [had] been cleared, the drawers were opened,

the paper baskets were emptied; No one should be put at risk by a letter or note left behind. We knew Hitler was about to stretch his hand to Prague.'

And so all the records of their proud organisation were burned in their basement furnace.

8.30 p.m. Polish Legation, Prague – 9 ½ hours until the invasion
The Polish vice-consul should have finished work three hours earlier, but true to his word, he patiently stayed put, waiting for Doreen. When she delivered the box of passports and the collective visa, he could have been difficult, insisting on checking each passport against those named on the visa. But instead, he simply stamped approval on the bottom, handed it back to Doreen and wished her good luck.

Wiping tears of relief from her eyes, Doreen was walking excitedly back to her car through the cold air when someone grabbed her from behind 'and seized all the passports from me by force'. She screamed out of fear and anger and fell to her knees as the box was torn from her grip.

Distraught, Doreen looked up from the snowy ground to try to get a look at her attacker. But she heard a woman shouting in Czech somewhere out of sight. Then, charging out of the darkness came Marie Schmolka, who Doreen had not seen since that night in Wenzel's flat when they trimmed the first list. What was she doing at the Polish Legation at that hour? Doreen never did find out. Instead, accompanied by Jaroslav Podhajsky, Marie shouted at the man, 'Return the passports!'

With no protest, he handed the box back and scuttled away. Marie and Jaroslav helped Doreen back to her feet and into her car, and she thanked her saviours before speeding off. The attacker and his motives have forever remained a mystery.

9 p.m. Wilson Station, Prague – 9 hours until the invasion
Robert Stopford was waiting anxiously at the train station, desperate to know whether Doreen had been successful at the Polish Legation. She duly arrived triumphantly, to be greeted by a crowd of women and children huddled shivering outside the barrier for the platform, where their train to the Ostrava Czech-Polish border stood poised.

Hilde Patz had set up a trestle table behind which she sat, with lists of names, train and boat tickets at the ready. The women and children queued patiently to be handed their documents. It took ninety minutes for the line to finish, by which time 500 people were now aboard the train. 'About 200 had not turned up; we did not know why,' Doreen said. The women waited for some stragglers to arrive, but only a handful turned up.

One of the women told Doreen it seemed certain that Ostrava was occupied while another said pessimistically that, 'The odds are that the train will run into the German army.' *What should the women do?* Doreen wondered. What is the lesser of two evils, sending 500 women and children into the hands of their enemy, or keeping them under captivity in Prague?

'It seems better to send them,' Doreen decided. At 11 p.m., the train pulled out of the station. Hilde and Doreen watched as it disappeared into the dark, hoping for the best because now that was all they could do.

Wednesday 15 March, 1939
1.30 a.m. Reich Chancellery, Berlin – 4 ½ hours before the invasion
When he arrived in Berlin, Czechoslovakia's President Hácha was made to wait in the Adlon Hotel while the Führer finished watching *Ein Hoffnungsloser Fall* (*A Hopeless Case*), an aptly named romantic film. It was another three hours before Hácha was summoned to the Reich Chancellery, Hitler's official office.

Hitler allowed Hácha to speak first, during which the elderly Czech pleaded for leniency for his beloved country. Hitler responded with an aggressive ultimatum, demanding submission to prevent an imminent invasion.

'A peaceful occupation would guarantee the Czechs autonomy and a certain measure of national freedom,' the Nazi leader reportedly told Hácha, before threatening, 'Resistance will mean extermination and total destruction.'

This aggression understandably charged the negotiations with emotion, which further escalated when Hitler and his aides, including Hermann Göring, pressured Hácha to sign a surrender document. At one point, Göring threatened to bomb Prague within hours, causing Hácha to collapse. Revived with medical aid from Hitler's personal physician, Dr Morell, Hácha ultimately agreed to the terms under duress, signing a document around 3:55 a.m. that read:

> *The conviction was unanimously expressed on both sides that the aim of all efforts must be the safeguarding of calm, order and peace in this part of Central Europe. The Czech President declared that, in order to serve this object and to achieve ultimate pacification, he confidently placed the fate of the Czech people and country in the hands of the Führer of the German Reich. The Führer accepted this declaration and expressed his intention of taking the Czech people under the protection of the German Reich and of guaranteeing them an autonomous development of their ethnic life as suited their character.*

4.00 a.m. Ostrava, Czech-Polish border – 2 hours until the invasion

As the train carrying the 500 refugees pulled in, the station had transformed. 'Guns were mounted in the station and German troops were on guard,' one passenger saw in amazement. They had left a free Prague and five hours later were now in what appeared to be a German-occupied district of their country. As one of the first regions of Czechoslovakia to be occupied, the Nazi war machine needed it to allow easy access for German troops to enter the Polish frontier, should that be required.

A message was passed in a whisper throughout the carriages. *Close the blinds and stay silent.* Elsa Brod who was on the train could not help but have a peak out of the window. 'The soldier looked like the statue of a Roman legionnaire,' she remembered. She was impressed. 'Truth be told, he was rather beautiful.' But as she looked beyond this hunky German, she saw what appeared to be hundreds of troops.

The handsome soldier, who it turned out was in charge, started walking along the platform, towards the driver's cabin. When suddenly, a BCRC representative from London called John Ingram opened a window as the soldier was passing and shouted in his most exaggerated English accent:

'You'll never guess what I've got here: A load of dirty Jews!'

The German was initially stunned, before bursting into a hysterical belly laugh. Other troops on platform started to join in on the amusement, before the officer made some antisemitic remarks, shaking hands with Ingram and waving the train on its way. Had it been discovered that the train actually contained hundreds of women and children, all of whom were related to wanted men, the results could have been disastrous for all on board.

'How well he carried out his mission!' Robert Stopford wrote in a letter about the events.

5 a.m. Czech Radio Headquarters, Vinohrady District, Prague – 1 hour until the invasion
The graveyard shift on state radio was the place where announcers either started their career, hoping to progress into daytime,

primetime slots, or it was where announcers were placed as a signal that their time with the station was soon to end. For thirty-eight-year-old newscaster Franta Kocourek, it was neither.

He was on air after the station received an urgent dispatch claiming it was from the President and the Minister of Defence. Staff initially thought it was a hoax, after all nothing interesting happened at this time of night. But the follow-up call from the Czech Presidential Office at Prague Castle, declaring that the statement be read without delay, showed them it was genuine.

Kocourek was summoned and with clear emotion in his voice, people still awake around the country heard the words they had been dreading for so long:

> *German Army infantry and aircraft are beginning the occupation of the territory of the Republic at 06:00. The slightest resistance will cause the most unforeseen consequences and lead to the intervention becoming utterly brutal. All commanders have to obey the orders of the occupying Army. The various units of the Czech Army are being disarmed. Military and civil aeroplanes must remain on their aerodromes, and none must attempt to take to the air. Prague will be occupied at 06:30.*

5.30 a.m. Hotel Alcron, Prague – 30 minutes until the invasion
Such was her state of anxiety, Doreen had been tossing and turning in her bed for the last five hours, unable to sleep even though she had not slept a minute the previous night either. The radio on her bedside table had been playing quietly, and she hoped it might coax her to drop off. But Kocourek's announcement of the inevitable invasion had sent a wave of intense heat through her chest, accompanied by a tightness in the stomach, as her body reacted physically to the weight of the news.

When she heard a gentle knocking at her door, she bolted straight out of bed and literally ran to answer it. A concierge stood apologetically with a tray upon which an urgent telegram was placed. Ripping it open, Doreen burst into tears as she read the two words sent from Ingram: 'All well'.

She returned to bed and collapsed into a deep sleep, still clutching the message in her hand. The invasion could wait, at least her latest transport was safe.

7.00 a.m. Berlin Hauptbahnhof, Berlin
Clare Hollingworth, a twenty-eight-year-old aspiring journalist, emerged groggily from her sleeper cabin after travelling overnight from Brussels to the German capital. Having left her husband back in London, Clare's work with the *News Chronicle* had put her in contact with Margaret Layton, who in turn had managed to recruit her to work for the BCRC. Clare had originally been looking for a job as a foreign correspondent, but having not succeeded, she accepted this was the next best option.

'As a result of a chain of administrative accidents, I was appointed as the senior official in Warsaw in charge [of] refugees from the Sudetenland,' she wrote in a letter to her parents from the train.

Having grown up on a farm, fascinated by economics and left-leaning in her politics, Margaret thought Clare would be the ideal counterpart to Doreen. She was also an ardent feminist, something that many of the women had in common.

'I gather I am about the eighth woman in England to have a passport in her [maiden] name,' she proudly told the German official checking her documents as she made her way to Tempelhof for a short flight to Gdynia.

Buying a newspaper from the stand, she learnt for the first time that Czechoslovakia was no longer a free country.

11.30 a.m. Gdynia, Poland

Clare arrived with metronomic timing in Gdynia at the same time 500 weary, scared and emotionally battered refugees were due, following their terrifying escape from Czechoslovakia. The snow was starting to turn to slush as temperatures finally began to creep above freezing. There was no time to acclimatise with her surroundings, let alone find somewhere to stay.

'The refugees had to be accounted for, organised, fed and housed,' she explained.

The exit from Prague had been so hasty, although all those who had travelled had the correct permits to continue on to Britain, no onward transport from Poland had been arranged.

'I was given a list of the names of the hundreds of women as they arrived for whom I was responsible,' she wrote, apparently unflustered by the scale of her task. She found accommodation for them all, before they travelled on to Britain to reunite with their partners, husbands and fathers.

Part Two
Occupation

Chapter Eight

Panic Stations

'What does a person do when his world goes to pieces?' Martha Sharp mused in her diary during the early hours of Thursday 15 March having heard the announcement of Nazi occupation.

Not being able to sleep, she wanted to put her thoughts onto paper. 'First, he cannot believe what his ears tell him. His mind does not yet comprehend. If he and his loved ones are apparently in no immediate danger for their lives he goes about his accustomed tasks, at the usual time. He arrives in his office [to] take care of the daily routine, even as he knows that his own situation will be changed by outward events beyond his control.'

And that is exactly what all the women did that morning. Doreen was already in her office, while Martha would make her way to the Ministry of Health building as soon as Waitstill was awake. In their taxi, the couple reflected on what had occurred on their way home from the opera the previous night where they had seen intense and frightening rioting, perpetrated by supporters of the German occupation. The couple fell silent after reliving it. The personal danger they now faced began to sink in. Up to that point, they had been so focused on helping other people, they had little thought for their own safety.

'There is a heaviness in the air,' Martha said, breaking the silence.

'Are you afraid?' Waitstill asked. 'Do you want to go home and let the Czechs fight their own battles?'

There was a long pause.

'I'd like to stay if you want to,' Martha said eventually, as their cab pulled up to their destination.

'Good, I want to stay too,' said Waitstill, opening the door.

Such was the crowd outside their offices, Martha needed to approach a policeman to ask for help getting inside.

'What office do you wish to visit?' the officer asked.

'American Relief for Czechoslovakia,' Martha replied.

'You must wait your turn. All of these people are waiting in front of you,' he explained apologetically.

'But that is our office,' Waitstill jumped in.

'Who are you?'

'Sharp!' Martha and Waitstill replied in unison.

The officer nodded knowingly and led the way, gently tapping people on the shoulder and saying, 'Please,' to create a pathway for them to get inside.

'These people have been gathering all night,' Martha's secretary Virginia Waistcoat informed her when she finally made her way inside. Having had the same issue trying to get in, she had asked the police to look out for Waitstill and Martha. One person had told Virginia that they thought 'this is American territory and if they can just get inside the office, they would be safe.'

How ill-informed they must be, Martha thought. But how determined they were. The only hope for these people – like so many others – was to escape the country altogether. The blizzard that morning had delayed the entire German Army from entering the city, but these people had soldiered through, waiting boldly in the cold. Robert Stopford remembered that day 'saw the beginning of a violent storm with wind, rain and snow,' which would last for the rest of the week.

After only about thirty minutes, the crowd, now resembling a mob, managed to break through the police barricade and into the warmth of the building. They were making their way up the stairs to where Martha, Waitstill and Virginia were working. They had been spurred on by the sight of the first German troops entering the city – under the command of General Blaskowitz – driving past the queue of people, on their way to Wenceslas Square. The invaders main objectives that morning were to secure Ruzyně Airport – where Martha had seen Trevor's plane with a group of children off the previous day – the War Ministry buildings in the Dejvice district, and of course, the Castle, where the Czech President resided.

Some of the scared Czechs who had been lining outside the Unitarian headquarters were now inside, up the stairs and banging on the door to the offices, begging in Czech, German and broken English for help. Martha could do nothing but sit at her desk terrified, while Virginia did the same. Waitstill had other ideas, swinging the door open to his inner office, he marched in an exaggerated fashion over to the outer door, on the other side of which the crowd were now howling. Shouting to stand back, he unlocked it, and bodies came flooding in, taking up every inch of space. Martha and Virginia backed up scared to Waitstill's open office door, as the crowd surged towards them.

Waitstill climbed onto a chair, and shouted, 'Quiet!' The room fell unnervingly to absolute silence, the men, women and children looking up at Waitstill with fear and hope in their eyes.

'The American Relief for Czechoslovakia is not an aid agency, nor a visa agency. We are not an official branch of the US Government,' he tried to explain.

The throng of terrified people listened, but as Waitstill spoke, single shouts of protest coming from the crowd quickly erupted again into chaos. As Martha watched her husband trying to calm the situation, she felt something cold pressing against the side of her neck. Raising her hands slightly as the internationally known signal that no resistance will be forthcoming, she turned slowly to see a man pointing a shiny silver pistol, now holding her captive. With his fingerless woollen gloves, long green overcoat and unshaven face, he looked more frightened than her.

'I came for help, so save my family,' he shouted at Martha. Such was the chaos in the building, no one noticed the unfolding hostage situation. 'Here are my wife and two sons,' he told her, gesturing his head towards a small woman with her arms protectively around the shoulders of her two you boys.

Martha managed to remain calm, showing no indication of the anxiety she was feeling.

'Come alone with me into my office,' she suggested to the man.

Still aiming the gun at her, the man lowered it to Martha's waist and then nodded. She quickly backed into Waitstill's inner office with him, closing the door behind them. It was now just the two of them.

'I am only one step ahead of the Nazis' he cried out to her. 'If you force me out of here, I shall shoot my family and then myself. I have no other choice,' he said, slumping against the wall.

Standing still and looking at the man directly in the eye, he was taken aback by what she said next.

'Cigarette?' Martha enquired, picking up Waitstill's pack from his desk.

Unsure what had happened, the man was immobile for a second but had no choice but to accept one. Lighting it and then one for herself, Martha suggested the two should sit down on the chairs facing Waitstill's desk. The American tobacco seemed to calm the man slightly.

Over the next fifteen minutes, Martha listened to him unload his worries. He sobbed quietly as he explained that he knew he had a target on his head. Formerly a leading lawyer, he had prosecuted pro-Nazis in the Sudetenland.

'They had vowed to "get" me,' he whispered, his voice cracking.

The more he spoke, the more composed he became. This man, so desperate, so out of control, so dishevelled, had until a few months ago been one of the country's most celebrated minds. Today he was homeless, hungry, cold, frightened and now being hunted. Martha was honest about what she could and could not do for him. But she told him about Doreen and how the BCRC would do all she could to help him. Asking how he could possibly repay her, Martha asked for the gun. Looking down at the gleaming device, the man paused, before slowly turning it around and passing it to Martha.

She stood up to shake his hand as he departed, ushering his wife and children with him. Closing the door once she was alone, Martha collapsed onto the desk, gasping desperately for air. It took her several minutes to compose herself, before she stood up, straightened her skirt, wiped away her tears and opened the door, to rejoin the crowd, clutching her handbag which was heavier than usual with the loaded revolver now inside it.

Waitstill's attempts to calm the crowd had garnered no results whatsoever, in fact, Martha thought it appeared even rowdier than before she stepped away. Holding her handbag as if her life depended it, she led her husband back into his office and closed the door, leaving Virginia to loyally try to keep the crowd at bay.

Cutting off Waitstill as he started protesting that no one seemed to understand what he was saying.

'This emergency demands aid of a different kind,' she explained. 'Maybe my old social case work training could be of help?'

For a week the previous year, Martha had spent time at Denison House, a settlement house in Boston, Massachusetts. As a place for refugees to be based while they are found permanent accommodation, most of her time there was spent being a shoulder to cry on, someone to listen and to offer pragmatic suggestions. Although she had never had a gun pointed at her head, the conversation she had just had with the armed man was very similar. He did not want to hurt her, he just wanted to be listened to.

'All these people want is to talk over their problems,' she went on. 'With someone who could find out what countries might be open to them and under what terms.'

'We've got to do something,' Waitstill agreed. 'Perhaps this is the answer. We part company. You take on the individual cases; I go it alone on the big relief projects and the financing.'

'Might this be the solution?' Martha asked.

Nodding, Waitstill replied, 'My God, I hope it works.'

With the decision made, Martha unlocked the door and as she did, it swung open violently, the Sharps pushed back into the room as a torrent of people were pushed in.

This time Martha took centre stage, climbing onto Waitstill's desk and screaming as loud as her lungs would allow for quiet. Amazingly, the sound of a woman's scream seemed to work and for the second time that morning, the room became hushed. Martha explained that she would need more information for each person before she could start to help them. But, she concluded, they needed to afford her twenty minutes to come up with a system. In order to do this, they needed to vacate the office and wait patiently outside.

Amazingly, the woman's touch worked. Word was passed down the line of people in the corridor who were out of earshot to step back. Slowly, the room started to clear, until eventually the last person had left.

The office looked like a bomb had gone off. Papers were scattered all over the floor, Martha's typewriter and telephone had been upended. No bother, though, as Virginia retrieved it from the floor and the two women set to work. They had a packet of Martha's calling cards and stamped each with the date, wrote a time for a ten-minute appointment the next day and numbered each one. It took them under quarter of an hour to create 200. They then went out into the corridor and started to hand the cards out, in order of the line.

As each family gratefully received their card, they started to disperse to wherever they were staying until the following day.

Among the chaos of their office, Martha then turned her attention to creating a form they would fill in for each family during their appointment. Meanwhile, Virginia started to phone around some of their contacts to help. She managed to enlist five people, who between them spoke English, Czech and German, to come to the office the next morning and start the process of meeting with the families. Virginia would be in charge along with one of the volunteers, Lisl Xall, a local girl who was highly regarded.

Of those who had received appointment cards from Martha, two returned to their places of residence and killed themselves, one by jumping out of the fifth-floor window of her room and the other by hanging.

Doreen Warriner was faced with another kind of chaotic situation that morning, finding the stairs up to her office packed with refugees, who were 'all desperate,' she later told Martha. Mr Schaffarsch, the tall and intimidating miners' union leader stood guard outside the front door. He was not only physically menacing, but highly respected. As a result, the people who arrived at the BCRC offices were far more ordered than Martha had experienced.

Throughout the morning, Mr. Schaffarsch allowed one or two individuals at a time into the office to see Doreen. In her top desk drawer, she had a substantial amount of money from the *News Chronicle* Fund and she gave small amounts to each person to assist them in leaving the country.

In the process of arranging the emigration of over 2,000 people up to this point, Doreen had collected a stack of redundant travel visas. There were instances where she obtained visas, but the recipients never showed up. Sometimes a name had been misspelled, and instead of returning it, Doreen simply requested a new one.

She had found that if she dabbed the name with a damp cloth dipped in alcohol, it would fade sufficiently to allow her to rewrite it with the name of whoever was standing in front of her. It was an incredibly risky tactic, and a forgery which would likely be discovered relatively easily, but with the situation being so urgent, it was a gamble she was willing to take.

She also wrote a short note for each person on the back of her calling card to the effect that they were under the care of the BCRC, specifically the Prague leader, Doreen Warriner. She believed this would give them the best chance of being allowed to get into Poland, where they should head to the British Legation in Katowice, where Clare Hollingworth had started to make connections. Doreen was, for the first time, directly and knowingly linking herself to people smuggling, a crime for which she could be arrested by Czech, Polish or British authorities, not to mention the threat from the Nazis.

After five hours of this work, Mr Schaffarsch poked his head round the door. He was concerned that people he did not recognise had joined the queue and there was chatter that they could be planted agents.

Doreen became concerned. She wondered if an undercover Nazi operative had been among the people she had seen, observing her forge a visa or provide money for their escape.

Collecting the few remaining visas, cash and calling cards, along with the only two boxes of papers she could carry, Doreen went out into the corridor and at the top of her voice shouted:

'You must get away!' she hollered. 'The Gestapo will come at any moment.'

On her way back to her hotel by taxi, Doreen collected an exhausted Tessa, who had only just got back from Bratislava and had with herself three additional boxes of documents. The pair would use Doreen's room as a temporary office. As they drove, the familiar sights they had passed so many times were now littered by anomalies. A tram – with businessmen leaning out of the door, straining to see what was causing their delay – had been stopped by a broken-down Panzer 1 tank. Further on, just past Wenceslas Square, they came across a six wheeled armoured Sd.Kfz. 231 truck that had stopped in the middle of Opletalova Street, blocking the road. As the driver asked for directions to the Italian Legation, a crowd of embittered but curious Czechs looked on in silence while the soldier in the turret sat huddled up against the driving snow, nervously fingering the trigger of his machine gun. Consultation with the taxi driver allowed the German automobile to continue on its journey, only for it to stop again further down the road. When they could not understand a Czech policeman on the side of the road who was trying to point them in the right direction, they dragged him forcibly into the vehicle to act as a guide.

Doreen and Tessa were heading to the Alcron Hotel, which, as one of the nicer hotels in Prague, was now filled with the most senior Nazi officers, all trying to establish it as their new home away from home. The change was astonishing. Only a few hours prior, Doreen had left the empty lobby of a quiet building on her way to help wanted individuals to evade the Nazis. Now, later that same day, she entered what had become in a matter of hours the nerve centre for the operations of the people she had been so desperately opposing. In fact, the Alcron was now the headquarters for General Blaskowitz, the commander of the Third Reich occupation.

Inside the hotel, the noise was overwhelming, with huge crates of posters being unloaded into the lobby for plastering around the city. Under the printed eagle and swastika read a message from General Blaskowitz:

Call to the people!
By order of the Führer and Supreme Commander of the German Wehrmacht, I have assumed executive power in the country of Bohemia.

As Doreen and Tessa walked past reception, a member of staff called out, saying there were three messages waiting for her. The first was from Robert Stopford asking for an urgent meeting at the British Legation at 4.30 p.m. Second, there was a request for her to call Margaret Layton in London. And finally, the man told her a lady called Miss Rathbone had been waiting on the line to speak to Doreen for just under an hour.

Doreen took the call from the politician in the phone box in the hotel lobby and Eleanor Rathbone was quick and to the point. Doreen should pass over any names she still needed visas for, and Eleanor would personally get them approved that day. Unlike most of the people Doreen spoke to in Britain, Eleanor agreed that 'the Government are acting with appalling slowness and unnecessary rigidity in respect of visas and immigration conditions.' The call had come too late, but Doreen was grateful nonetheless.

She needed to pinch herself at what was happening. Here was an eccentric British politician giving orders from her Westminster office to Doreen, who was now completely surrounded by the German General Staff, who were making a racket as they tried to check into one of the best hotels in a country they had invaded that morning. It was surreal.

Next, Doreen called Margaret Layton. The secretary of the

BCRC was concerned. 'Why not come home?' she asked Doreen, after explaining how worried she was for her team's safety.

'There is still too much to do for me to leave,' Doreen replied, before making excuses that she could not talk any longer.

Up in her room, Doreen and Tessa locked themselves in. Tessa began going through the papers organising them into two piles – destroy or keep. The former was a messy stack on the floor, while the small, neat pile of 'keep' documents were limited to correspondence with London where no names were included. But how to destroy the incriminating papers? 'We spent about a day tearing them up and flushing them down the loos of the grandest hotel in Prague,' Tessa recalled with a chuckle.

While this was happening, Doreen called around from her bedside telephone asking for others to attend the meeting at the Legation in the next hour.

Martha was still in her office when she received the call.

With under an hour to cross the city, she left with Waitstill to head to the British Legation. As they stepped out into the street, Martha was shocked with what she saw. It had been snowing non-stop for the day, leaving ten inches on the pavements. The centre of the road was being continually cleared by the thousands of Nazi soldiers – apparently oblivious to the piercing cold and slippery ground – goose-stepping in time for their first parade in the occupied land. Every building Martha could see down the street now flew the Czech tricolour flag out of their windows. In an attempt to show that the residents of Prague welcomed their invaders, each house had been visited and ordered to hang a flag, otherwise they would face arrest and join in custody the few men who had been apprehended by soldiers for slashing the tyres of some German lorries, the only minor sabotage that had happened so far.

As the invading soldiers marched towards the centre of the

city, residents slowly plodded through the thick snow in the other direction. Trying to make her way along the crowded pavements, some whispered under their breath to Martha, 'Staroměstské náměstí'. She waded on, until another person said the same to her. Then another, then another. Although Martha spoke almost no Czech, she knew this meant Old Town Square in the centre of the city, home to memorials and statues of the infamous people who had died in pursuit of freedom for the country.

'As if drawn by a tide, we joined the crowd,' Martha said. Leaving the Nazi procession, they followed the masses. No one spoke a word to each other, each person simply walked with their head bowed. As Martha entered the square, she was met with the sight of thousands of people either standing or kneeling, apparently praying in silence. Small bouquets of snowdrops and violets were scattered all around. The only noise was occasional sniffling and sobbing. A country which had been a beacon of democracy and equality for over a decade was now shattered, its people now literally and figuratively on their knees. 'I realised for the first time how much harder it is to live one's principles than to die for them,' Martha reflected.

But she could not reflect for long. Waitstill tapped her shoulder and gestured that they needed to get to the British Legation quickly. Looking at her watch, it was now 4 p.m. They would need to rush across the city in the conditions to make it on time, which they did by a whisker.

Doreen had left Tessa in her room destroying documents by painstakingly ripping them up into small enough pieces to flush down the toilet. Two German guards stood on sentry duty with fixed bayonets outside the hotel, as they now did at most public buildings across the city. Doreen opted for a taxi, but was stopped by Charles Bridge, as the German Army were marching across ceremonially. She could not stand the sight of it. Leaving the meter running, she got out of the warm car. The temperature was so cold and the snow falling so heavily that she was forced to take refuge in the large church by the roadblock. Inside, she was stunned to see it completely packed. No mass was taking place, the lights were off, but the building was full of men and women, almost all kneeling in silence. In a similar scene to the one Martha had just witnessed, the only sound was wails of despair, which echoed around the walls. Doreen stood in there for a few minutes, unable to move and overcome with a tide of emotion.

As she left to return to her taxi, four immaculately dressed soldiers were sauntering along the one-way walkway in the wrong direction towards her, oblivious to the system. An indignant older Czech woman walking the correct way in front of Doreen pointed her umbrella at the soldiers and shooed them back across the bridge, as if they were stray dogs.

By the time Doreen was back in the taxi, her driver was allowed to cross the bridge and drive to the Legation.

Present with Robert Stopford were Doreen, Martha and Hilde, along with British Ambassador Basil Newton. Stopford explained that he had received word from the Government in Britain that he should try to bring several anti-Nazi leaders to the Legation for sanctuary. They had put word out and some had already made it into the building, including the Jewish deputy leader of the DSAP Siegfried Taub and his wife.

Stopford said there were two men on the list for whom it was too dangerous to try to get there on their own. Stopford would not reveal their identity, only calling one Mr X and the other Mr Y. It would be less conspicuous, he told the group, if they could be accompanied by women, thereby appearing to observers as couples rather than being men walking alone.

Martha volunteered to act as Mr X's chaperone and Stopford handed her a piece of paper with an address written on it. He would call the Alcron Hotel and ask Tessa to collect Mr Y.

Worryingly, he had also been unable to make contact with Marie Schmolka, so Doreen agreed to go to her house and bring her to the Legation. Her phone could not connect, but perhaps the lines were being cut off by the invaders.

Doreen took a taxi to Marie's residence. Upon arrival, she observed that the door was slightly open. Proceeding with caution, she entered and discovered that the house was in disarray and unoccupied. The wind blew through the building from the broken windows at the rear of the house. In a state of shock, Doreen exited and walked down the street aimlessly. How had Marie been arrested already? And would they be able to get Mr X and Mr Y in time?

As Martha left the British Legation, it was pitch dark. A booming voice announced through loudspeakers that Martial Law had been implemented and a curfew would be imposed from 8 p.m. Anyone seen out after that point would be shot, the announcer warned. Martha was appalled.

Flagging a passing cab, Martha was worried she could be followed, so gave an address several streets away from that written on her piece of paper. Although she had now taken dozens of taxis since being in Prague, this was the first time that the driver appeared to have an accomplice sitting next to him. The passenger turned around and asked in a thick German accent whether Martha was British, flashing a white smile. Good god, Martha thought. *Was this a Gestapo agent?* Trying to make polite conversation, as the man continued to probe Martha, she began to worry for her safety. As his quizzing intensified, the driver stopped the car, announcing they had arrived at her destination. Telling him to keep the change, Martha thrust a koruna bank note onto the man's lap and quickly exited.

She walked away and turned a corner out of sight of the car but waited to see if she was being followed. Peeking back around, she saw to her horror that the passenger had left the car and was now walking briskly in her direction. But worst of all, she made eye contact with him. He had seen her spying back on him – she could not have behaved any more suspiciously. They locked eyes for what felt like minutes but in reality was less than a second, before Martha bolted down the street away from him. Although he had physical advantage over her and would likely outpace her running on the ice, Martha had spent enough time in this part of the city to know her way around and was confident she could evade someone less familiar with the streets. She recognised a small side street which she darted into, taking refuge in a doorway.

Sure enough, 'I flattened myself against the entrance, and in the darkness he walked right by,' she said. The man stopped and as he was about to turn back to retrace his steps, the taxi screeched to a halt in the other direction, with the driver honking his horn and shouting for the man to come back. After which, the car sped off, presumably to search the streets further down for Martha.

Trying to walk as quickly but nonchalantly as possible, Martha came out of the doorway and headed to the rendezvous address.

It was a five-story apartment block and, stopping to scan the flats on the sign by the door, to her dismay, Martha saw that the one she wanted was at the top of the building. She sprinted up the stairs so quickly that by the time she reached the correct door, she needed to lean on the frame to stop herself feeling like she was going to pass out. The bell was answered by a woman.

'I am here to pick up Mr X,' Martha managed to say, struggling for breath.

The woman tried to slam the door in her face, making some mumbled comment to the effect that no such person lived there. Using her foot to stop it closing, Martha begged the woman, but she did not give way. Producing her American passport from her coat pocket was the only thing that she thought might reassure her, so Martha stepped back and opened the passport to show the photograph page.

After observing for a few moments, the woman took the document from Martha and said, 'A moment,' in a thick Czech accent, before slamming the door shut.

Great, Martha thought. Had she just had her passport stolen on the day Czechoslovakia was invaded?

Her concerns receded as she heard a rustling on the other side of the door. It opened ajar and a man's voice from within said in good English, 'Mr X can be given a message.' Martha started to explain that the British Ambassador had sent her, that she had been followed but had managed to lose her tail, that time was running out and they needed to leave now. Oh, and please could she have her passport back? The man grunted, before slamming the door again.

Martha barely had a chance to smack on the door, before it was flung open – this time with the chain removed – and in front of her stood Wenzel Jaksch, Prague's most wanted man.

'I am Mr X,' Wenzel told her softly in the same excellent English, before handing back her passport.

The bitter temperatures around the city proved helpful to Wenzel's efforts at disguising himself as he could wrap himself in a long coat, scarf and hat without being conspicuous. Standing outside the building together, Martha flagged down a passing taxi, but she was horrified to see that, like her previous ride, the passenger seat was occupied by another man. Apologising to the driver, she stepped back and it drove off. The next taxi to pass also had two people in the front, then the next, then the next. It seemed every taxi in Prague had an agent accompanying the driver, as she explained to Wenzel. 'We'd better walk to the embassy,' he suggested.

She nodded, and the two started the brisk hike. By now, not only was it completely pitch dark with the streetlights turned off, but the falling snow had turned into hard sleet, which slapped Martha's exposed face painfully. It took them twenty minutes to reach Charles Bridge, and the medieval stone arch structure linked the city over the River Vltava looked more menacing than usual. A lone Nazi soldier stood guard at the entrance to the bridge, with icicles forming on his helmet. He stepped out of the shadows and put up a shivering hand.

'Americans ... on our way to the U.S Embassy,' Martha shouted out, putting on a German accent in the way so many people do when they are speaking English to foreigners, in the hope it might help with their understanding.

The soldier did not look impressed. 'Identity cards,' he requested in German.

Martha pulled out her passport once again, saying over and over 'Passport?' before adding again in an attempted accent, 'I don't speak German'.

Wenzel remained in the shadows behind her, not daring to move a muscle, even trying to muffle the sound of his chattering teeth.

After a pause, the soldier barked 'Go!' and stepped aside.

Martha linked arms with Wenzel as they started to cross the famous bridge. She was staggered that it seemed to get even colder as they were over the water, her hands and feet now completely numb. Another soldier on the other side of the bridge waved the two of them through as soon as he saw Martha produce her passport. From there, it was only another ten minutes before they reached Thunovská Street which led to the Legation.

As they approached their final destination, she saw two Nazi soldiers standing guard outside. They had not been there when she left.

'Are we to fail with the doorway to safety in view?' she asked herself.

Martha would do everything possible to stop that happening. She had successfully evaded an undercover German operative, navigated her way through the city without being followed and smuggled the most wanted man in the country through two checkpoints. She could get across this last hurdle.

With Wenzel now just behind her, she turned around and loudly started to complain to him about having to walk all that way. 'We would never have accepted the appointment with the secretary of the embassy,' she told her confused companion, hoping the guards would hear her.

As they got to the doors, Martha tried to make out that she thought these guards were in fact Legation staff, so nonchalantly asked, 'Will you please tell Mr Swanson that Mr and Mrs Sharp are here?'

'Oh, I am not the British Embassy guard,' the Nazi replied politely in perfect English. 'He is there,' he continued, pointing to the actual Legation member of staff. 'You should ask him.'

And with that, Martha and Wenzel were allowed into the Legation.

Tessa was there to greet them, offering a much need hot cup of tea to the arrivals.

'We have been chilled to the heart and bone,' Martha explained gratefully as she warmed her hands over the fire.

Tessa had had a much easier time collecting the Senator for the Czech Social Democratic Workers' Party, František Václav Krejčí, who had viciously attacked Hitler in his journalistic capacity for the last six years. 'There was no time to be scared,' she reflected courageously. She had not needed to travel as far as Martha, so had simply walked to the address, met up with the seventy-two-year-old Krejčí and the two had strolled at an almost leisurely speed back to the Legation.

Having helped them settle in, Tessa left the Martha and Wenzel in the room alone. A few minutes later, Doreen, Hilde and Waitstill came in, the former falling into an uncharacteristic embrace with Wenzel, kissing him several times on the lips out of relief.

Waitstill and Martha were stunned. They had no idea that the married Wenzel was anything other than a professional acquaintance with the Prague leader of the BCRC. Somewhat awkwardly, Waitstill coughed, looked at his pocket watch before telling Martha that they should leave.

'We have barely enough time to cross the city and reach the hotel before the 8 p.m. curfew,' he explained to Doreen and Wenzel, who were still locked into each other's arms.

The Sharps backed out of the room, closing the door behind them. Waitstill had been masterful in allowing the couple to extricate themselves from that strange situation, although it was only 6.30 p.m. and they had plenty of time to make it to the Hotel Atlantic. Holding hands they walked slowly through Prague to their hotel, arriving just as the clock ticked 7.30 p.m.

Chapter Nine

Trapped

In the British Legation, Ambassador Basil Newton took stock of everyone he now had under his care. He sent a telegram to London:

> *At their request I have given provisional refuge in the Legation to the following persons: Jaksch (and) Krejčí, leaders of the German Social Democrats, Miss Patz [of] Miss Warriner's Secretariat ... I believe all these persons to be in particular personal danger. I should be gratified for immediate instructions as to whether these persons should be allowed to remain in the Legation and as to the attitude I should adopt if the German authorities request their surrender.*

They were safe for now, but if Newton received instruction that they must leave, he would have no option but to turf them out into the bitter cold.

Doreen's uncharacteristic public display of emotions with Wenzel was only in part because of his safe arrival into the safety of the British Legation. She was also showing how worried she was about the piles of documents which were still in her office. She had been so concerned about the potential of German agents being in the queue earlier that day that she had not had a chance to destroy anything. There was also a box of passports which she was looking after while visas were being requested. Doreen was desperately worried.

'We must go back to the office and collect our papers!' Hilde suggested, making the other two jump, forgetting they were not alone.

'Even if we got to the office in Vinohrady on the other side of the town, we would never get back in time,' Doreen said.

Hilde was clear-headed. 'I know exactly how these things go,' she responded, referring to her experience from the occupation of the Sudetenland. 'So long as it is only the army, it is all right; they are too busy to interfere,' she said. 'Later, when the Gestapo come, we shan't be able to move'.

She was quite right, and Doreen knew it. Clearly it was too dangerous for Wenzel to go anywhere, so the two women set off alone. Unaware of Martha's experiences earlier, Doreen did not think it strange that there was a man sitting in the passenger seat of their taxi as the driver took them directly to the door of the BCRC.

The office was eerily quiet. Despite having heating, it also felt unusually cold. Doreen had often complained that it was too warm. It was as if the arrival of the German army had caused the whole city, indoors and out, to drop in temperature.

The women immediately set to work. Doreen's private office became the nerve centre, as it had the largest fireplace, which she stuffed full of papers, before pouring Slivovitz – a plum brandy adored by the Czechs – onto the pile and setting it on fire. The two ladies then ran between rooms flinging papers into the fire.

Doreen had three large packing trunks which had for some reason always been in the office, where they were used as seats for visitors waiting to see her. The pair now used these to load up with anything they wanted to keep.

Worried that these cases might be too big for a taxi, Doreen telephoned Jaroslav Podhajsky, the Czech Commissioner for Refugees, who was still madly in love with her, to ask if he would drive over. He willingly agreed and appeared at the office in an alarmingly short space of time.

So heavy were the trunks, now full of papers and typewriters, it took all three of them to carry each down the three flights of stairs. They were loaded into the boot and back seats of the car, before Jaroslav put the car into first gear and slowly started to splutter along to the end of the snow-covered road.

'Stop!' shouted Doreen from the back seat. Jaroslav slammed on his brakes, but despite them only just moving at a crawl, the car skidded several yards before hitting a lamp post.

Hilde and Jaroslav looked round quizzically at Doreen. She had forgotten the box of passports which were still in her private office. Before anyone could say anything, Doreen was out of the car and wading quickly through the snow back to the front door. Passing the empty reception desk, she sprinted up the flights of stairs until she got to the familiar BCRC offices, where she froze.

Though the door to her private office was shut as she had left it, she could see light coming from the gap by the floor. And she thought she could hear something moving around inside.

Slowly edging towards the door, as if she were walking on the ledge of a tall building, she put her hand on the knob, but just before turning it, someone from within shouted 'Hier!' followed by more intense movements.

Doreen did not wait another second, she turned and sprinted out of the office, down the stairs and into the street, where she slipped over on the snow, landing painfully on her side. Managing to stagger to her feet, she clambered into the back of Jaroslav's car and shouted for him to drive, hitting the back of his seat furiously.

They sped away to the Legation as fast as Jaroslav could drive in the icy conditions. Doreen fired a daggered look at young Hilde when she innocently enquired where the passports were. She had been right to flee when she had, for within her office were two agents working for the Nazis. They had been tipped off about the location by the taxi driver's passenger who had travelled there with Doreen and Hilde. Such was the efficiency of the Nazis; they had acted on the information immediately. Unaware that anyone had come back into the office, the two agents had searched the building, before walking out onto the street, a box under one of their arms containing 300 passports.

Doreen looked out of her window in silence. The streets were lined with Czech people with despair written all over their faces. Some sobbed into their handkerchiefs, while others looked on in horror as giant plush swastika flags were risen above the castle, a building so meaningful to the people of Prague. As the car, flanked by German army vehicles, crept further into the heart of the city, the more the invaders were making their presence known. Signs were already erected in German and any visible symbol of Czech nationalism seemed to be in the process of being removed, as if the country's soul was being taken apart one piece at a time.

All three looked directly ahead as Jaroslav pulled the car past the German sentry at the front of the Legation, who did not make any attempt to stop them from driving into the courtyard. They unloaded the cases, this time with others helping to lug them all the way to the top floor and into the ballroom, led by Doreen. As she flung open the doors, the vast room, now cold and empty, looked back at her. Apart from the grand piano, which appeared tiny given the size of the room, there were only eighteenth-century portraits of British dignitaries watching from the walls and great chandeliers hanging from the ceiling.

Jaroslav and Hilde, followed by Robert Stopford, Wenzel and Tessa pushed past Doreen, dumping the packing cases onto the oak floor with a thud.

Stopford pulled Doreen aside, looking her straight in the eyes and said, 'Patz cannot stay.'

Basil Newton had received word back from London:

Persons mentioned may remain in Legation until arrangements can be made for their safe departure from Czechoslovakia. If possible, I should prefer that you should not admit any more refugees, but realise that in a few exceptional cases you may feel it impossible to refuse asylum.

Stopford was consulted on the reply by the Ambassador. The Legation needed to keep capacity for British Nationals who might need to seek refuge. For example, Doreen, Tessa, Jean and Mary might all need to live there until they could get out.

Of those who were now there, Stopford wondered if any reasonably able to leave the country without fear of arrest. He felt, on balance Patz – Doreen's Sudeten assistant, whose husband was already in England – would not be known to the authorities. She could go.

Doreen did not know whether to scream, cry or punch Stopford. While she was contemplating, he explained that the Ambassador wanted Hilde to return to her residence before the curfew started.

'But she has stayed on in Prague to work for the office, when Hilde could have joined her husband and he his wife in England long before,' Doreen protested, not wanting her to hear the hushed conversation with Stopford. Nothing Doreen could say would change the situation; she knew that. And in reality, any protestations now would just waste valuable time.

Doreen insisted on telling her. She was, as always, taken aback by Hilde's pragmatism. There were no tears, no shouting. She listened and then asked for a few minutes to digest the news. She went off to the corner of the room and leant on the grand piano alone. Doreen watched her with a mix of pride and sadness flowing through her veins.

The young woman decided that she would go to the border town of Ostrava, where her husband had family. There, she would try to cross into Poland illegally. Doreen hugged her, before turning to the others in the room and explaining the situation.

'We must go at once and do not wait,' Jaroslav said, offering to drive them to the station. 'For the moment, everything is safe,' he concluded.

Doreen felt a deep sense of responsibility for her whole team, but Hilde was particularly important to her. She was young, pretty and only recently married. She had had the option to go to Britain at any point in the last four months to be with her husband but had flatly refused, insisting on staying with Doreen.

Jaroslav drove them to the travel agency, where they bought a ticket for a train which was due to leave just before the curfew would come into effect. The train was far from fully booked, Doreen was told. What about the others in the Legation, she thought, such as Wenzel? Could they not try to leave now and cross the border with Hilde?

Telling her to wait outside the office until they returned, Jaroslav and Doreen raced back to the Legation. 'I panted up the four or five flights of stairs to the ballroom and urged the others to escape.'

Wenzel had made up his mind that he could not stay in Prague any longer, but he was such a well-known face, he felt it would be impossible for him to leave now without a decent disguise.

He was, of course, right. Thinking on her feet, Doreen turned to Tessa and asked: 'You wouldn't mind lending him your passport, would you, if I dressed him up?'

Wenzel and the others looked at Doreen with astonishment. Was she being serious?

'Of course!' Replied Tessa, fishing around in her bag for her documents. But before she could produce it, Taub stepped forward and asked for quiet. They needed a diplomatic plan to get out. For now, they were safe in the Legation. It would be foolish to try to smuggle anyone out that evening.

Doreen let out a frustrated *tut* to emphasise her disagreement. Her return trip to the Legation was completely wasted, but deep down she understood she had been too impulsive. Back they drove to pick up Hilde to take her to the train station as agreed. To Doreen's horror, the place she had left her was deserted. 'We walked up and down, and drove around, but she did not come,' Doreen remembered.

She did not want to go anywhere until she found Hilde. 'It was getting late,' Doreen said. 'And every moment was more dangerous.' She knew the jeopardy they would be in if they did not make it back to the Legation in time for the curfew. They would be trapped outside in the freezing cold with nowhere to go. Deciding to split up, Doreen kissed Jaroslav goodbye, thanking him for all he had done that day. She then trudged through the empty streets of Prague towards the Legation.

As she turned up Thunovská Street with her destination now in sight, speakers across the city barked: 'Achtung, Achtung, anyone on the street will be shot on sight ... Achtung, Achtung.'

Doreen broke into a sprint, racing into the courtyard. She kept running until she was back in the ballroom. Exhausted, she looked out through the window up to the Castle, where swastikas were lit up, there to welcome Hitler, who was on his way for the night.

On the other side of the city, Martha and Waitstill had arrived back at their hotel in plenty of time. The couple had stood in stunned silence after walking through the revolving doors into the lobby they now knew so well. It was bustling with Nazi officers, standing around with drinks and cigarettes in hand, chatting and laughing together as if they were at a cocktail party.

Despite having no appetite, Martha wondered whether forcing herself to eat something might ease the constant nausea she had. But the dining room was a sea of Nazi uniformed men. The *maître d'* embarrassedly apologised to Waitstill that there were no free tables, but said he would prepare the next available one for the Sharps, as soon as it was vacated.

Hearing the conversation, a monocled Nazi officer stood up, came to attention and offered Waitstill and Martha to join his table.

'We wish to be alone,' Waitstill replied curtly.

The officer was not insulted, he clicked his heels, turned to Martha and winked, before sitting back down. It only made her feel sicker.

Just at that point, a waiter approached and said a table was now free. But after their food arrived, neither had an appetite. 'The food somehow tasted like straw,' Martha reflected. So they made their way to their room and without saying a word to each other, got ready for bed.

Outside, they could hear the roar of German military trucks being loaded with food from the warehouses around the city and driven back to Germany. Sometimes convoys of over forty trucks raced their way back to Berlin, with looted stocks of steel, timber, textiles and food. The looting went on every night for months. Supplies for the refugees were going to become even more scarce, Martha thought, before she fell into a light sleep.

As Martha slept in her hotel room, Doreen was ensconced in the British Legation, where she slept in the ballroom with Wenzel. She looked out of the window from where she could see across the city up to the castle, where Hitler was currently accommodated along with Reichsführer SS Heinrich Himmler, the head of Nazi security police Reinhard Heydrich, foreign minister Joachim von Ribbentrop and Deputy Führer Hermann Göring, all of whom had accompanied the Führer to Prague. Their train to the Sudetenland and then car into Prague had been escorted by a group led by Karl Hermann Frank, a Sudeten German notorious for his hatred of the Czechs. Hitler's entrance into the country was kept secret, and thanks to the strict curfew, no one saw his motorcade arrive.

Hitler arrived before the Czech President, Emil Hácha who was also travelling back from Berlin, and when Hácha finally got there an hour later, he was forced to use the servant's entrance, a symbol of the new relationship between the Germans and the Czechs. He was not invited to Hitler's candlelit supper, which had been hastily prepared by the Castle staff. Despite being a vegetarian teetotaller, the Führer tried some local ham, washed down with a small glass of Pilsner beer.

When he complained the following morning that he had slept badly, blaming his foray into Czech alcohol, the residents of Prague spread a rumour that the ghost of Tomáš Masaryk had kept him awake.

*

Doreen's dream of being rocked gently as she sat on train came to an abrupt end when she awoke to find a Legation member of staff trying to stir her. He apologised profusely, but his knocking at the door had garnered no response. He passed her an urgent message that a group of women and children were gathered at Wilson Station asking for her.

Thanking the departing messenger, Doreen rolled over and shook Wenzel awake. She needed to leave immediately. She dressed and raced through the cold morning to the station where she found over thirty families. Some had gone to her office that morning but had walked into what felt like a scene from a novel, with officials in Nazi uniforms swanning around.

Huddled in the crowded station waiting room, these were some of those who had not managed to get back in time for the train which left a few nights prior. These poor souls were not yet aware that many of them no longer had passports.

They were so exhausted and hungry that Doreen paid for them all to have a hot meal at the station restaurant. She got a message to Tessa to find some accommodation for these families. This immediately proved problematic, as all the central hotels, hostels and guesthouses were being used by the German soldiers. However, she managed to find some rooms in the northern outskirts of the city – Roztoky – where an elderly innkeeper was willing to house the refugees for a week's payment in advance in British Sterling.

By 11 a.m., Hitler was parading proudly through the streets of Prague, the pavements crowded with people, many of whom turned their back on his car as it passed. The Nazi procession sent the city into complete gridlock, with Wenceslas Square entirely shut. The Führer made a display of greeting a staged column of German students. Adorned in Nazi uniforms and heavily bandaged, they were there as the supposed victims of Czech brutality. Hitler's official photographer, Heinrich Hoffmann, was on hand to snap several shots of the Führer comforting these so-called distressed men, all of whom grinned uncontrollably.

The theatrics meant that Doreen and her throng of women and children needed to go all the way around the city through the backstreets in order to get a bus to their new accommodation which Tessa had hastily arranged. Scared of attracting unnecessary attention to themselves by walking in large groups, they tried to walk separately – not an easy task with so many children in the group. Eventually, after a couple of stops for food and coffee, a fainting woman and several crying children, Doreen was relieved when she found a taxi rank full of cars, paying for them all to be driven to the bus and then on to their hotel.

Upon her return to the Legation, another message awaited her. More people had arrived at Wilson Station. She went back and forward for most of the day, finding hotels and hostels where they could on the outskirts of the city. Each one was grubbier and dirtier than the previous, but luxurious for the refugee women and children, who had been living in squalid camps for the past six months. By the end of the day, Doreen had amassed a total of 240 women and children who were living in six establishments in and around the city. Only a handful had their passport; the rest were now technically stateless.

After his parade, Hitler appeared on the balcony of the Castle to address the people of Czechoslovakia. 'I now proclaim this state the Protectorate of Bohemia and Moravia,' he barked. Martha looked up from the crowd, thinking he sounded even wilder than she had heard on the radio. She had spent the morning in her office with her new staff meeting families who had appointments. Following advice from Doreen, she was now also encouraging people to cross the border illegally if they could, taking one of her calling cards to present in Poland. Next to her in the crowd, Tessa shook her head as Hitler spoke, in disbelief that this was the second time she had been present at one of his speeches.

He finished by introducing the new leaders he had appointed to lead the new protectorate. Baron Konstantin von Neurath was to assume the post of Reichsprotecktor, effectively the country's leader. As German Foreign Minister until he was replaced by

Joachim von Ribbentrop, he was a known name to Martha. Although a member of the Nazi Party, she viewed his appointment as a diplomatic move to lend a veneer of stability and legitimacy to German rule over the occupied Czech lands. 'He was so old he had been in virtual retirement,' she mused, and was now resurrected to be a figurehead. She hoped there might be time to get more people out while the elderly man got a grip of the mechanics of the city.

Taking solace from the fact that all was not yet lost, Martha returned to her office. In a quiet moment she telephoned Clare Hollingworth, who was just starting to get up to speed on the situation from Poland.

Born on 10 October, 1911, and having grown up in a modest but comfortable household near Leicester, Clare's attendance at boarding school from a young age gave her the independence and confidence she needed to be able to take on this assignment with the BCRC. Martha was struck by her reason for doing so. While studying at Zagreb University in the summer of 1934, Clare shared a house with a Jewish refugee called Otto. Having escaped Germany after the rise of Nazism, Otto impressed on her 'how unbearable life had become in Germany for anyone who the Nazis disliked'. She wanted to help people like her dear friend Otto.

Following a few days in Gdynia, Clare had taken the train to city of Katowice in Upper Silesia. This was where Bertha Bracey and Margaret Layton had envisioned she would be the most effective. Thanks to Doreen's ingenuity in sending people illegally over the border – a tactic Martha had now adopted – hundreds of people were now showing up at the British and American Legation offices in the city with calling cards, saying they had been told to report there for onward travel to London. The officials were getting frustrated by the queues of desperate men, women and children, all of whom believed that they were expected.

The appointment of Clare was an inspired choice by Margaret. With over five years working at the League of Nations Union (LNU), she was knowledgeable and well connected in European affairs. British Consul General John Thwaites – who was deluged with requests for help from hundreds of refugees waving calling cards in his face – had heard of her by reputation. He took to her immediately. Clare impressed him not only with her hard work and understanding of the political environment, but also with tales of her brief fling with Irish writer, James Joyce, which she was sure to drop into conversation.

Thwaites offered her an office next to his, and Clare set about trying to meet more than fifty refugees each day. She would compile lists of those who had travelled there illegally, requesting visas for Britain. For those who had got there through legitimate means, she would organise their onward travel. With two female secretaries working for her, within two weeks of being in Poland she reported back to Margaret Layton that her feet were well and truly under the table.

Mirroring the scenes to those in Prague, each morning Clare would arrive at work at the Legation offices in Poland and to get to her desk would need to push through the throng of people queuing down the stairs and spilling out onto the street. The building had two large waiting rooms which would also be packed. One of her recently appointed secretaries had devised an efficient system of each person collecting a number. Then a blackboard would show which number was being seen at that point.

Clare believed Poland was only one step behind Czechoslovakia, and firmly in Hitler's sights. People who had fled Czechoslovakia found little comfort in getting over the border without knowing if onward travel would be possible. There was also a general sense of antisemitism in the air, with mutterings of disapproval at the number of Jews now travelling to Katowice. Clare estimated that over 100 refugees would arrive from Czechoslovakia every day, most of whom were Jewish.

Her efficient and industrious presence was immediately felt by the women in Prague, who were struggling with the bustling workload, now having been thrown out of the BCRC office.

Following the departure of Hilde Patz – and Jean Rowntree who had left with 'I don't know how many rings on all my fingers!' belonging to Czechs desperate to get their valuables out of reach of the Nazis – Margaret Layton had jumped into action to find some more people to help. Digging out an old letter recommending the two women, she booked them on the next available flight to Prague, without speaking to either of them first. She dashed off a telegram to Doreen:

MARGARET DOUGAN AND CHRISTINE MAXWELL ARRIVING TODAY BY PLANE STOP WIRE IF YOU NEED MORE STOP LAYTON

Both women were enigmas, giving little away about themselves. Little was known about their backgrounds and even less about their motivations, but nevertheless, they were effective workers. Margaret Dougan, who immediately became known as Miss Dougan to avoid confusion with her namesake in London, would act as another courier, supporting Tessa. Meanwhile, Christine was given the job of interviewing refugees who came to the British Legation or American Relief offices.

Although Martha had been relying on her local staff of women from among the refugees, their situation was becoming more precarious by the minute. Her loyal assistant Lisl Xall left the office on the evening of 15 March, exhausted. Her country had been invaded, her Jewish family were at risk, and her new work for the relief organisation would do nothing for her own safety.

Martha had often pondered on the question, what does one

do when one's country is taken over in this way? For Lisl, she tried to carry on as normal. A days' work and then something social in the evening. For the last few months, along with her husband David, they would meet her beloved brother Friedl in Kavarna Artia, a café popular with Jews. Lisl had always been so grateful for not only finding a husband, but a best friend for her brother. David and Friedl adored each other. And the three of them spent many happy evenings in this bar. But as they sat dejected at a small corner table, looking out of the window into the dark street, it was not the same. Kavarna Artia had produced some of Lisl and her family's happiest recent memories, rare among the suffering they were enduring. But after the invasion, it immediately felt completely foreign. Lisl wondered, was it the fact that – like her – everyone in there was drinking away their sorrows? At least, she supposed, they were united in grief.

The mellow tone of the room on that evening of 15 March was suddenly changed after Lisl heard screams from the door just fifteen feet away from where she was sitting. A man had kicked it open and was standing with his right arm in the air, holding a grenade aloft.

He paused for a beat before throwing it into the bar. As people scrambled to get away, clambering over tables and chairs, the explosive device hit the counter, bounced off an overturned table and rolled towards Lisl. She was frozen in fear.

Her brother Friedl, with no thought for himself, grabbed it and ran to the door, hoping to toss it back where it had come from. He had only taken a couple steps before a huge blast erupted. In front of her eyes, Lisl saw her beloved sibling blown into tiny pieces. She was thrown back by the force of the explosion and knocked unconscious.

She awoke with ringing in her ears, dizzy and with so much debris in her eyes she could hardly make out where she was. But the smell of burning flesh told her she was still in the bar.

Feeling a familiar hand grabbing her, her husband David led her through the mayhem of smoke, fire and people screaming in agony, towards the front door.

'Come, we need to get out of here,' he shouted to her. 'Friedl is beyond our help.'

Those ahead of them ran out onto the street, gasping for air, only to be met by a barrage of shots. Two women who had managed to escape the blast, were cut down by machine gun fire. The snow of the pavement was now being melted by blood. On the other side of the road, a dark green requisitioned Škoda Superb car had its back window rolled down, and a man was firing indiscriminately on those trying to get out of the known Jewish establishment. In the passenger seat sat the man who had thrown the grenade, a small notebook open on his lap where he drew five bar gates, counting the number of victims from the attack.

In a stroke of ingenuity which saved their lives, Lisl's husband dragged his wife in the other direction, further inside the building. Clambering over the fallen tables and the smashed glass crunching under their feat, the couple ascended the stairs to the second floor. Climbing through a window at the back, they ran along the snow-covered roof tiles of the next-door building, then across several other rooves until they made their escape.

When Lisl arrived in the office the next morning, punctual as always, she wore black to mourn her brother. Her left eye was completely lost beneath the dark purple bruising that covered one side of that face. Her cheeks were full of crisscross patterns of cuts and grazes. The piece of glass that had lodged itself in her scalp throbbed terribly.

It was a shocking sight for Miss Dougan and Christine Maxwell, who had been in the country for a matter of hours. Martha was stunned seeing the state she was in. When inquiring what had happened, Lisl simply said that she had be involved in an accident. And yes, she was fine to work that day. 'I am so happy to be working here. I get so absorbed in other people's troubles; I sometimes manage to forget my own,' she told Martha despondently.

Attacks on Jewish establishments such as Kavarna Artia, where Lisl's brother had been killed, became a regular occurrence in the coming weeks. Opposite Robert Stopford's flat, another little café was wrecked by a bomb which had gone off in a room used as a Jewish club on the same evening.

Anecdotally, Martha had been told that the Nazis believed that of the refugees, ninety-nine percent were Jewish or part-Jewish. Whether this was true or not, the danger to the residents – permanent or temporary – in Prague was becoming more real by the day.

Chapter Ten

Defiance

Later on the morning of Friday 17 March, Martha and Doreen were sitting in a small café on Nerudova Street, a short walk from the British Legation. Martha was shaken by the attack Lisl had suffered. Doreen had heard a rumour of the incident, but since the occupation, radio broadcasts were now blocked – except for the propaganda messages – and with newspapers censored, it was impossible to verify what news was real. When Waitstill had turned on the wireless in their room that morning, all Martha heard was 'the deafening buzz of jamming filled the room'. Therefore in the absence of reliable news, gossip was rife about the goings on in Czechoslovakia and further afield.

'I have also heard that the Chamberlain government in Great Britain has fallen, and Sir Anthony Eden is now Prime Minister,' Martha divulged.

'Wishful thought,' Doreen replied, knowing that the British Legation would have told her if that was true. Yet this was also something which she had heard already. It was being talked about around the restaurants in Prague as if it were fact. These conversations became normal in the weeks after the occupation. *Have you heard that this person was killed? No, I had heard they were arrested for killing that person.* Having no way to verify what was and was not true was difficult to endure.

By the end of the weekend, they were able to gather some small shreds of news, thanks to ingenuity of Mary Penman. She began partaking in some passive resistance, having had a radio fitted in her car which could access the BBC. The Nazis had a system for pinpointing such machines which were hacking into banned stations, so Mary took to driving around the city while listening to the news. She did not know that her activities had attracted the attention of the Luftwaffe, who, now the weather had improved, were flying over the city trying to find the vehicle, instructing military police on motorcycles to intercept Mary's car. Martha in particular appreciated getting some snippets of information. 'So far she has eluded discovery, but it was getting more dangerous every night.'

Martha had wanted to meet Doreen in a public place that morning, as she had some serious concerns she wanted to discuss. Over the last two days, low-ranking youthful German soldiers had begun standing guard outside all noteworthy establishments in Prague, including the offices of American Relief, the Alcron Hotel and Hotel Atlantic where both women were staying. But Martha's concern was more pertinent. The previous day, the Sharps were told that a telephone engineer had been sent to their hotel room to fix the handset, which they were unaware had any issues.

That morning, Waitstill whispered to her as they walked from the taxi, ascending the steps into their offices, the only time they were outside alone together. 'I found my bed wired for sound,' he said as quietly as he could. 'There is a machine hidden underneath. I disconnected it. We must be careful.'

Doreen's heart missed a beat. Yes, she had noticed for the last couple of days an off-putting tapping sound that could be heard whenever she would call someone from her hotel room. And the chit-chat of agents bugging as much of the city as possible was common. But something which had been puzzling her, suddenly became so clear. She had called Margaret the previous morning to ask for some additional funds to allow her to buy hundreds of postage stamps. When Margaret politely questioned her reason for such a purchase, Doreen told her it was the best way to bribe Polish border guards. Upon her return to her hotel later, a large bowl of flowers had been placed in the middle of the table in her room. In the card, someone had written: 'You are a brave girl.' She now suspected the anonymous admirer had not sent them through admiration, but as a threat.

Moving forward, the only option was to meet somewhere secret or a public place, such as the street or hotel lobby. But gathering in a clandestine location would put the women in higher danger and so Doreen and Martha agreed they would meet for a walk each morning. Martha had heard that a group of German police had pounced on two people speaking together, separated and questioned them to test if their versions of the discussion topic matched. They would therefore agree a 'subject' in the first few minutes of the walk, before moving onto true business matters.

With the telephones being tapped, rooms bugged, telegrams and letters intercepted, they also devised a new technique to communicate with London. For example, a telegram would be sent to England asking for sixty feet of carpet. Carpet being the code for refugee visas. If they expressed concerns about five pieces of jewellery, this was five Jews. Their telegrams and letters from the 18 March are filled with cryptic sentences, many of which have never been deciphered by anyone other than the intended recipient.

Clare invented the code in Poland, using her remarkable creativity which would make her the talented writer she turned out to be. She first used it when writing to Margaret's secretary:

Dear Miss Allen
300 feet of carpet is by no means long enough for the size of the houses out here. I shall therefore be extremely grateful if you will double the order.
When you have done this, I shall be very glad if you

> *will inform me immediately, as a house without carpets is slightly noisy.*
> *Yours sincerely*
> *Clare Hollingworth*
> *P.S. I shall have to return to England [soon] and would like the house as much as possible in order before I go.*

It was not just communication methods that were changing for the women in Prague. The Nazis were making their presence known in peculiar ways. For example, the Czechs drove on the left of the road, but the day after the invasion it was announced on the state-sanctioned radio that traffic would shift to driving on the other side of the road, to align with the rest of Third Reich. Robert Stopford immediately spotted at flaw. 'It was pointed out that the trams could not negotiate the points the wrong way and so the order had to be suspended for several days.' However, that did not stop the chaos that followed. With only a handful of drivers aware that the order had been delayed, there was a sharp increase in traffic incidents across Czechoslovakia. Prague reported twenty-six car crashes and one fatality in the aftermath. The Nazi leadership in the city were unhappy that it took a further ten days for the change to actually take place.

Baron Konstantin von Neurath, the new Reichsprotecktor, was in all but name the country's leader. His deputy, Karl Hermann Frank – who had escorted Hitler into Prague on the day of the invasion – was the enforcer. Described as 'one of the worst horsewhipping bullies of the upstart type' by a former colleague, he was determined to make the Czech people pay for what he believed had been twenty years of German oppression.

Frank wasted no time in implementing 'special courts', with ultimate power over any existing Czech legal systems. In these, the three German judges decided what evidence was admissible, there was no appeal against sentence and no interpreters or legal representatives were allowed. Convictions were guaranteed. The 'special courts' were used to administer new decrees imposed for offences such as hoarding food, breaking blackout rules, making political jokes and listening to a foreign radio station. The Malicious Offences Law stated its purpose was to make 'grumblers, carpers and faultfinders into criminals'.

In such a supressed environment, everyone became paranoid towards each other. That was, after all, the intention. 'I found myself so disturbed by the pressures and the potentially serious consequences of making the slightest mistake,' Martha recalled. The occupiers relied heavily on malevolent denunciations, with nearly a quarter of the arrests in those first few days arising from this source. It became impossible to know whether the person you were talking with could be trusted.

The Czechs, a people usually so willing to speak their minds, were being silenced. And their free press was now completely censored. For the brave few who still tried to listen to overseas programmes, such as Mary in her car, there was little information of note to pick up. Scenes following the occupation of Czechoslovakia were appearing in newspapers and on newsreels in Britain, but the impact on the general public was mixed. *Had Hitler actually been invited into Czechoslovakia? Or was this an act of war?*

The attacks such as the one which Lisl witnessed were kept from the international eyes, but press briefings were prepared anyway, blaming Czech terrorists, in case the news leaked. Even some officials in Prague were so oblivious, they started to believe the propaganda. 'I am encouraged to hope that [the Nazis'] attitude towards the mass of the Czechs may turn out to be more hopeful than many had anticipated,' one American Legation official wrote with naïve optimism.

This incredible gullibility was far from the truth of what was actually happening. The new 'special court' in a trial room at

Pankrac Prison started to hand out thousands of sentences each week, ranging from hefty fines through to long imprisonment with hard labour and death. Offences varied, but in a randomly selected five day period under German rule, the court was told of offences such as over-pricing washing soda, listening to a foreign radio broadcast, hiding a pig, unauthorised slaughter of cattle, booing in a cinema during a newsreel and over-charging for the extermination of rats. For cases where a death sentence was handed down by the judges, convicts had ninety seconds to address the bench before being taken into the adjacent, white-tiled slaughterhouse-styled execution room to be hanged.

There was also a guillotine with a sixty-five kilos knife in case the fourteen hooks for nooses were full. Karl Hermann Frank would boast that at their peak, his men were executing more than 150 people each week.

Martha was relieved that Alice Masaryk had agreed to leave the country and was now on her way to the safety of the United States. She had nightmares of this women she respected so much, being killed in the same way in Pankrac Prison. Doreen had tried unsuccessfully to persuade Františka Plamínková to do the same, but she flatly refused. Having stood up to Hitler for the last ten years, she would be damned if she was going to run now. She remained, always looking over her shoulder because there was no one from the establishment she could trust anymore. Rather than being disbanded, the Czech police were forced to cooperate with the commands of the Nazi leadership under the threat of death. On the first day of the occupation, four policemen were arrested on trumped up charges and executed that evening by firing squad. Leading police officers were brought to witness the event, ensuring that they knew their fate should they not carry out their orders.

They were used for a variety of tasks, most of which were seen to be too trivial for the German invaders. A special unit of detectives was set up to process all exit visas from the Protectorate following the occupation. These Czech men bravely did all they could to ensure that as many permits were issued as possible, something which went unnoticed by their new masters for some time.

It was therefore a pleasant surprise for Doreen when she was informed on Friday 24 March, less than two weeks since the occupation, that 100 people had been cleared to leave. They had also been given their visas from the United Kingdom, albeit delayed by British officials for nearly a month. All that was needed now was to book travel as quickly as possible.

Doreen had a covert task which meant she needed to remain in Prague indefinitely, so she asked if Tessa and Martha would act as the couriers; Tessa taking the first group at 4 p.m. and Martha the second at 4.30 p.m.

With the Germans having issued legitimate exit visas and travel permits, one advantage of the invasion – if there was such a thing at all – was that the refugees could now travel through Germany up to the Hook of Holland as there were no longer any official borders to cross. The border to Poland was closed indefinitely because of the unmanageable volume of illegal crossings, meaning that the normal route was no longer an option. Clare was relieved that she could get things under control in Poland without yet another transport adding a further 100 people to her books.

Tessa was happy to go, but Martha worried about leaving. She was busy without Waitstill, who had taken a train to Geneva on 22 March to cash two cheques they had brought from America, hidden in his money belt, worth $10,000 ($225,000 in 2025). The banks in Czechoslovakia had all been taken over by the German invaders, making transactions of this amount impossible.

'Nobody can do it as well as you, Martha,' Doreen said persuasively, as she saw the American lost in thought. 'A clergyman's wife and an American!'

Doreen explained, with a wink, that Martha and Tessa would primarily be escorting 'household workers.' This was code for people who needed to escape urgently. There would be known anti-Nazis within the group, and if the women were caught attempting to assist the enemy of the Third Reich in this way, prison would be the lightest sentence they could expect, no matter their nationality. Torture and death were the usual punishment. Having listened to Doreen, Martha instinctively thought of her children, trying to imagine what they would be doing at that moment. The truth was that after being apart from them for two months, she was struggling to picture them without the help of some faded photographs.

'Saving endangered people seems worth the risk,' she stoically told Doreen after a few moments' thought.

Martha and Tessa had to go to their respective Legations to get urgent travel visas, which they did with no trouble. Then they went to the police headquarters, where they found the Czech Criminal Investigation Department – which strangely had been made responsible for coordinating travel permits – closed as their new Nazi boss was out for lunch. So much for German efficiency, thought Tessa. They waited over an hour until a young German soldier opened the door. Martha explained their travel plans and asked to see one of the Czech detectives.

'Why do you want to leave Prague?' the private asked with genuine confusion in his voice. 'Now that we are here, everything is so wonderful!'

'We only want to see some old friends in London,' Martha replied, before adding 'And since we live here in Prague, I must be sure you give me a re-entry permit too.'

'I am afraid that I shall have to ask you to wait for my captain,' the soldier said. 'He is a bit late trying out a new cuisine.' The women were by now used to the occupiers' lavish use of Prague's restaurants. A new order in place stated that German 'liberators' should be served first, meaning that by the time anyone else were eligible to eat, the only dish left tended to be soup and dumplings. Conversely, hospitals in the city had seen a spike in stomach-related ailments caused by the invaders' excessive feasting.

The women waited an hour. It was nearly 3 p.m. and Tessa's train was due to leave in another hour. Eventually the captain arrived, having clearly enjoyed his liquid lunch. Rather attracted to the two smiling women, he was happy to stamp them a visa and re-entry permit which lasted for ten days.

Successful in that quest, they split up. Tessa heading to her apartment to collect some belongings, and Martha to go to her office for some papers and leave a note for Waitstill. 'Gone to see some friends in London. Back soon,' she wrote, hoping he would read between the lines. As she left the office, just outside she bumped into Lydia Buschova, a wealthy refugee she had befriended. When Martha explained that she had to rush to the station as she was going to London, Lydia started to pull off bits of jewellery and handed them over, piece by piece to Martha. 'My mother needs a cancer operation and the sale of these could take care of the clinical costs,' she said.

'Fine,' Martha replied, pocketing the valuables. Tessa had had a similar request, with paintings by a world-famous artist stashed in her rucksack, along with a ring hidden in a needle case. Tessa never divulged the identity of the artist, taking the secret to her grave. She only offered the teaser that the drawings were 'by someone in the same league as Van Gogh!'

Martha got a taxi to her hotel where she threw some possessions and a bit of money into a bag, asking the taxi to keep his meter running while she was inside. Then she went to the station, arriving at 4.15 p.m. where she was met by Doreen. Tessa, she explained, had just left with fifty refugees.

Martha was given a handwritten list of another fifty she would be taking. 'Some of your group have not yet assembled,' Doreen told her. 'Some will come out of hiding just in time to board the moving train.'

Excellent, thought Martha. 'Household workers' would not be in hiding ... she recognised in her group a famous Jewish surgeon who had managed to escape from German concentration camp Buchenwald, a well-known actor who had played a satire of Hermann Göring the previous year, and a renowned female scientist who had been publicly anti-Nazi.

Martha found her seat in fourth class among the others she hoped to escort safely to Britain. Doreen came into the carriage with three more women and asked for the list back. Borrowing the pen of the man sitting next to Martha, Doreen wrote the three new names on the bottom of the list, before handing it back. The fresh names in green ink stood out from the others, which had been written in black.

As the train pulled away – with its ear-piercing whistle and great exhale of smoke – people started to sob, whether out of relief or sadness, Martha could not tell. Their instincts were telling them not to go into Germany. But they had no other option.

As the train started to pick up speed on its way out of the station, two men sprinted along the platform and clambered in through the door, collapsing on the floor.

'They're yours!' Doreen shouted from the platform, unsure if anyone could hear her.

The men introduced themselves to Martha. They were Jewish journalists from the *United Press* and *Associated Press*. Despite their physique that enabled them to jump like gazelles onto a moving train, their 'poor health' apparently required a change of scene and warmer climate. The many words they had published supporting communism meant they also happened to be in a lot of danger.

As the train made its way towards the border, people started to get up and move around, stretching their legs, peering out of the windows or finding someone else to converse with to pass the time. Martha found herself sitting next a twelve-year-old boy and his fourteen-year-old brother.

Pointing to a tall man and women on their other side, Martha asked in German if they were their parents, but neither boy answered. She asked again in German, but getting no response, she thought maybe they only spoke Czech.

'Their parents were a double suicide last week,' the tall man told Martha quietly in English, putting his arm on the shoulder of the younger boy. 'They have relatives in England,' he continued.

Martha sat with them quietly until the Czech conductor walked through the carriage asking for tickets and breaking the silence.

'Where are you going?' he asked the tall man.

'To London,' was the reply, not being able to conceal his excitement.

'Don't forget us poor Czechs when you get there!' the conductor replied, before punching the tickets and moving on.

It took hours to get to the German border. The passengers watched out of the windows at the stunning countryside. 'Lovely valleys, streams, scattered villages and hamlets; hills and mountains crowned with chapels, churches, castles, and widespread fields,' one woman wrote in her diary.

The outside beauty contrasted with the inside of train, which was so busy that luggage kept falling off the racks at the slightest jolt. The fourth-class seats were painful on the bottom and there was no running water in the toilets. By the time the train did arrive at the border, the carriage was cramped, hot and stank of sewage.

The crossing to Germany was busy. Everyone got off the train, while Martha and her fellow travellers' carriage was unhitched and put in a siding, while the rest of the train and its passengers went on. Martha tried to find out more information, but nothing was forthcoming. There was a small food stall where she could buy some sustenance for everyone with her limited funds. They were also able to wash their faces and drink from the faucet on the platform.

It was not until dawn the next morning after they had left that the carriage was hitched to another locomotive, and they moved off again. For three hours the travelled slowly through Germany before being put into another siding, with the rest of the train going on. This happened several times, each adding further anxiety to the refugees who were desperate to just get out of Nazi territory. They were also meant to be getting their boat from the Hook of Holland to England in the next hour, and they were still in Germany.

When the train stopped at Reine in Westphalia, only half an hour from the Dutch border, everyone was again ordered off. Martha was by this point wearing Lydia's diamond bracelets, neckless and earrings. She had never felt so grand.

Taking her luggage for customs inspection, her bag was searched but no one batted an eyelid at all the fine jewellery she was wearing. Her American passport certainly added weight to her status. The refugees' bags, on the other hand, were emptied, while anything valuable such as a silver spoons, plates, jewellery and money was all confiscated. The Nazi guards even insisted on taking wedding rings, forcing women to prize them off their fingers in tears.

Martha ensured she was last to get back on the train, and

thinking everyone had boarded, from behind she heard desperate shouting.

'Mrs Sharp! Mrs Sharp!'

She jumped off, back onto the platform, dodging the conductor who tried to stop her. The two newspaper men who had arrived last on the train were stood on the platform, one stripped to the waist, both their bags laying empty on the table. All their possessions were strewn all over the floor, including all their travel documents.

'What is the meaning of this?' Martha bravely confronted the German policeman. She gave no time for them to reply. 'Have you orders to arrest these men?'

'No but we must get special permission from headquarters before they can leave.' The train started to blow its horn behind them, signalling its imminent departure.

Noticing a letter from the United States Legation – which Martha had collected from her office earlier that day to distribute to everyone in her group – laying on the ground, she picked it up and handed it to the German. The grand seal of the United States made him take notice.

'Does anybody here read English?' Martha asked in German.

When her question was received with shrugs and head shakes.

'Very well, I shall translate,' she said. 'This letter puts this man under my protection as an American citizen. He and the others are members of my group going to London and I will not leave without them.' She flashed the signature of Wilbur Carr, United States Ambassador in Prague, at the bottom of the letter. The man seemed genuinely impressed, Martha thought. 'I will call my officials if you insist on holding these men,' she added for good measure, before the train blew its horn and let out an impressive puff of steam.

After a quick look to his colleague, the Nazi started to ask: 'If you will give us the letter to show that they are under United States protection ...'

'Yes, you may have the letter to show to your superior,' Martha interrupted, handing it over. She looked to the other newspaper man who was frozen topless where he stood. He did not register immediately, and then suddenly dropped to his hands and knees, searching through the pile of his possessions for his own letter, which he duly found and handed over.

The officers conferred in low voices together, while the train guard behind was rushing up the platform shouting and slamming the doors closed.

'They may go,' the German officer finally said.

The two journalists and Martha scooped up as many of the possessions from the floor and dashed to the moving train. Martha literally threw everything she had in her hands through the window before being pulled onto the train through the door.

It did not take long before the train pulled up at the border with Holland. Although the Dutch officials were far more courteous than their German counterparts, they were no less thorough. Hitler was trying to insert agents across Europe, so vigilance was essential, and no one was above suspicion. By the end of 1939, up to 20,000 of Hitler's undercover operatives were active across the continent.

The Dutch passport official who boarded their carriage was visibly taken aback by the stench from the blocked toilet. Asking in German who was in charge, Martha stepped forward and explained that her group were under American supervision. She handed over her handwritten list of the group Doreen had given her, written on Legation headed paper. The official then walked down the aisle checking each passport and visa against the list. Martha strained her neck around to watch, but after a while it became too uncomfortable, so relaxed facing forwards.

'Mrs Sharp! Mrs Sharp!' Martha heard from behind almost instantaneously. She took a breath, closing her eyes in frustration for a second, before turning around and painting the famous smile back on her face. It was the two journalists again.

'What is it now?' she asked.

'They say our names are not on your list. They say we must go back into Germany.'

Martha's heart sank. The list Doreen had given her, and then added to, never had the two last arrivals on it. She looked at the journalists, one of whom was literally trembling with fear. *Think. How could she bluff this?*

Getting up and going over to the passport officer, she asked to examine her list. She then walked anxiously back to her seat, all the time looking frantically around for the man who's pen Doreen had used in Prague. *Which one was he?* They had all moved seats so many times since their journey started. Before she could make her mind up, a man pulled his pen out of his top pocket triumphantly and presented it to Martha as she passed. If it had been of any value, it would have been confiscated by the Germans, but thankfully it had been spared. And now perhaps the journalists would be as well. Martha turned her list over and scribbled the two names on the back.

'These two men are in my party. You should have turned over the list' she told the officer. She flashed the reverse of the sheet in front of his face, and then waved it around as if to show everyone else. In truth, she just wanted the ink to dry, so fanning it might speed that up. Everyone nodded in agreement.

The officer grabbed the paper and looked on the back. In disbelief, he said, 'I am sure the names were not there before'.

Martha just stared at him, right in the eyes, trying not to blink. He started to shake his head, let out a small chuckle and okayed the journalists' passports. He knew exactly what she had done but admired her for being so audacious. He also could not stand the aroma for a moment longer.

Free to go, the train sped on, for the first time out of German-occupied territory. Martha was physically and emotionally drained. A second near miss had sapped her of any remaining energy. Plus, the uncomfortable seats were tiring her out. It was now safe for her to leave those she was escorting, so took herself to the dining car alone. Having spent all her money at the food cart at the German stop, she looked at the remaining coins in her hand to see what she could afford.

A charming British man queuing behind her tried to drum up conversation. When Martha explained her journey so far and the reason for her travel, the man casually handed her a £50 (over £3,000 in 2025) note, asking if it would be enough to get everyone something to eat. He had more if it was needed. Martha flung her arms around the unexpecting man, squeezing him tight.

'Thank you,' she whispered in his ear, before running back down the train like a child on their way to a sweet shop, to her carriage. She led her group back, where they queued to get their first real meal since they had left the previous day. Such acts of kindness against a backdrop of so much despair can be overwhelming. The emotions around the tables on that train turned from elation while desperately scoffing down their meal, to solemn sadness. Their country had been invaded, they had managed to escape leaving their homes and many loved ones behind, been bullied throughout their journey through Czechoslovakia and Germany. But now they were being treated like royalty by a complete stranger.

At 10 p.m. the train rolled into its final destination at the dock at Vlissingen. The group had travelled non-stop for nearly thirty hours to that point. They wearily lined up in the cold for the night boat, which was waiting, due to depart in an hour.

'Is Mrs Sharp here?' someone called in an English accent. 'Does anybody know whether she and her party got through?' the man continued.

'Here I am,' she answered unenthusiastically.

'Come into my office,' the man said. *What now?* Martha thought.

She entered his small office, housed in a hut next to the dock. A little fireplace made it cosy and welcoming.

'Now, I'll go over your accommodation for the boat,' the man said.

'We haven't any accommodations. The British Committee provided fourth-class tickets and we were only allowed to take out money barely sufficient to buy food.'

'But your people look dead tired,' he replied. 'Wait just a minute, while I check the number of passengers please.' He disappeared outside the office, before returning with a small stack of tickets. 'I can put you all in berths with a little doubling up.'

When Martha tried to interject, he added, 'And this will be at the company's expense.' For the second time that day, Martha stood up and threw her arms around a stranger, hugging him tight. She could have wept, if she hadn't been too tired to do so. The English accent was so reassuring, the kindness and consideration for those in her charge meant so much. There *were* still good people in this world.

Once everyone was on board in one piece and the boat moved off, Martha took a group of children onto deck, and they watched the shores of mainland Europe disappear into darkness. It was a beautiful, clear night, which accounted for the bitter coldness. She started to point to the stars and name them in German. Some she made up, but her audience knew no better. One member of the group remembered that, 'Nearly all of us had never seen the sea before so quite a few got seasick on that cruise.'

The next morning, the entire group gathered together on the dock to watch the boat enter the port of Harwich. They were huddled together, bound by the kind of unity which is bred by intense shared experiences. People started to whoop and holler as the boat docked, embracing each other at random. The child of one family escorted by Martha commented after her arrival in Britain: 'It was probably not necessary for an American to have been charming and beautiful to help refugees. It was just necessary to have been brave and persevering, but Martha was all of these.'

The fourteen-year-old orphan from the train came over to Martha and hugged her. 'Thank you,' he said in German, the first words she had heard either child utter since they left Prague.

The welcoming party on shore of members of the BCRC and the British Unitarian Women included Margaret. 'My dear, your face looks as if you have been in a coal bin, but your diamonds are glorious,' Margaret teased Martha. She had completely forgotten that she was still wearing all of Lydia's jewellery. Checking into a nearby hotel, Martha ran a hot bath before collapsing into bed.

She awoke the next morning to a letter that had been slipped under her door:

Dear Mrs Sharp
We shall never forget what you have done for us and wish to thank you from the depths of our hearts.
Yours and gratefully.

It was signed by twenty members of the transport. Martha broke down in tears. The personal risk she had taken had been worth it.

The refugees headed on to London with Martha, who treated them to a bus tour of the city. 'We admired all the bus and car drivers,' one remembered. 'How they managed to drive their vehicles through a labyrinth of traffic!'

For the following two days, Martha spent time meeting anyone willing to listen to her about the urgent need for more action in Czechoslovakia. Some of the British officials she met – accompanied by Tessa – felt affronted to be spoken to by an American in this way. But her message was clear. 'In some respects,' she told each of them, 'the outflow of refugees is more effectively impeded by the circumlocutions of the British Passport Control Office than by the heavy fist of the almighty German Gestapo.'

Any delays through squabbling and bickering, as Doreen witnessed daily, was costing lives. The 100 people they had brought to England on their most recent journey could have been doubled, if not tripled.

It has never been understood exactly why, but after these meetings, Bertha Bracey received a letter from the British Foreign Office, informing her that the decision had been made in London that Tessa would not be allowed back into Czechoslovakia. Whether it was a disgruntled official exacting revenge, or for genuine reasons, Tessa's work for the BCRC came to an abrupt end.

Chapter Eleven

The Great Escape

One person who would never be allowed to leave German territory was the chairman of the Social Democratic Workers Party, the ruggedly handsome Wenzel Jaksch. He was by now one of the most wanted men in Czechoslovakia. According to the *Daily Herald*, a price was placed on his head and the Gestapo were ordered to 'get him dead or alive'. He had been so critical of Hitler, that it would be an embarrassment for him to not be made an example of. When the Czech newspaper *A Zet* had printed a picture of the Führer which was deemed slightly unflattering in their 18 March edition, they were shut down the next day and their editor arrested. Someone with Wenzel's reputation and history was thus a top priority. Wanted posters with his moustached face on them began to appear throughout the streets of Prague. Despite the campaign to find him, his whereabouts were a complete mystery to the Nazis, although they had their suspicions.

The British Legation, where he had remained in hiding since being collected by Martha, was situated in the grand five-storey Thun Palace, boasting a large courtyard and gardens in the heart of Prague's Mala Strana district. As the crow flies, it was less than a five-minute walk to Prague Castle, where Hitler himself had been staying, much to Wenzel's amusement. 'Hitler had been my neighbour,' he joked.

The location of the British Legation in the heart of the city might have been enviable to some, but it was less than ideal for a man on the run. When leaving the courtyard of the complex through the imposing brown gates, one enters a narrow-cobbled path framed by two high buildings that go for twenty yards before turning onto Thunovská Street. Where this path meets the street today stands a magnificent brass bust of Sir Winston Churchill, looking defiant with his hands gripping the lapels of his jacket. In March 1939, however, his place was taken by two poorly disguised secret police officers, leaning against the stone wall smoking an endless supply of cigarettes, and failing to look inconspicuous.

The Germans had correctly suspected that the disappearance of Wenzel was somehow related to Doreen. As she was now practically living in the Legation, they believed he was there as well. They had gone to the extreme lengths of trying to persuade the British to surrender him, promising no harm would come his way. This was something nobody ever entertained as being true. According to Doreen, her lover had already decided to escape, 'because he knew that they would never let him go.'

Describing himself as 'the uninvited guest' at the Legation, Wenzel lived for a week in a makeshift bedroom, sleeping on what he recalled as 'the red plush bench of the ballroom', and sharing it with Doreen. He would divulge his anguish at night-time when they were alone together.

'You must give me the *gnadenschuss*,' he begged her one evening, referring to a *coup de grâce*, or mercy killing.

The idea of death as his only way out was not something Doreen would entertain. While he settled into his new surroundings, she was busy planning a daring escape mission, even though such an operation would be far from straightforward.

There was only one way in and out of the Legation – down the cobbled path, which was now under constant surveillance night and day. Then to get across the city to the train station – the only viable mode of transport – one needed to navigate multiple checkpoints, only to be subjected to endless searches once on the train. If they managed to make it this far and leave Prague, they would next be greeted at the border by Nazis guards, who were on high alert for the distinctive looking Wenzel Jaksch. None of this deterred Doreen, who continued to construct her elaborate plan, which was the reason why she needed Martha to take the transport of refugees to London with Tessa.

Early on the morning of Tuesday 21 March, the spring weather was starting to appear and the snow showed signs of thawing, finally signalling an end to the bitter winter which had engulfed Prague. A middle-aged man who called himself Mr Kminek was making his way to work, dressed in his usual overalls of blue dungarees, a buttoned up grey shirt, boots and a large trench coat to keep out the cold. He wore a waxed flat cap, pulled low over his eyes and creating a shadow across his face. Weighed down by a heavy bag of tools slung over one shoulder and several six-foot copper pipes balancing on the other, Mr Kminek blended easily into the backdrop of a busy Prague morning.

The two German officers watching the cobbled path leading to the entrance of the British Legation took little notice of this man who was clearly on this way to work as he knocked on the towering black gates of the complex and was then swiftly allowed in. They paid him even less attention when he exited from the courtyard a few hours later after his mornings toils and walked back onto Thunovská Street and disappeared into the crowds of the city. Such little attention was given by the German soldiers that they did not notice that in the space of a few hours the workman had grown a moustache. In fact, it was a completely different person beneath the overalls. It was Prague's most wanted man.

Doreen wrote later how she had chosen the disguise for Jaksch as 'he looked like a workman, because he had in fact once been one when he was younger,' making it an easy role for him to briefly play. As if heading to his next job, he quickly made his way to Mary's apartment where his escape party waited. It consisted of an older loyal Sudeten German known only as Mr Sacher and two women, one of whom was Czech and other German. Such was the concern of the repercussions for helping a wanted man evade the Nazis, the identities of his conspirators were guarded so closely that to this day their exact identities are still unknown. Mr Kminek was the only one who is recorded in Doreen's diary, where she writes of him 'throwing up his job and leaving his flat, to which he would not return in order to help'.

With no time for Wenzel and Doreen to be alone one last time, the remainder of that day was spent preparing for their up-and-coming adventure. Mr Kminek joined them later that night, having been able to slip out of the Legation in the dark without causing suspicion. He had decided to wait until nightfall, as the agent's task of trying to account for everyone would prove tricky under darkness given the sheer volume of visitors queuing outside the building, desperately trying to get a permit to escape to Britain. 'It was chaos,' one female refugee remembered. That Tuesday was particularly busy, as Doreen had deliberately arranged for as many of her contacts to descend on the Legation, to the extent that at points the crowd created lines stretching so far down the road they blocked cars.

To be able to leave the city, Wenzel and his accomplices would need to travel on false passports and travel permits. To obtain them, Doreen enlisted the help from her underground network, befriending a German member of staff who had 'for a consideration been forging passports.' A considerable sum of Protektorátní koruna – the new currency just introduced by the Nazi invaders – bought five counterfeit passports.

Because scrutiny was so intense at Prague's main train terminal, Wilson Station, the escapees were likely to be searched on multiple occasions before they could leave. It was common by now for trains to be stopped from departing, everyone forced off and then searched. This ritual would sometimes be repeated up to five times before they could eventually proceed. It would therefore be impossible for any one of the travellers to carry their genuine identity cards with them, as they would almost certainly be found. However, it was equally important that Wenzel had his real documentation to get into Britain, as a German man risked not being allowed to enter the country with fake documents, no matter his status. What Wenzel needed was someone who was willing to smuggle his real documents separately across the border, into Poland and meet them in a pre-agreed location. There was only one person he knew he could trust and who would be up for the task no matter the personal risk – his lover Doreen.

By this point, not only was she resolute in her commitment to the ideals of the German Social Democratic Workers Party, but her affection for Wenzel was growing deeper. The man who she had started a sexual relationship with some months before, had developed to something far more than just a physical connection. But to be complicit in his escape to England would mean an end to their fleeting love affair. Her help in his getaway would, therefore, come at a price to her happiness.

The following afternoon, on Wednesday 22 March, the escape party of five left Mary's flat and headed to Wilson Station to catch a train east in the direction of Moravia.

Disguised as well-to-do winter sport aficionados, the two women wore bright knitted jumpers, and the three men dressed in smart all-in-one ski outfits. They carried sets of Flexible Flyer-styled vintage skis over their shoulders and large backpacks full of supplies.

At the station, the last of the evening sun shone through the front of the stained-glass semi-circular window towering over the front entrance, just enough to light up the German soldiers on patrol inside. The group of supposedly wealthy skiers were given surprisingly little hassle by the guards as they sat patiently in the waiting area before being searched and then let into their train compartment, aboard the 11 p.m. train from Prague to the Polish border. To add to his nerves, Wenzel noticed six men with knapsacks also waiting on the platform when they arrived, and standing out from the crowd. After two weeks of Nazi occupation in Prague, the escape party had become expert in spotting undercover members of the German secret police. These six men were indeed Nazis, and to their dismay, they were 'steered straight to our carriage by the [conductor] and filled the compartment next door.'

The ritual of the train being stopped and searched was skipped on this occasion, most likely because even the regular German soldiers were afraid of the secret police, daring not to delay their journey.

Mr Kminek, Mr Sacher, Wenzel and the two women felt both relief and terror as the train drew out of the station on the dot of 11 p.m., as although they were at last on their way, only the thin wooden partition of the carriage separated them from the Nazis next door.

As the train trundled out of Prague, for an unknown reason, these officers began to get suspicious of the five people in the next-door compartment. Was it the fact they looked shifty, sitting completely still and had not muttering a word? Or was it because they had been given such an easy exit from Wilson Station? Maybe the officers were bored, and this was a way to pass the time. In any case, their leader stood up, placed his fedora hat on his head, and walked through the corridor and entered the escape party's cabin, where he began asking questions to the terrified occupants about their business, their intended destinations and the reason for their journey.

Mr Kminek immediately took the lead, explaining how they intended to ski near the border, as the snow was fresh and nearly completely untouched. This pricked the interest of the officer, who was himself a keen skier and it transpired that he intended to try the same slopes as well. Within a few minutes, he had invited his secret police subordinates from next door into the adjacent compartment and the eleven men and women began sharing stories about winter sports with each other. Wenzel recalled that 'from our backpacks we took oranges, ham sandwiches and schnapps,' the latter they shared with their new Nazi travel companions, who in turn produced a bottle of vodka.

Soon Mr Kminek had a large map unfolded on the floor of the compartment, using his index finger to show the best slopes for the Nazi officers to try when they were off duty. Little did they know, Mr Kminek was guiding them on the exact route he intended to take Prague's most wanted man, who was sitting in that very compartment. Wenzel went undetected, marvelling to Doreen afterwards that 'they took me for a winter-sports enthusiast', and paid him 'little attention in comparison to Mr Kminek, who had charmed them'. By this point, the skiers were laughing merrily, sharing drinks with one and other and scribbling down map references for their favourite winter hobby. After some hours of this, the train drew into the Nazi group's stop, where they all shook hands with Mr Kminek and his companions, before leaving the train.

A sense of pure relief descended on the escape party, quite possibly magnified by the fact they were all so inebriated after hours of drinking the Nazis' seemingly endless supply of vodka. Wenzel described years later how in response to each of the Nazis' jokes during their journey, he would force himself 'to laugh, which sometimes came a little roughly from the throat.'

Now back on track and not in the sights of their enemy, the group changed onto a small regional stopping train, heading for the Moravia-Slovakia border in the early hours of that Thursday morning. At the train's final stop, they were the last people to get off and were left standing on the platform in the pitch dark. It was too late to travel any further, and they tried to find shelter in a nearby tourist hut close to the train station. As they approached it though, they saw men inside in black leather jackets and matching forage caps with black tassels. This was unmistakably the uniform of the Hlinka Guard, a merciless Slovakian Nazi-sympathising militia group.

Luckily, the escape party were able to retreat from the hut unnoticed, as the Hlinka Guard were notoriously ruthless and would likely have caused the escape party some considerable inconvenience. Seeking refuge in an abandoned peasant's house, the group settled down for a night's sleep, made easier by the copious amount of vodka they had consumed that day, sharing body heat for warmth.

*

'I felt particularly relieved at his escape,' Robert Stopford wrote in his diary after he came to the Legation only to find the Sudeten German leader not there. Stopford was not only fond of Wenzel, but a conversation the two had had the day before his escape had stayed with the diplomat. Calling Stopford to one side, Wenzel had produced a revolver from his pocket – the gun which Martha had confiscated from the desperate refugee earlier in the month – and whispered, 'I will shoot myself on the doorstep if the Gestapo come to take me away.'

A man of his word, Stopford did not doubt for a second that Wenzel would follow through with his claim if necessary. Going up to the ballroom on the top floor of the Legation, Stopford was thankful to see the gun lying superfluous upon the unmade makeshift bed he had shared with Doreen.

But his relief was short lived. Although Wenzel was out of

Prague, he was not across the border. He could be arrested at any point. He also had other concerns.

'My main preoccupation is the position of the women and children,' he told Legation staff as they fretted about Wenzel's disappearance. The group who had failed to get to the train station on time the night before the occupation were now living in hostels around the city without their passports and by now there were also many more. Arrests were taking place regularly; it seemed almost daily that Doreen and Martha would receive word that someone in their network had disappeared.

As a senior British representative, Stopford had arranged to meet the new German Foreign Ministry representative, the man responsible for displaced people from the Sudetenland. Dr Karl Ritter had been Ambassador for Germany in Brazil, before being sent to Prague. The fifty-six-year-old diplomat was receptive to Stopford's approach and just after Wenzel's escape, they met together at the German's office on 24 March.

The conversation started off in a positive manner. 'No one will be detained unless they are a vicious enemy of Germany or had committed some crime,' Dr Ritter reassured him after his concerns were raised.

This was not strictly true, but his department was under such strain with the sheer magnitude of work which needed doing to secure Czechoslovakia that any emigration would ease the burden. He saw little problem in people leaving. Stopford said, 'His only Nazi-ish remark was a polite query why England wanted so many Jews.'

Dr Ritter stipulated that women and children would all receive safe passage. Men would also receive safe passage as long as they were not charged with High Treason, espionage or political offences. Stopford rolled his eyes at this final point. The Nazis could just invent charges of political offences against anyone they chose. He would, however, allow the Jewish deputy leader of the DSAP Siegfried Taub, his family and the others in Legation to leave safely.

'Finally, Herr Jaksch cannot have an exit permit,' Dr Ritter said firmly. But he added, 'You will receive an assurance that nothing will happen to him.'

Stopford was somehow able to keep a straight face. Wenzel had left the Legation three days earlier. All the officials from the British Legation who knew about the escape had agreed a reasonable period should be allowed for him to get into safe territory before the Germans were told. Dr Ritter would not have put this condition about Wenzel into his negotiations if he suspected he had escaped. It was therefore clear that the Nazis had no idea he was no longer in the Legation.

*

That morning, Wenzel had in fact strapped his boots into ski bindings and was beginning his journey through the snow. His head hurt and his mouth was dry thanks to all the vodka he had consumed with the German officers the night before. But the exercise soon cured his hangover.

For the next three days, he and his escape party skied across the mountains of Slovakia, heading east towards Poland. One member noted that the group were 'not practiced winter sportsmen and in particular Jaksch, who having broken his leg recently in a car crash, put in an incredible performance of stamina.' They would ski almost non-stop for twelve hours each day, from sunrise before 6 a.m. through to dusk at 6 p.m. As darkness descended over the mountains, they would plead with locals to allow them shelter for the night from the elements. During the daytime, temperatures would reach a comfortable ten degrees Celsius, but then rapidly drop off to well below freezing when the sun went down.

For the first two days, their skiing was uninterrupted, and they were never stopped or questioned on the almost completely abandoned mountains, although this did mean they regularly got lost. However, by day three, as the Polish frontier neared, they ran into potential trouble. The further they headed out of Bohemia, the more open the terrain there was, leaving them exposed. At around midday, they skied up a ridge to find a track at the top, which led to what appeared to be a large tourist inn. The ground around the barn-like wooden building was not the untouched white snow they were used to, instead it was dirt brown and clearly well trampled. Concerned that the inn could be a German army station, Mr Kminek crept ahead to do a recce alone while the other four remained below the ridge to avoid being seen. Keeping to the side of the track, Mr Kminek had only been gone for a few minutes before a convoy of military trucks came into view, heading towards them.

What Wenzel, Mr Sacher and the two women left behind in the ridge did not realise was that, although hidden from view from the inn, they were completely exposed to anyone on the other side, from where the trucks were now emerging. Clearly in sight of the approaching convoy, the four remained crouched as any attempts to run would now be futile. When the lorries were parallel to them Wenzel observed that 'the colourful composition of our group turned out to be an advantage with two women with bright sweaters and two ski uniformed men, as the Nazi soldiers simply waved to us and passed on to the inn.' Once the vehicles had come to a halt at the building, Mr Kminek crawled back, reporting what the others already knew, that the inn was swarming with soldiers, probably on their way to reinforce the Polish border.

With no other option, the group simply reattached their snowshoes into their ski bindings and headed past the inn and on towards Poland. This was now the second time Wenzel had come face-to-face with German soldiers without causing suspicion. As he passed some soldiers, he imagined them thinking how wonderfully the Czechs live, enjoying their hobbies with such vigour and commitment, unaware what one of these skiers would be worth if captured.

The convoy of trucks now parked behind them at the inn would soon be on the move again, and as they were also heading to the Polish frontier, they would be right behind the escape party.

For the remainder of the third day on the slopes, the skiers pushed forward relentlessly. As they entered the last few hours of their journey, Wenzel recalled that 'the tiredness [of] the day made itself felt to the group.' Food supplies were now completely exhausted, and energy levels were rapidly falling. Mr Sacher, the oldest of the group, began to fall behind and break away from the rest of the group. With a long history of cardiac troubles, the strain was becoming too much for him.

Mr Kminek told Wenzel that he was concerned that the German soldiers would be fast approaching them, thanks to the advantage of their more efficient mode of motorised transport. The skiing party were leaving tracks which were impossible to conceal and easy to follow. Now was not the time for the group to slow down. They tried their hardest to encourage Mr Sacher by telling him they were only a matter of hours away from the Polish border, but every time they would start to regain momentum, Wenzel would hear from his rear 'Sacher's pleading voice not to leave him behind.' To do so would almost certainly mean his death from the elements.

The final hours of that third day were therefore sluggish, but the group agreed they must remain together and all cross the border as one or all be caught together. They decided to deviate from the open slopes into the dense forests, knowing that the military convoy behind would be less likely to be able to follow them through such tough terrain. As dusk fast approached, navigation once again become harder. 'For eight hours we skied on, over very difficult going, up and down steep slopes, through forests, avoiding the paths, a way that no skier would have ever taken for sport,' Mr Sacher said. Fortune was on their side, as they stumbled across a bemused Slovak forest worker who agreed to take them to the Polish border for a small sum of money.

By this point, they were getting slower and slower, but the journey was nearly over. Their new guide took them deeper and deeper into the forest, before holding his hand up and bringing the group to a halt. Wenzel vividly remembered him lighting a cigarette and then pointing to the marked spot on the trunk of a tree and saying, 'here is Poland.'

Their remarkable three-days skiing had ended in the most unremarkable way. 'We then came down in the hot evening sun through the snow-covered forests and into the valley,' Mr Sacher wrote happily. With visions of high barbed-wire fences, countless numbers of border guards and menacing German Shepherds, the group were surprised, albeit in a positive way, that they had been able to simply pass a marked tree trunk and were now out of Nazi-occupied land.

It was not yet the time for celebration, as border guards on either side could still make their efforts be in vain. The weary group pushed on until it was completely dark, settling in the small Polish town of Bohumín, which the Poles had recently occupied thanks to the Munich Agreement. Exhausted, they found a tiny inn which was able to accommodate them, where they used their last drops of energy to remove their soaking clothes before passing out into a deep sleep. 'We should either have been arrested or lost and frozen to death in the forest,' Mr Sacher said reflecting on their good luck.

The next morning, Mr Kminek managed to muster the strength to dash off a telegram to the architect of the last three days in Prague, Doreen Warriner, simply saying, 'Monday in Bohumín.' This was the secret code she had been waiting for. Doreen booked herself on the overnight train to Bohumín leaving Prague at 11 p.m. on Sunday 26 March, with a bag packed with the real passports, visas and entry permits required to get the five escapees through Poland and on to Britain – the final hurdle needed to get Wenzel out of harm's way. Knowing now that her phone was tapped and she was being followed, Doreen had told no one – even the women in her organisation – of her involvement. She had gone to the extent of telling Margaret that she was taking a transport to Poland, causing panic in London when there was no record of her, or the transport ever crossing the border. Sent to investigate, Clare reported back, 'I motored to Ostrava and we enquired for Miss Warriner. In the book with the names of all people who had crossed the old Czech frontier, there were only three British subjects and Miss Warriner was not amongst them.'

Unaware of the shockwaves she had created among the leadership of the BCRC, who now classed her and the non-existent group of refugees as 'missing', Doreen was on the train having bribed the guard to keep her sleeper cabin door locked for the whole journey, which he did. The next morning, she emerged from Bohumín Station to be greeted by five exhausted but thankful people. 'As I walked out of the station, a skiing party of three men and two women, brown and dirty and very fit, came across the street to meet me,' she wrote in her diary. They spent the day recounting the ordeal they had been through, describing their three days of exhaustion and exchanging the necessary documentation as well as destroying the fakes.

In an emotional farewell, Doreen saw Wenzel and the others off, as they continued through Poland. In a letter from a relieved

Clare to Margaret in London on 27 March, she updated that Doreen was indeed not missing:

> *Dear Miss Layton*
> *Miss Warriner has just been here with a party of people including J. I have already arranged travel visas for these people, and they are now settled for the night.*

Wenzel departed the following morning for Great Britain, while Doreen returned to Prague on the night train, arriving early on 28 March.

Upon her arrival, she went straight to the British Legation to find Stopford anxiously waiting for news. No words were needed – the grin on her face told him the mission had been a success.

The timing was impeccable, as he was on his way to see Dr Ritter's assistant, Dr Mitis. Now that he was out of the country, Stopford would tell the Germans that Wenzel had escaped.

The meeting again started off positively. Dr Mitis had good news. 'Apart from Mr Jaksch, none of the other Legation refugees are charged with any crimes,' he told Stopford. He handed over their exit permits.

Stopford quickly pocketed them, before confessing, 'Mr Jaksch has disappeared.'

Dr Mitis was shocked. He instantly became frighteningly angry, gripping the desk so hard the ends of his fingers went white. He shouted, 'Disappeared? How?'

'Just disappeared,' Stopford replied, shrugging his shoulders, then adding, 'without informing us.' His relaxed attitude only made the German sitting opposite him angrier.

'This alters the whole position with regard to the others,' Dr Mitis hissed across the desk. 'I will have to refer this situation to the Gestapo,' he threatened.

Stopford's experience as a negotiator came into play. 'The

Legation is not a prison,' he replied matter-of-factly. 'We extended our hospitality to Mr Jaksch, and if he no longer wished for it, he was free to go at any time ... the promise of safe conduct for the others had not been made conditional on Mr Jaksch remaining.'

The room fell silent. Dr Mitis stared at Stopford, as if he were trying to look inside him. Stopford looked back, attempting to appear calm. Beads of sweat were forming on his forehead. He saw Dr Mitis's mouth start to twitch slightly, bracing himself for a screaming match. Stopford was flabbergasted when the German suddenly burst out into uncontrolled laughter. Dr Mitis struggled to breath he was in such hysterics, that feeling of hilarity that can cause stomach cramps.

'The Gestapo will be furious,' he blurted out when had recovered sufficiently. 'I will be in great trouble, but it is really rather funny that the Gestapo wanted Jaksch so badly but let him escape!'

As if he were a headteacher gesturing to his pupil, he waved Stopford out of his office.

Stopford considered the meeting a success. He left with visas for all those who were holed up in the Legation. They departed Czechoslovakia safely later that week, with Stopford escorting them onto the train to ensure there was no funny business. Miss Dougan acted as their chaperone, seeing them legally across the border into Poland.

Chapter Twelve

Enter the Gestapo

Martha stopped off in France on her way back from London to Czechoslovakia, and when she arrived, she had a cunning scheme ready to put into action. An introduction in London to the French Ambassador had resulted in a meeting with several leaders of the Ministry of Foreign Affairs in Paris. Martha was able to get them to sign an agreement which stated that she personally had 'the right to name persons in Czechoslovakia who should receive visas for France'.

She was also invited to give a talk at the meet of the American's Woman's Club in Paris and decided to give her speech a provocative title: 'What It Would Be Like to Have Paris Occupied by the Nazis'. There was such horror at the concept, many people came up afterwards offering donations to the relief work in Prague.

With two busy days in Paris complete, Martha travelled on an almost completely empty Orient Express back to Prague on 5 April. She had had an eventful time since she had been out of Czechoslovakia. In particular, during her meeting with Alice Masaryk's brother, Jan, in London, he had given her a dozen tubes of toothpaste with rolled up papers hidden in each one. Martha was to give these to Alice.

The prestige of the luxurious Orient Express was compromised by the five French military transport carriages added to the back of the train. The soldiers, who were being taken to reinforce a section of the border, were rowdy, loud and very drunk. Martha had dealt with sly spies, uncompromising secret police agents and antagonistic German border guards in the last week, so wolf whistles and sexual gestures from these Frenchmen did not intimidate her as she walked through their carriages to the dining car. Perhaps it was because she was so tired, or she was too blasé, but on Martha's return from dinner along the gauntlet of inebriated men, she did not notice the four who followed her back to her compartment.

Locking her door, Martha undressed and put on her nightdress and silk dressing gown before getting into bed, turning off the lights and falling into a deep sleep. The next thing she knew, she was being woken up by a key turning the lock on her compartment door. She watched in terror as it was pushed open by just a crack, only stopped by the flimsy chain bolt she had remembered to put on. Backlit by the bright corridor lights, Martha saw a crowd of the drunk French soldiers all trying to get in. They were kicking at the door, pushing their shoulders into it, punching at it with their fists. A man's face was pressed into the open crack, with one hand reaching in, he succeeded in grabbing Martha by the leg. She managed to kick his hand away, but he pulled the covers off her, much to the audible delight of the mob.

Martha frantically pressed the call-bell, hoping desperately that a steward might hear it and come to her aid. She had shifted out of the bed and had now pressed her back against the door, using all her might to try to support the four small straining screws that held the chain anchor in place. The men eased off the door, to the great relief of Martha, but threw themselves at it all together. She screamed in fear but the noise was drowned out by the laughing, shouting louts, who only seemed to be spurred on by her panic.

Mercifully, the pushing suddenly stopped, and the soldiers fell silent. Martha waited, sitting on the floor, breathing heavily and with her back pressed against the door. She did not move for half an hour before she plucked up the courage to stand up, unhook the chain and peer into the empty corridor. Something must have spooked the crowd of intruders, and they had scarpered. But someone had used a key to open her door, so they might be back at any point. She locked herself in, put the chain back in place and sat on her bed staring at the door for the rest of the night until they reached the German border. The Nazi officials who boarded the train to inspect passports seemed friendly compared to her earlier experience of the French soldiers.

She fell into Waitstill's arms the next morning as he met her at Wilson Station.

'I'm just tired,' she told her husband when he asked if everything was alright. She never told anybody about her ordeal on the train, keeping the incident secret until she wrote about it in her memoir.

*

Lots had changed in Prague since Martha had left. The might of the German army had started to dissipate. There were fewer Panzer Tanks and Opel Blitz Trucks carrying troops on the streets than there had been the previous week. But their reduced number was far from comforting.

'For a short time after the invasion,' Stopford said, 'the military were in control and it was not for several days that the Gestapo really got to work.' But within a few weeks, they were beginning to make their presence known, taking over from General Blaskowitz. Deputy Reichsprotecktor Karl Hermann Frank had overarching responsibility for security in the country, and he set up his SS and the Gestapo headquarters in Prague at Petschek Palace, the former bank building now requisitioned by the Nazis. Czech teenager Nikolaus Martin remembered seeing among the army soldiers, Germans dressed differently: 'From their black uniforms, red and white swastika armbands and a skull and crossbones emblem on their caps, I immediately recognised them as SS officers.'

The SS had broader responsibilities than the Gestapo, encompassing military operations, ideological enforcement, and eliminating enemies of the state. The Gestapo operated under the SS, with specific responsibility for investigating and suppressing opposition to the Nazi regime, including political dissidents, resistance movements, and other 'enemies of the state'. Despite their differences, the SS and Gestapo worked closely together. Their shared brutality and terror would make them central to the Nazi regime's control over Czechoslovakia.

The Gestapo had been operating agents in the city for over a year, but they had been doing so as foreign agents. They were now the official secret police. Taking over the control of security from the military in late March, the number of arrests began to dramatically increase, in an exercise codenamed *Operation Fence*. Many people went into hiding, only daring to come out at night to get some fresh air. The curfew was lifted from 8 p.m. to midnight, making it slightly easier for these wanted people to get outside. 'One saw them lurking in the shadows of the public gardens,' Stopford remembered.

Herr Kriminalrat Karl von Bömelburg was appointed as the Gestapo leader in Czechoslovakia. Joining the Nazi Party in 1931, he initially served in the regular army before transitioning to the SS and then the Gestapo, where he held various roles, including directing criminal police operations in Berlin. In 1938, he joined Joachim von Ribbentrop's staff in Paris, where he unofficially establishing Gestapo operations in France. His activities, which included supporting extreme-right French groups, led to his expulsion by French authorities in early 1939, after which he was sent to Prague. Aged 54-years-old, he was an 'elderly, smiling gentleman, far from sinister,' one British official reflected. He provided great humour to Doreen and Martha, who referred to him as 'the criminal rat' from the moment they heard his title.

Bömelburg had secured himself a room in Hotel Alcron, only a few floors away from Doreen, meaning she was being even more careful than usual, expecting everything she said to be recorded. It was therefore a surprise when the secretary of the Communist Federation of Trade Unions, Emmi Döllin, appeared outside her room. Her husband Rudolf, a leading Czech Communist, had managed to evade arrest, escape Czechoslovakia illegally thanks to Doreen's help and at that point was making his way to Moscow.

Emmi had a reputation for dressing in a fashion Doreen described as 'café communist'. A long plain bell skirt, tucked in shirt of the same colour and a large handkerchief tied into her hair made up the only outfit she was ever seen wearing.

Doreen did not initially recognise her when she answered a knock on her hotel door because Emmi was dressed in elegant black furs, high heels, lipstick and a veil – she was in disguise. She had come through the lobby and up in the lift with a group of German Generals, who all stood to one side to let the dignitary out first. Little did they know who she really was. While Miss Dougan was couriering those released from the Legation, Emmi had been working for Doreen at the British Legation, helping Christine Maxwell.

So good was her disguise, Emmi suggested the two women should go downstairs for coffee, as they were afraid to speak openly in Doreen's room in case it was bugged. 'We sat in the lounge among the Nazi officers, making conversation like German matrons,' Doreen happily remembered. Emmi adopted the alias of Ilse, confidently introducing herself to one SS officer, shaking his hand firmly and looking straight into his eyes.

It might appear unnecessarily risky, but small acts of control when one had lost one's freedom can be a huge boost. The Germans might have taken Emmi's country and forced her husband to flee, but she was still able to make fools of them. In hushed tones, the women discussed their plan for the coming days. Doreen had a group of women and children without passports scattered all around the city. There were also thousands more families who were in great danger.

Now that Stopford had received confirmation from the German authorities that women and children would be allowed to leave, Doreen and her team had successfully applied for travel permits for another group of seventy women and children.

'It is high time to get the transport away,' she told Emmi.

'When?' replied her helper.

Doreen replied excitedly that it would be the following night.

Emmi left the hotel to pass on the news to those selected to leave. Meanwhile, Doreen went to her room. Hidden behind a drawer in her wardrobe was a pile of Czech passports with their distinguishing faded pink covers. Collecting them for the past month, they had belonged to people who had escaped on forged documents or those who had died. Some of the women who had had their passports taken could travel with these instead, Doreen surmised.

She wanted Elisabeth Baier, a woman pregnant with her fifth child whose health was starting to deteriorate; young Emma Goerlich, a single mother with her one-year-old baby; Marie Greiss, who was struggling mentally since her husband left at the end of 1938; and communist Wanda Bauernfeind, to leave now. None had passports, but flicking through the small pile she had, she believed they could be smuggled out. It would just take a small amount of forgery and quite a lot of guts. Doreen had already offered a passport to Emmi downstairs, but she refused as she did not want to jeopardise the safety of the other travellers.

At 9 p.m. the following evening, 31 March, having spent the previous few hours making sandwiches and packing supplies for the journey, Doreen arrived at Wilson Station. All seventy women and children were present according to Christine, who was checking them off. Miss Dougan had only been back in Prague for a few hours, but she would be escorting them on their journey. The illegal travellers – Elisabeth, Emma, Marie and Wanda – had assumed their new identities. They were now Božena, Marta, Helena and Emília, and, with documents in hand, boarded the train. The sight of Emma's son sleeping peacefully in her arms seemed to calm everyone.

As the clock ticked round to 11 p.m., Doreen and Christine stood back and waved off the group of seventy. As the carriages began to strain out of the platform, there was a huge commotion from behind the guard hut, and the train suddenly juddered to a halt, having only moved a few yards. Four large men in leather jackets sprinted down the platform, flinging doors open, banging on windows and ordering people out of the train in German. Dragged from their seats, all the passengers were ruthlessly searched on the platform. The unhappy screams from Emma's baby were piercing as the poor infant protested about being woken up, and they only increased in volume as his baby sling was shaken out to ensure there was no contraband inside.

Bags were emptied and the belongings kicked across the platform. Doreen was shocked at the way these women and children were being treated. It reminded her of the sheep farm she grew up on. The passengers were lined up along the platform in single file. One of the men in a leather jacket – presumably the leader of the group – started to check each person's passport. After only inspecting a handful, the man gestured towards a woman. Doreen strained to see who it was in the dark. One of his underlings grabbed her from the line by the arm and pushed her down onto a bench, where she sat alone and with her head in her hands. When she looked up, Doreen's heart sank. It was Wanda, one who had a forged passport.

All she could do was watch on as passports were inspected down the line. The man got to Marie, where he looked at her counterfeit passport for only a few seconds, before handing it back and moving on to the next person. The same happened with Emma and Elisabeth. Why had they taken Wanda? A few minutes later, a man was also pulled from the group, with his wife screaming frantically after him, and placed next to the woman.

She could not stand this anymore. A red mist came over Doreen, who marched across the platform to the man making all the decisions.

'Who are you?' she demanded, firmly prodding the man on the back of his shoulder repeatedly.

She recoiled as he swung around so aggressively, he almost knocked into her.

'Secret State Police,' he retorted moodily, pulling a badge from his pocket. He looked her up and down, and then demanded: 'Passport?'

Her protests that she was not herself travelling was met with a blank expression and a more aggressive request to see her passport.

Producing it from her pocket, Doreen handed it over. He then spent the next five minutes looking through it, page by page, comparing the picture with her face time and again, supposedly checking the authenticity with his flashlight light. He pulled a notebook and pen from his pocket, before coping down Doreen's details.

He gestured to Christine, who had remained where they had been standing. Her passport was checked, her details also written down.

'This woman has a visa for England,' Doreen insisted, following the man as he worked, gesturing to the shivering Wanda perched on the bench. He stopped and look round causally. 'And she has an exit permit signed by the Gestapo themselves.'

'I have ...' the man tried to reply before being cut off.

'Why can't she leave?' Doreen asked.

'The Gestapo gives no reason,' he said back coolly. His response sent chills all through Doreen, who stood silently, defeated. Christine slowly guided her by her waist back to where they had been standing.

The man continued to the end of the line. He then shouted an order to his men in unintelligible German. They started to run up and down the train, kicking down the lavatory doors, clambering underneath the locomotive with their flashlights and then ordered the train to be shunted forward and backwards a couple of times. Doreen recalled it lasting for hours. Were they looking for a particular person? Wanda and the man might just have been collateral damage. In reality, they were just there to terrorize them. Reduce everyone to a state of helplessness and fear. In particular they wanted to send a clear message to the BCRC. Transports will no longer be as easy as they were before.

Finally, everyone was allowed back on into their carriages. It was a sorry sight to see people scooping up their belongings that had been strewn all over the ground. Two of the men in leather jackets had also boarded the train and were now sitting either side of Miss Dougan. One looked past her to the other and started jeering about 'the lying and traitorous English'. They laughed, while she just sat looking straight forward. Doreen wanted to get a message to her telling her to get the other three women with fake documents off the train as soon as possible. These men clearly knew something was going on. Doreen was sure they would be searched at every station from here to the border, and once there, the real trouble would start. But Doreen could not say anything. The train was allowed to leave in the early hours of 1 April, some three hours after it had first started its departure. The platform was eerily silent after it had left the station.

The two remaining men walked back to the bench were the two lonely figures sat. Pointing at Wanda, the leader said, 'Communist muck,' and to the man, 'Dirty Jew,' then gestured to his colleague to bring them.

Doreen did not know the man. But she had got to know Wanda well, which meant that being unable to do nothing except watch as she was led away was agonising. Wanda was never heard of again. She had turned twenty-five that month and, as happened to so many, her fate would never be known.

The Nazis' immense brutality towards the people of Prague had started. In August 1961, the trial of Stefan Rojko – an SS officer based in Czechoslovakia – heard specifics of the atrocities carried out against the innocent people of Prague in those first few weeks. The summary of charges against him is the only detail required:

A Viennese film producer, beaten by Rojko with the handle of a shovel and finished off with a thick branch; a parish priest from western Bohemia who had his head dunked in a barrel of water until he drowned; a school director from Prague and a Czech colonel, clubbed to death by Rojko in their cells in front of other prisoners ... twelve elderly inmates, hardly able to walk, whom Rojko ordered to jump a ten foot ditch, and shot as they lay inside it.

Sitting terrified on the train, Miss Dougan had no idea what to do now. She had two members of the German Secret Police sitting next to her. She needed to get the three remaining women with forged documents off. When the train stopped at a signal and did not move for more than ten minutes, the men either side started to speak across her in German, suggesting reasons why they were delayed. After another five minutes, one got up and walked towards the front of the train, the other soon following. They left the carriage, and Miss Dougan assumed it would take them a few minutes to find the conductor or make contact with the driver.

'Quick,' she whispered to the silent group around her. She ordered Elisabeth, Emma and Marie, along with their respective children, to follow her towards the back of the train, trying the doors as they went. On the last carriage she found one unlocked, flung it open and climbed out. Handed the children one by one, she then helped the women out. Elisabeth groaned with pain as she clambered out, clutching her bulging stomach.

The women and children found refuge behind some shrubbery. Miss Dougan fished out a small piece of chocolate from her pocket for one of the children in the hope it would stop her crying. The train let out a puff of steam, strained, before starting to pull away again. It was completely out of sight before the hideaways emerged. They were in the middle of nowhere, in the freezing cold. Elisabeth was hardly able to walk and there were five young children to take care of.

All they could do was to make their way slowly up the train tracks back in the direction of Wilson Station. Although the train had only been going for ten minutes, the walk back took several hours. When they finally reached the station, they were able to sneak around, ending up back in the waiting room they had been many hours earlier. Elisabeth collapsed into one of the chairs, clutching her midriff in agony.

Miss Dougan called Doreen's hotel room, who was surprised to hear her phoning from the station. 'Her determined cheerfulness seemed to indicate disaster,' Doreen wrote in her diary.

Miss Dougan simply suggested they meet for a drink near the 'American', code for the train station which had been named after President Woodrow Wilson. Doreen raced to the group and was greeted by an exasperated Miss Dougan. 'The Gestapo,' she said, 'really are tiresome.' She piled Elisabeth and her children into a taxi and drove her to the YWCA building where she could be looked after. Due to the curfew just coming into effect, Doreen also spent the night there. After a week of pain and bleeding, Elisabeth miscarried and only just survived.

'It was obviously too dangerous to try and organise any other transports without official approval,' Doreen concluded after this ordeal.

It is hard to balance between being gung-ho, as Doreen instinctively was, and cautious. The former can mean too much action is taken, the latter, too little. Waiting a few more days for the correct documentation could mean someone leaves legitimately and therefore supposedly, safely. But the longer people wait, the greater chance they will have of being arrested, usually on jumped up charges of being an 'enemy of the state'.

Arrests were happening daily. It was rare for Martha and Doreen to not receive two or three distressed phone calls each day telling them someone had gone missing. When Emmi disappeared suddenly, there was panic. As the days went by, Doreen had that all too familiar sinking feeling in the pit of her stomach, assuming that like so many others, Emmi must have been arrested. But then out of the blue she received a telegram from Poland saying, 'Best wishes, Ilse,' Doreen knew she was safe. Her alias was still proving useful.

However, many others were not so lucky. Rumours were rife around the city of interrogation, torture and murder. People said they heard screams coming from the basement of the Gestapo headquarters Petschek Palace. Relatives who were brave enough for wanting details about their loved ones who have disappeared, were harassed to the point that they stopped asking.

Legal transports continued – while underground operations were paused for the time being – with a party of sixty women leaving on 31 March and a further 108 people leaving on 5 April, which meant Doreen and her group had now helped more than 4,000 people to escape. Very few people were entering the country, so it was a complete surprise when a Canadian woman named Beatrice Wellington appeared at the American Legation unannounced, offering her services.

Born into a progressive family in New York in 1908, Beatrice grew up surrounded by people with a strong sense of social responsibility and intellectual curiosity. Her father, a journalist, and her mother, an advocate for women's suffrage, instilled in her a commitment to justice and equality from an early age. Beatrice excelled academically, earning a degree in social work from Barnard College, before pursuing further studies in European politics and humanitarian law. The similarities in her background and interests to Martha were astonishing. The only thing that they really did not have in common was religion as Beatrice was a devoted atheist.

By 1939, she had already established a reputation for her tireless dedication to humanitarian causes, having spent the previous decade working with displaced communities across Europe, including aiding refugees fleeing the Spanish Civil War. Impressed by her multilingual abilities, pragmatic nature and deep compassion, Doreen snapped her up, and Beatrice joined the BCRC and American Relief immediately.

Her brown hair, piercing eyes and build was remarkably similar to Doreen. 'In appearance we were rather alike,' the Englishwoman agreed. A resemblance which nearly cost Beatrice her life.

After only working with the BCRC and American Relief for a matter of days, on 14 April, she was dragged from her bed in Hostel Elf at 6 a.m. and driven by four Gestapo agents to their headquarters. Beatrice was taken into the interior courtyard of Petschek Palace, where she was hustled from the car down the stairs and into 'the cinema', a dark blank walled room with long wooden benches. It was crowded with people sitting in absolute silence.

'Any movement or attempt to talk will bring three days' solitary confinement without food or water,' a guard warned Beatrice as she took her seat to await her interrogation.

When she was eventually taken to a cell, as was common practice for the Gestapo they made her stand through the whole ordeal, facing the wall while two interrogators behind her fired questions without taking a breath and answering their queries themselves before she had a chance to respond.

Their questions went around in circles, trying to confuse her into answering incorrectly. But Beatrice was tough and stood up to the interrogation admirably.

When the officer asked, 'Where is the British Legation?'

'Look in the telephone book,' was her response.

They went on to accuse her of hiding many of the women they were looking for in the Legation, which Beatrice denied. Their knowledge was nearly accurate, as the women were not actually being hidden *in* the Legation itself, but rather by those inside. But Beatrice could quite honestly say she had no knowledge of this, which was the truth. She had only just got there. They kept trying to catch her out by calling her Christine, hoping that she might give away a knowing look. The ruse did not work, but it was clear who the Gestapo were looking for.

When the officers accused her of illegal activity, she simply said, 'Everything that you do is illegal.' Her heroism was admirable, but she was aggravating her captors to the point that she would soon be put in front of the four German judges in the 'special court', with its adjoining execution room. She was given a small sip of water following six hours of interrogation, during which she fainted repeatedly.

News of Beatrice's arrest was a terrible shock to the women. People were being taken regularly, but they were always natives. 'Every day I wondered whom they would take next. I never imagined that it would be Beatrice,' Martha wrote in disbelief.

Robert Stopford was already in his car, racing to Petschek Palace. He waited there all morning, demanding her immediate liberation. 'She was not released to us till 12.30 p.m., after hard grilling, but with no physical ill-treatment,' Stopford told Legation staff when he arrived back with her that afternoon.

'I will take you to the train station,' he had told her when they were in the safety of his car.

'I am exhausted,' she replied, 'but still full of courage. I need to get back to work.'

Any further attempts to get her to leave for own safety failed. At the Legation, she warned Doreen of the insinuations that she was Christine Maxwell. She was clearly now wanted.

'They have probably caught one of the refugees to whom she had given money and a card – or possibly Maxwell had contacted someone who had informed on her,' Doreen surmised. Robert Stopford was insistent that Christine should leave immediately, and upon calling her to the Legation, she protested violently. Threats by the Ambassador were the only way to persuade her to depart that evening. She was still objecting in Stopford's car on the way to Wilson Station.

After a hot drink and some food, Beatrice was able to think straight. *What else did she remember from the interrogation?* They had asked about Miss Dougan, which was unsurprising as she had escaped from their officers on a train, taking Elisabeth Baier, Emma Goerlich and Marie Greiss on 31 March.

With the arrival of Beatrice in Prague, Doreen had the opportunity to send some further help to Poland and get Miss Dougan out of harms way. She sent a telegram to Margaret instructing a change:

ARRANGEMENTS IN GDYNIA ARE MADE STOP
INSTRUCT DOUGAN GO THERE AT ONCE STOP
WARRINER

Beatrice warned Doreen that during her interrogation, the Gestapo had raised Doreen's name. The women already knew they were looking for Doreen, but Doreen disregarded the warning, replying that Beatrice should relocate to another hostel. She moved herself to a new location and refused from that point to use a telephone in her room, relying on more old-fashioned communication techniques.

Martha was amazed when a boy, waiting on the street outside her offices, called out her name. Acknowledging the lad with a quizzical look, he handed her a note. 'Come at once. I am free,' followed by an address. The boy had disappeared while Martha read the brief note.

Swapping taxis twice to ensure she was not followed, Martha was dropped off several blocks from the address she had been given, and walked the rest of the journey.

'The reason I asked you to come at once, Martha,' Beatrice told her, 'was to warn you so you'll be prepared. The Nazis asked a lot of questions about you.' She sombrely recalled their plans to arrest the American as well. 'Be ready for it any morning at 2 a.m.,' she said grimly.

All through that night, Martha would suddenly jolt awake. What was that sound? Did she hear someone? She had nightmares of being attacked in bed just like she was on the Orient Express.

Her paranoia was justified. When she walked out into the corridor of her office the following morning to call the next refugee due in to see her, she had an almighty fright. Martha froze when she saw the woman sitting at the front of the queue. She looked exactly like the Gestapo agent Trevor Chadwick had pointed out to her on the morning of the invasion at the airport.

She was now dressed in rags, a bundle in her arms that Martha had initially assumed was a baby. But now, on closer inspection, she suspected it was a bundle of cloths. Many legitimate refugees she had met would turn up with what appeared to be a baby but was actually a rolled-up towel, which would be handed from one woman to the next before they went to see Martha.

The woman smiled at Martha, before standing up and walking hurriedly out of the door, down the stairs and onto the street. As Martha shouted from her office window after the woman, she started to speed up, before breaking into a run. The bundle she had been holding was left on the bench on which she had been perched. As Martha suspected, there was no baby.

This type of infiltration became a regular occurrence. Even within the British Legation, days after Wenzel's escape, Stopford reckoned the Gestapo 'put one or two spies into the building and they spread rumours that they were going to break in and seize our "guests".'

That evening, Martha returned to the Hotel Atlantic only to find all their belongings in a pile on outside the front entrance. The concierge she had got to know so well looked at her apologetically.

'Our old Atlantic has been requisitioned by the Nazis,' he explained, looking over his shoulder nervously.

Martha hailed a taxi, packed their things in the boot and went in search of a new hotel. She managed to get a room at Hotel Pariz, checking in under her maiden name Dickie, in the hope that she might be able to keep their new location secret.

The feeling was that nothing and nobody was safe anymore. Each morning before they met for their walking meeting, Martha and Doreen would search their respective buildings for bugs and spies. Then it would then be business as usual. The women were resolute. Keeping themselves protected was secondary to their singular focus of rescuing those in far worse predicaments.

In amongst all the bad news, there were some threads of positivity coming from the home front. People now seemed generally aware of the situation in Prague and in a vast number of cases, were welcoming of refugees into England. It was helped by Eleanor Rathbone, who in one of her infamous letters to *The New Statesman and Nation* at the start of April 1939, alluded to the extent that Doreen and Martha, along with their teams were working: 'Densely over-crowded offices with too few telephones and workers result in preposterous hours. Ringing up one of the principal workers [in Prague] at 9 a.m. and one usually finds that she *(it is always a "she")* has already gone to her office. Ring up again at 11 p.m., and she has not returned'.

Even the most ardent advocate for appeasement Neville Chamberlain capitulated. 'I am afraid that such faith as I ever had in the dictators is rapidly being whittled away,' he wrote. The negativity felt in Britain only worked to benefit those trying to escape Prague. For the first time, Stopford was now being questioned by his superiors in London as to the fate of the women and children trapped without their passports.

Chapter Thirteen

Doreen's Farewell to Prague

Over the telephone, Robert Stopford had made an appointment to meet Gestapo chief Bömelburg during the afternoon of 19 April. It took place at their headquarters in Petschek Palace in the New Town district, the Gestapo's terror centre where they interrogated, tortured, and detained political prisoners, resistance members, and anyone suspected of opposing the Nazi regime.

Walking up the grand concrete steps to the front door, Stopford later reflected, 'It sent shivers down my spine.' The only other time he had been in there was to try to secure the release of Beatrice. He believed she was one of the only people to enter under arrest and then leave a free person.

Once he was inside, however, Stopford was surprised by the normality of what he saw. Despite the chilling atmosphere, nearly 1,000 people worked in the building, and it seemed, upon entry, like any other office block.

Stopford told the blonde teenager in a spotless uniform on the front desk he was there to see Bömelburg and received a suspicious look in return.

'What is his room number?' the lad asked in German.

Stopford was dumbfounded. How on earth could he know which room the head of the Gestapo was occupying?

'I do not know.'

'If you do not know, then you may not see him,' the German shot back.

Stopford was furious. This mild-mannered diplomat was

renowned for his ability to keep calm under pressure. Yet, this cocky German boy was treating him with absolutely no respect.

'I have an appointment with him,' Stopford shouted, shocking even himself with his sudden temper. 'If I do not get taken to him immediately, I will return to the Legation and telegraph to London today that I was being impeded by the Gestapo in carrying out an agreement made between the British and German Government.'

Like a punctured tyre, the chap seemed to shrink in size and his cheeks flushed. Not wanting to cause a diplomatic incident, he picked up the telephone, and within minutes Stopford was being shown into the office of Bömelburg.

Immaculately turned out, Bömelburg was a short, stout man with a stern, imposing persona. He wore a stark black tunic with silver piping and the Gestapo's ominous insignia, including the silver death's head and the swastika armband on his left sleeve. As he looked up at Stopford, offering a hand to shake, his slicked-back hair fell to one side, revealing the worst combover the Englishman had ever encountered.

The Gestapo officer was so straight-faced, so composed, it was unsettling.

'Robert Stopford,' he introduced himself.

'You are Herr Stopford himself?' the German asked taken aback.

Was he mocking him?

'Yes,' Stopford replied cautiously.

A smile appeared on Bömelburg's face for the first time. His demeanour changed completely. He took Stopford's hand again in both of his, shaking warmly.

'I apologise. I had been told you were sending a representative. It is so nice to meet you!'

He continued to fuss about the misunderstanding as he poured Stopford a drink and offered him a seat on the comfy sofas in the corner of his office. Sensing his opportunity, Stopford did not miss a beat. He jumped straight in. There was a group of women and children, none of whom had done anything to warrant arrest, who were stuck because their passports had been taken.

Bömelburg knew exactly what Stopford was talking about. He had been shown the box of passports when he first arrived. They were in fact sitting in a pile of other items confiscated from the Czechs in his secretary's office next door. He drained his drink and stood up.

'They can leave by train tomorrow,' he told Stopford. As he tried to reply, Bömelburg continued. 'But I would like to visit the women myself first.'

Stopford's confused expression needed no words. 'I want to tell them that it is quite unnecessary to go, neither they nor their husbands are in danger if they return to the Sudetenland.' He added for good measure, holding his hands up in surrender. 'I will give them back their passports if they still insist on going.'

Stopford was perplexed as he walked back to the British Legation. His belly was warm from the glass of forty-year aged cognac he had been served. But he was anxious. This could all be a trap set by the Gestapo to arrest these women.

But, the only feasible option Stopford could think of to get the passports back was to allow the Gestapo to visit all the women and children. They would try to persuade them to stay in the Third Reich, and maybe even suggest they bring their husbands back. It was seen as a loss of face for the Nazis that a group of strong Aryan Germans would want to live anywhere else, Stopford surmised.

He strangely felt confident that Bömelburg would honour his word, assuming none of the women agreed to stay. Even if he did not, what other option did they have? These women and children were still trapped.

He broached the idea with Doreen, who was initially resistant. But she was feeling the pressure of the deadlock so much that she conceded this might be the only option left to them.

'I will put it to them as a question to decide, since to face an ordeal by your own deliberate choice is a very different matter from being driven into a decision by someone who can stand aside,' she told him.

That evening, Doreen was driven by Stopford around all the hotels and hostels, where she put the idea to all 120 women and children still without passports. The pair came up with a novel way of ensuring that they did not give away the locations of the women's hideouts to the spies who were likely tailing them. Stopford would turn down a side road when he neared one of the lodgings, and Doreen would jump out almost as the car was still moving. He would then drive off in circles for another ten minutes, before pulling over and waiting in his car. He would go back an hour later to the same spot he had left her, where he would pick Doreen up and they would head to the next location to repeat the exercise.

Each time, she told the women their remaining options. They could either stay in hiding, they could try to leave illegally, or they could be visited by the Gestapo in the hope they would be granted their passports back.

After some discussion at each, every single woman agreed to have their details handed over. Doreen told them that they should not believe any of the propaganda they would be told about returning to the 'fatherland'. She feared that some of the women had spent so long in ghettos and then in hiding that their exhaustion would mean they could cave in under the slightest pressure.

After the decisions had been made, Doreen and Stopford created a new list of everyone in the hotels, along with their addresses. He then delivered it by hand to Bömelburg's office.

Promptly the next day, on 20 April – Adolf Hitler's fiftieth birthday – Bömelburg visited the first two addresses on the list. He spilled an endlessly charming propaganda campaign to the women, promising them and their children written assurances of their safety. He knew they were all longing for home, why not go back now to live happily ever after? Everyone bravely resisted his advances, to the point some even started to jeer at the Gestapo leader.

After visiting the first two addresses, Bömelburg gave up. These women were not for turning.

Upon his return to their office, following what was a very unsuccessful morning for them, Bömelburg was greeted by Stopford. He was waiting for them to honour their word of passing over the passports and exit documents. The Nazi officer tried to protest, but Stopford was prepared. 'I quickly learnt the technique of dealing with German officials ... so I spoke to him with some heat and banged the table vigorously with my hand.' Remarkably, this seemed to do the trick, and Bömelburg produced a carboard box containing all the passports and exit permits.

As Stopford was leaving, Bömelburg called him back. From his drawer he produced another folder and placed it on his desk as if to offer the British man a chance to look at it. Flicking through, Stopford's heart sank. There was a picture of Doreen, covertly taken outside the Alcron Hotel. The details from her passport were included – which had been taken by the German Secret Police at Wilson Station – along with many, many pages titled 'intelligence report'. There were several of Doreen's calling cards, which she had written for the men who were going to leave the country. They were pinned to mugshots of the arrested 'criminals' who had them in their possession. There were even pictures of Doreen leaving the British Legation on the day that Wenzel escaped.

Stopford looked up from the file. Bömelburg looked back apologetically. 'It would be best if she went,' he told the diplomat in a hushed voice. 'Quickly.' He snapped the folder closed and placed it back in his drawer.

Thanking the German, Stopford ran straight to the British Legation. There was some commotion on the street outside its front gate, although it was passing by the time he got there, as a car sped away into the city. Earlier that day, Doreen had asked Emma Goerlich – who along with her baby had tried to leave unsuccessfully on fake documents with Miss Dougan – if she would help with the administration of the next transport, assuming the passports were returned. Christine Maxwell and Miss Dougan's departures from Prague had left Doreen with no secretaries. Emma enthusiastically agreed, bringing her baby and a friend, Frau Schnabel, to help. They worked all day in the British Legation completing the necessary paperwork for the women and children to leave. Emma took particular pride in filling in her own form.

Unbeknown to anyone in the British Legation, as the two women left after a successful day's work, a car was blocking Thunovská Street leading away from the building. Two men were standing with the back door open, ordering the women in. Schnabel got in first, while Emma gripped her baby tightly and followed her friend into the car. Schnabel was sent to Pankrac Palace with its execution room, while Emma and her baby was taken to a woman's concentration camp at Ravensbrück. Neither the women nor the baby was heard of again. 'The Kriminalrat was not a strong Nazi,' Stopford reflected, 'but the machine around him was working.'

Oblivious to the arrests, Stopford was worried about how he should break the news to Doreen that she needed to leave. The two of them had been working together in Prague for over half a year, and they had grown close, coming to respect each other tremendously. Doreen's initial jubilation at the passports being returned, quickly turned to sadness as Stopford explained her predicament.

At first Doreen refused to leave, and stormed out of her office in a fury. She bumped into Beatrice who was going the other way. The Canadian's calming presence was much needed. Doreen had done so much for the Czech and Sudeten Germans, but now she could make an even bigger sacrifice. By leaving, Beatrice explained, it would take a lot of the spotlight off the BCRC.

Doreen took herself to the ballroom alone. Looking out of the window, she saw Prague Castle loom as a dark silhouette against the night sky, the faint shimmer of the Vltava River which mirrored flickers from the streetlights. What beauty, she thought, against the backdrop of so much evil. She reluctantly made up her mind. She would leave, acting as the courier for the next transport. Having spent a month desperately trying to save the women whose passports she had lost, it was fitting that she should escort them to Britain. Accompanying them would be a further group of endangered refugees who had recently had their visas issued.

One of the women she would be taking was Marie Greiss, who had tried and failed to leave with Miss Dougan on a forged passport. Desperately waiting to be reunited with her husband, who had been of the first men to leave with Tessa, she was in a state of extreme anxiety.

But as Doreen flicked through the visas that had been prepared that day in the British Legation, she noticed that Greiss's name had been spelled with a 'z' rather than 'ss'. It was a simple mistake, but one which would be instantly spotted in the rigorous border checks. It was a race to get the permit corrected before the next train was due to leave the following evening.

Doreen telephoned Marie to explain the situation, telling her she might not be able to travel after all. But she was working hard to see if it could be changed in time. Marie was understandably despondent. Doreen finally managed to get her hands on the updated document the next day, which she took round to Marie's hostel room to surprise her.

When no one answered the door, Doreen's heart sank. Maybe she had been arrested. There was no one in the reception area and the dank building felt abandoned, so Doreen put her shoulder to Marie's door, and it opened easily thanks to the feeble lock. The room was dark with the curtains drawn, and there appeared to be no one in there, but after reaching for the light switch and flicking it on, Doreen froze. In front of her hung Marie's stiff body dangling motionless from the ceiling light. The strain of waiting had become too much.

Not wanting to cause panic among the other women, there was nothing for Doreen to do but back out of the room, closing the door behind her. The rest of the morning was spent in the car with Beatrice, driving between all the hotels and hostels. Doreen could only produce a sad smile when Beatrice asked what the matter was. This normally chatty, bossy lady was suddenly so subdued. Beatrice inferred Doreen's mood was sadness that she was leaving Prague. At each stop, they would congregate the women and children, handing out the passports and visas to those who would be leaving with Doreen that evening. Anyone whose travel permits had not arrived would be looked after by Beatrice, they were told. 'It was misery to have to tell them that I was leaving, though they knew why,' Doreen reflected.

There were other loose ends to tie up. Within the YWCA, there were several children Doreen had found wondering the streets, whose parents were either arrested or dead. These were put under the charge of Trevor Chadwick, who promised they would leave on the next transport he was organising with Nicholas Winton.

Despite the deep sadness Doreen felt, the beauty of that afternoon was breathtaking. Spring was coming to Prague at last. It is amazing how good weather can boost a person's mood, almost no matter their personal circumstances. Doreen felt optimistic about the situation, even though she knew there was no strong reason to.

But in a black saloon car driving down Keplerova Street, in the Hradčany district, there was a very different atmosphere. The three men in their familiar black coats, black fedora hats and leather gloves were so-called undercover Gestapo agents. But by this time people in Prague knew exactly who to look out for. Their disguise did nothing to hide their identity, which was perhaps the point. They instilled terror wherever they went.

The fourth man in the car was a petrified thirty-eight-year-old Jewish tailor, who had been arrested a few minutes before. He had been told he was being driven for questioning at the Gestapo headquarters.

The reputation of the Petschek Palace infused the city's residents with dread. Talk was rife of the brutal methods used there to extract confessions, including beatings, psychological torment, and the use of advanced interrogation techniques designed to break even the most resilient individuals. Those summoned to the palace rarely returned, and for many it was their last known location before execution or deportation to concentration camps.

The Jewish tailor knew this only too well. He was sitting on the left-hand side of the car in the back seat looking aimlessly out the window. Was this the last time he would see the city he had come to know so well?

The car slowed on the turning onto Úvoz Street where a roadblock was now a permanent feature. Being members of a secret police meant the car would usually just be waved through. But the bottleneck of cars trying to cross meant there were always traffic jams. As the car pulled to a halt, the Jewish tailor could see a group of children making their way along the pavement, holding hands. How normal, he thought. He wished he could transform into an innocent child, who did not understand the horror he now recognised. Those children, he thought, knew nothing yet of the evil in this world.

For some reason, the sight of them gave him a sudden injection of confidence. The Gestapo had not bothered to handcuff the gaunt man, and his seatbelt was not on. Was the door unlocked as well, he wondered? In the haze of being snatched a few minutes before, it would be hard to remember if the Gestapo men had done so.

As the driver punched his car horn at the vehicles in front, in a single movement, the Jewish tailor reached over and yanked the door handle. Mercifully, it opened, letting a cool spring breeze into the car. Before the officer sitting in the back could grab him, he leapt out of the car, and sprinted down the busy street, screaming at the top of his voice for help.

His captors were hot on his tail, their Lugers drawn, firing indiscriminately in his direction. Noticing someone leaving a building to his right, he darted through the closing door under a sign which said 'Sveriges Ambassad', just making it inside just as it shut behind him. This was the Swedish Legation. He ran up the grand staircase, past enormous oil paintings of dignitaries, his dirty shoes marking the plush red carpet. Trying every door he came to, he found one unlocked, darted inside and began pushing the two single beds against it to barricade himself in.

Folke Malmar, the Swedish Ambassador – known as the Envoy – had already had his share of drama over the last few months since the Nazis' arrival in Prague. It had been a busy time for all diplomats in the city as they tried desperately to get their people out of the occupied territory. Malmar was now in the process of closing down the Legation altogether, an exhausting task.

Thus, when he was told by his staff that a man had broken into the building and was now barricaded in one of the bedrooms, he could do nothing but let out a groan. Ordering a lockdown, he went from his office to the front door, where the Nazi officers chasing the Jewish man were now assembled and shouting to be let in.

Despite the array of threats thrown his way, Malmar valiantly refused to open the door. This was sovereign Swedish territory, and he would be damned if they thought they could intimidate their way in. Eventually, the Gestapo withdrew from the doorstep, creating a boundary around the building, cordoning off Úvoz Street and clearing away the crowds within a matter of minutes. Backup had been called, some already arriving. Ten minutes later, there was a mass of German military vehicles parked haphazardly all around.

This was escalating quickly, Malmar thought. The last thing he needed was a diplomatic incident. It now looked like Legation may itself be invaded. He opened one of the windows at the front of the building, his hands visible, showing he meant no aggression. With the growing number of soldiers having their rifles and machine guns trained on him, he explained calmly that he would speak to the Jewish man to see if he would come out peacefully, but he made it abundantly clear none of them were to enter the building. He would also not use force to remove the man either.

Malmar then went upstairs to the blockaded room where he knocked gently on the door. He said in his best German who he was, that he intended no harm, and he wanted to help. He explained that the Jewish man simply could not stay there indefinitely. The Legation would after all be closing down for as long as Czechoslovakia was part of the Third Reich. Maybe, he suggested, if he were to give the man a positive reference, it might mean the Germans would look favourably upon him. But neither man believed this was ever going to help. People do not leave Petschek Palace unharmed, and that was where the Jewish tailor was being taken.

The man sobbed back that he was meant to be leaving the country. He had been to his appointment with the BCRC. His train was leaving that evening. He was so close to getting out. He just needed time to think, to find a way to the train station.

The Ambassador returned to his office, picked up the phone and dialled Robert Stopford's number. Before long, Malmar was speaking to the BCRC's Prague representative directly. Doreen was in the British Legation at the time, packing up her things. She collected some belongings from her desk, put them in her bag, and hurried to the Swedish Legation. The German guards blocking off the roads initially would not let her through.

Malmar had to shout out of his office window that she should be allowed through, and after some discussion, she was permitted. Doreen went through that same entrance, up the stairs, past portraits, and tapped calmly on the barricaded door. The man on the other side immediately knew who had come. A great sense of relief came over him, and he agreed to let Doreen in, as long as she was alone.

Doreen sat on one of the beds now pulled away from the door, while the Jewish man sat opposite, his head in his hands. She gently broke the news to him that there was no way he could get out of this. Escape was impossible and the Nazis would never allow him to leave. She knew he was a dead man already.

After ten minutes, Doreen emerged from the room closing the door behind her. She told Malmar waiting anxiously at the foot of the stairs that the Jewish tailor wanted a few minutes on his own, before he would surrender to the Gestapo.

'Well done!' Malmar said, as if he was congratulating his secretary for bringing him a cup of coffee. He went back to his office to telephone the German negotiator he had been speaking with the good news.

Doreen was out of the building, past the roadblock, walking back to the British Legation, when she heard a single shot ringing out from behind her. Breathing in deeply, she had to steady herself on a nearby lamp post as tears filled her eyes. Not looking back, she walked stoically on.

Hearing the shot, Malmar, several of his staff and security with their weapons drawn ran up to the third room, rammed the door open. Lying back on the bed was the Jewish tailor, his blood painted over the wall behind him and soaking into the fresh sheets.

His right hand was gripping a shiny revolver, the same one Martha had confiscated from the desperate refugee on the day of the occupation. The same one Wenzel had threatened to use on himself had he have not been able to escape. The same one which, since his departure, had been in the bottom drawer of Doreen's desk in the British Legation.

It is difficult to comprehend how enabling someone to take their own life, in a strange way, was the kindest thing that Doreen could have done. Malmar allowed the Nazis into the Legation later that evening, and the man's body was unceremoniously removed. The arresting Gestapo agents were reprimanded for allowing him to escape in the first place and for not searching him properly when he was picked up. It was assumed he had been carrying the gun the whole time.

By 8 p.m., along with eighty women, children and a few men, Doreen was standing on the platform of Wilson Station. A place she had got to know so well. But this time, she would not be waving the train off and returning to her hotel, she would be making the journey herself. She wondered if she would ever see it again.

From the entrance, Jaroslav Podhajsky appeared, a bunch of flowers in hand and eyes puffy as if he had been crying. Being head over heels in love with Doreen meant this day was particularly poignant for him. Linking arms, he guided her to his car and the two drove up Petrin Hill, where one can get the best view of Prague. As she looked back on the place nicknamed the 'City of a Hundred Spires', with its endless array of churches, the last six months suddenly seemed so vivid in her mind. 'I had got to know Prague well, this winter better than ever,' she reflected. How it had changed since the Germans had invaded. Not only from making their physical presence known, with all the uniformed officers sauntering around and the swastika flags strewn everywhere, but in the atmosphere that seemed so foreign compared to when she first visited more than ten years earlier.

The pair chatted joyfully as they returned to the station, reminiscing on some of the happier times they had spent together. But it was an emotional farewell for Jaroslav, who had to fight back teers when Doreen finally got out of the car and walked away. She turned back to give him one more wave, before disappearing through the giant arches of the train station.

That was the last time she would see Jaroslav.

In the station, chaos greeted her. In the brief period she had been away, the Gestapo had arrived. As usual, they were making a nuisance of themselves. Doreen recognised the leader; he was the man who had been at the station a few weeks ago causing problems with Miss Dougan.

'You are traitors to the race,' he was barking at one terrified woman. She just stared directly ahead, not saying a word.

He glanced towards Doreen and seemed to immediately recognise her. Mercifully leaving the woman he had been berating, he marched over to the Englishwoman. Snatched the bag she was carrying which contained all eighty passports, he began an inspection of its contents.

'Mr Stopford is on his way,' she said softly as he began to sift through the passports.

This seemed to instantly subdue the man. In a stark demonstration of the power of Robert Stopford's reputation by this point, the Gestapo officer sheepishly handed back the passports. In what would be her final interaction with the Nazis, Doreen complained that he had returned the passports disarranged from the alphabetical order they had been in and asked for an apology, which he reluctantly gave.

She then turned her back on them and ordered the women onto the train. At 11.00 p.m. on 22 April, 1939, like clockwork, the train steamed out of Wilson Station.

Doreen sat in a compartment looking out of the window. The dark city started to race away from her one last time.

*

Two days later, the bellboy at the Alcron Hotel was startled when he answered the bell being continually rung on the reception desk and saw eight uniformed members of the Gestapo standing in a line. With their high-collared black overcoats dripping with water from the rain outside, their leader demanded the key for Miss Warriner's room.

They made their way up to the third floor, crammed into the elevator with a terrified lift attendant. Their disappointment was palpable as they unlocked the room only to find it empty. Bömelburg's tip off to Stopford had paid off. Both parties were happy, as Doreen had escaped safely. And although Bömelburg did not have her under arrest, he believed the problems she had been causing around the city would cease.

Little did he know that there were still a few women left behind who would carry on her work with just as much determination and courage, spearheaded by Martha Sharp.

Chapter Fourteen
Keeping Going

The Gestapo and the SS were proud of the fear that they instilled. It was their ruthless and unrelenting reputation that made them so effective. It was well-known around Europe that they could not be negotiated with. Whatever argument was put forward, no matter how rational, it was prone to being ignored. And the Nazi leadership in Berlin expected nothing less from their enforcers.

In May 1939, word started to spread among the upper echelon of the secret police leadership that things in Prague were too lenient. Under his watch, Bömelburg had allowed thousands of people to escape the city. He had actively supported the BCRC with their quest to get as many people away as they liked. And he had collaborated with British officials, not least Robert Stopford, who seemed to have a hold over the Nazi. One of Bömelburg's assistants had reported back to Berlin his leader's terror when he heard Stopford shouting at him down the telephone. The Englishman's version was that, 'during all this [shouting], I was banging the table, holding the telephone close to it so as to be sure that he could hear!'

Doreen's departure just before she was meant to be arrested was not quite the last straw but rather was a contributing factor in Bömelburg's downfall in Prague. There was already scrutiny on his leadership and questions about his toughness. Was he up to the task? It was decided in the early summer of 1939 that he was not, and he was unceremoniously replaced by Adolf Eichmann, someone who insisted he would not be intimidated by anybody, let alone an English diplomat.

The ambitious and methodical SS officer was sent to Prague to oversee Gestapo operations. Eichmann was also tasked with the brutal implementation of Nazi policies concerning the Jewish population in Czechoslovakia. With a background in business and administration before joining the SS, he was known for his cold, bureaucratic approach to implementing the Third Reich's programmes. With a somewhat nondescript appearance – blond hair, fair skin, and a reserved, almost unremarkable demeanour – Eichmann's temperament was rigid and impersonal, focused on the efficient execution of orders rather than emotional involvement. He made his intentions known to Stopford upon their first encounter.

Arriving at his weekly meeting with Bömelburg, Stopford was surprised to see Eichmann instead. For a change, no cognac was offered to the British diplomat. Eichmann was implementing a new regime, he told Stopford. No more leniency towards him and certainly no more deals to be struck. The BCRC, in Eichmann's mind, was clearly conducting illegal activity. It would end right there and then, he insisted.

When Stopford protested, saying that the BCRC was a legitimate British organisation who had been working in collaboration with the German authorities, Eichmann was having none of it. Not only did those who he suspected of illicit activities need to leave immediately or face arrest, the BCRC should cease in its existence.

The German leadership in Prague had been so generous, he told Stopford, in allowing and helping the organisation to succeed. But they were being taken advantage of and Eichmann would stand for it no more. Anyone who was associated with the BCRC would need to be replaced before he would consider issuing any further permits. He was now ranting uncontrollably, jumping between topics. Stopford was baffled when the issue of Doreen Warriner's office then came up.

Eichmann stated how disappointed and surprised he had been with what they had found, claiming that although it was known her work had been underhand, they were shocked and confused by her activities. As the German ranted on, Stopford was becoming increasingly worried that she had left details of the American's collaboration with the BCRC, or worse.

In fact, they had found something much more peculiar. Pornography. And lots of it. There were bookshelves all around Doreen's office, filled with thick, red, leather-bound books containing German pornography. The reason boiled down simply to the fact that the building the BCRC had requisitioned for their headquarters used to belong to a publishing company, who were not your everyday publishers. They were focused on post-World War I erotic photography. Doreen had adopted one of their storerooms as an office, which happened to be surrounded by a lot of leftover stock. She had asked on several occasions for these to be removed, but given the urgency of their other tasks, this one soon fell to the bottom of the priority list.

The agents who found them took several away for thorough examination, checking them page by page in the privacy of their own rooms, apparently to make sure there were no messages hidden within – one of their more enjoyable tasks that winter.

After that revelation, the meeting was over. Refusing to shake his hand, Eichmann suggested that Stopford let himself out of his office.

As Stopford walked through the cobbled streets back to the British Legation, he knew the end had now come. Martha was not part of the BCRC, so maybe she could continue. But Beatrice, as the new leader of the BCRC, would need to shut it down.

Doreen Warriner's stoic and selfless attitude towards her work set a lasting precedent. Following her lead, no one truly showed the strain their emotionally and physically exhausting work was putting them under. After her arrest, Beatrice had not taken time to recover and now she was carrying the weight of responsibility of the entire BCRC, making her accountable for who should be saved and who should be left behind. The enormous load was taking its toll on her and, unknown to most of those around her, Beatrice was having a breakdown. It was evident from Martha's letter to Margaret: 'We work with Beatrice Wellington whenever her nearly-deranged nerves allow her to. But she is pretty nearly a case herself.'

Hence, when Robert Stopford burst into the ballroom at the British Legation to enlighten her on Eichmann's ultimatum, he found her sitting in the dark, dejected and lethargic. He called Margaret, who in turn wrote an urgent telegram to Beatrice to come to London immediately to discuss the future of the BCRC.

Beatrice refused to obey, believing that the fuss was all a conspiracy from her peers to get her out of Prague. She wrote in a telegram to Margaret: 'I doubt the motives of my recall.' She then produced a rambling seven-page report which she sent out to anyone she thought might be of influence, including Sir Walter Layton and Eleanor Rathbone. She ended the note: 'Whatever might have been the cause, and whoever may have engineered this move, it was not due to local interference or antagonism on the part of the Gestapo.'

A new battleground was forming within the BCRC, fought between London and Prague. Although she was not averse to the odd skirmish herself, Doreen had managed the extreme pressure of operating on the front line admirably. Now part of the London team, she worked closely with Margaret on more of the bureaucratic activities, which gave her an understanding of the very different anxiety her counterparts had been dealing with.

Along with Margaret and Eleanor, the three women made

presentations to the Home Office to make the mechanics of granting visas easier. 'The obstacles created by the Passport Control Office are almost greater than those created by the Gestapo,' Doreen explained, with the benefit of her vast and unimpeachable on-the-ground experience.

Having built a good working relationship with Martha, Doreen was able to liaise with her directly, while the situation between Stopford, Beatrice and Eichmann unfolded. Things ran relatively smoothly, and another 320 endangered people were able to leave in May. Issued with individual visas rather than on a mass transport basis, Martha hoped they would be less conspicuous.

At the same time, Waitstill had put in place a financial system that was not only helping people escape Czechoslovakia and take their money with them, but was also generating huge sums of Czech korunas which American Relief could use to keep the remaining refugees alive. He had the idea after Martha told him how often she was being told of people's concerns about not being able to convert their currency when they left the country.

Waitstill had considerable sums of US dollars to spend on Czech aid, and so he deposited this in banks outside Czechoslovakia, in places such as Geneva, Paris and London. Then, back in Czechoslovakia, when someone came to him with korunas, he would work out an exchange rate and write an IOU on his calling card. The person changing their money would then leave Czechoslovakia and present the card in one of the banks where Waitstill had deposited the US dollars, and take out their money, while back in Czechoslovakia, Waitstill had a growing pile of korunas to use inside the country.

He would not have been able to deposit the cash into banks in the Protectorate, because even if banks were allowed to make such a big transaction, the money would have been seized by the Germans. His simple but ingenious scheme became very popular because now anyone leaving the country could convert their money into other denominations, which was forbidden under Nazi rule, and because, given its instability, Czech korunas were not accepted in banks outside of Czechoslovakia.

Those looking to leave Czechoslovakia would bring the cash they wanted to convert, and Waitstill would consult the unofficial exchange rates he had written in his notebook. Major landowners and farmers would get the highest rate as he felt they could afford it (160 korunas to the dollar), followed by a lawyer or certain people in industry, such as senior skilled factory workers, supervisors and business owners (seventy-five korunas to the dollar), then a social worker rate (thirty-seven korunas to the dollar) and so on. In exchange for the cash, Waitstill would tear one of his business cards in half, writing the amount in dollars that was owed to that person on both. One he would keep as a receipt and the other he would give to the depositor. The torn card would be accepted in any branch of the bank where Waitstill had deposited the US dollars. He had arranged this directly with his banker, to whom he signed off his letter with a stern warning that, 'Absolutely no word of this arrangement should ever come into the Protectorate.'

This allowed people, whether they were wealthy or not, to get at least some of their money out of the country which would often be used to pay for onward travel or repay the cost of their visa. At the same time, it meant Waitstill was quickly sitting on a huge amount of cash. Two million koronas to be precise, which he hid in the safe of the American Legation.

He and Martha needed to decide what to do with all this money. It was not as simple as just paying it to relief organisations. Such was the political tension with the German government, no such funding arrangements could be official. Martha would therefore drop off bags of cash to the Salvation Army, paying for two hot meals per day for 350 homeless refugees for six months. Many of these people were ones Martha was trying to arrange visas for. Funds were also handed out to the YWCA who were housing orphaned children.

The church's chief accountant had provided Martha with three large ledger books to keep track of their spend. But when the Sharps returned to America later that year, the books remained completely empty and unused. Auditors for the church had to rely on the couple's memory – and Waitstill's pile of torn business cards – to do the accounts, which turned out to be accurate to within two nickels. This explained why, when Martha was escorting a transport to England in March, Waitstill had been in Geneva depositing tens of thousands of dollars.

One of the uses Martha put the money to was paying for train tickets for those who had received exit permits. Her strategy – unlike Doreen's successful operations with the BCRC – was to send out a few people each day, and this continued into June and July, with more than 300 people going out through legal means to London, many of whom travelled on to America.

Waitstill left Prague on 1 July, basing himself in different cities around Europe, including Geneva and Paris. He was desperately worried for Martha, but he had to attend a series of conferences as part of his schedule. He hoped to return to the Czech capital, but ultimately he never would. In the same way, Robert Stopford was forced to leave the country for meetings in London, but as the situation escalated, he was unable to return.

Martha, meanwhile, remained in Prague and oversaw the ongoing success of drip-feeding exit permits, which also meant she no longer needed to act as courier, a task which was fraught with more and more danger by the day. The only travelling Martha did outside of Prague that summer was to the border where she met Františka Plamínková , not to get her out of Czechoslovakia, but to try to prevent her from re-entering. Martha had received a surprise visit from one of Františka's supporters, who had initially been relieved that Františka had left the country for a lecture tour but was now beside herself after finding out that she planned to come back.

'We must prevent her from returning,' the woman told Martha. 'She has turned aside every effort which I have made personally, in letters, to dissuade her from coming back … she does not understand how difficult and changed life is here now.'

Františka was in unimaginable danger. Her anti-Nazi rhetoric was infamous around the country. Martha could not believe she was planning to come back to Czechoslovakia – if she hadn't left she would surely have been among the first arrested and if she returned, she would be in extreme danger. Martha travelled to the German border, where she was recognised by one of the border guards who had searched her while she was acting as a courier.

'Don't you remember me?' he asked the bemused American. 'I checked your American passport!' he said proudly. Although travelling on an American passport allowed certain privileges when it came to passing through checkpoints, as this young guard emphasised, it was so rare to see an American it was hard for them to go undetected.

'Why are you here?' the guard asked.

Worried about her safety, Martha tried to reply casually. 'Just to collect an older woman,' she said.

'What is her name?' he inquired back.

Martha knew she could not lie. If she gave a fake name, he would later be checking their passports anyway. 'Františka Plamínková.'

'That's a funny name,' he replied with a chuckle, and went on his way.

As she waited for the train to arrive, Martha noticed a huge block of houses which she had seen on her last visit to this border had somehow disappeared. Wandering around to get a better look, she saw they had been completely destroyed by fire.

At that moment, the train signalled its arrival. Františka was mystified when she climbed out of her carriage to be greeted by Martha. Taking her by the arm, the American woman tried to put forward her best case as to why Františka should not cross into Czechoslovakia.

'Shall I stay in comfort on the outside, while my women are suffering?' she asked. 'I must go back and fight!' And with that, Martha knew there was no way of persuading her, even though Františka must have known she was likely to be arrested and executed on her return.

They joined the queue to re-enter Czechoslovakia. Upon reaching the guard, Martha pointed to the burnt-out buildings. 'What happened to them?' she asked.

'We blew them up!' the guard replied proudly. 'They are the houses Jews lived in.'

By now tens of thousands of people – mostly Jewish – had been rounded up, their property confiscated and homes taken, if not destroyed. The numbers of those who were able to escape thanks to Martha and Beatrice, who was still refusing to leave, were dwindling. Those who made it to Poland were then stuck as the local government struggled with the burden of the influx of people, along with their own growing tensions with Germany. It got so bad that Clare wrote to Margaret on 26 July describing the situation: 'There are some hundreds of refugees in Poland who will never obtain a visa to the United Kingdom.' Several were now being sent back to the border and forced to return to Czechoslovakia.

On 3 August, after a direct ultimatum from the Gestapo, Beatrice Wellington finally left. She took the last of the 445 people who had got to England through the BCRC and American

Relief since Doreen had left Czechoslovakia. When Beatrice's train arrived in London two days later, along with the tired souls she had evacuated, they were met by the familiar face of Doreen on the platform.

With Beatrice now gone, Martha found herself alone, the only foreign refugee worker left in Czechoslovakia. Her bravery was remarkable. For the past two weeks she had been followed constantly by a man, wherever she went. Nicknaming him her 'protector', he now slept in the room next to hers in Hotel Pariz. To begin with, it became a game for Martha trying to lose her 'protector'. She found it exhilarating and something she was very good at. Twice, she found him standing at the front door of the hotel, having lost her earlier in the day.

But after two weeks of this, it was starting to eat away at her. 'His evil face and burning eyes began to appear even in my dreams,' she recollected. 'I believed he was capable of killing his own grandmother to serve his cause.'

Her nerves were in tatters when on Thursday 3 August, after a night of tossing and turning from sheer terror, she eventually drifted off as it was becoming light outside. When she opened her eyes again it was 8.30 a.m. She had overslept. Rushing to get the tram – her protector in hot pursuit – she came to a halt. Her notebook was still in her room.

Hurrying back, as she burst through the door, it was full of men. One had her mattress on one side, another was rifling through the chest of drawers, searching among her undergarments. The third was sitting at her desk, looking through her papers.

Everyone fell silent. Martha frozen, the men staring back at her, unsure what to do next.

'Oh, excuse me,' Martha said, backing out of the room. 'I will just be in your way,' she continued once she was in the corridor.

She carried on with her day as if nothing had happened.

On Tuesday 14 August, she received a call from a man with a thick Czech accent in broken English. 'I have heard that you to be arrested on the Thursday,' he said.

'Who is this?' Martha asked.

'If you leave tomorrow, you can escape,' he continued.

Martha had no idea who she was talking to, nor whether they were credible. This could be a crank call to just scare her into leaving. But she calculated, if the Nazis wanted to frighten her to flee and it did not work, then they would just arrest her anyway.

Sensing the pause, the Czech man said, 'You have helped many peoples. Do not wait.' The telephone then went dead.

With no options left, Martha booked herself on the Orient Express leaving Prague the following evening. She was speechless from the outpouring of gratitude from those she was leaving behind. While she felt she was turning her back on people she cared for so much, they appeared just thankful that she was among the few who had come to assist them.

It was lucky that she was the only passenger on the train bound for Paris that left the next night on 15 August. Her washbowl and the entire adjoining compartment were filled with gifts, mementos and flowers which had been presented by the hundreds of locals who had turned out to the station to see her off.

Two weeks later, Clare found herself behind the wheel of a borrowed diplomatic car, driving along the quiet frontier between Poland and Germany on the warm, sun-dappled afternoon of 28 August. The peaceful serenity of the moment contrasted sharply with the eerie sight that greeted her eyes—a vast concentration of German military forces, their tanks, troops, and artillery camouflaged under nets, all waiting, poised for action.

The enormity of what she had just witnessed hit her like a thunderclap, and as she returned to her hotel in Katowice, the weight of the moment pressed down upon her. Without hesitation, she picked up the phone and called Margaret Layton in London, her voice trembling with urgency as she relayed what she had seen. Then, she made the call to *The Daily Telegraph*'s London office, warning them that war was imminent.

On 1 September, when the deafening rumble of German tanks rolling across the Polish border reached Clare's ears, she contacted London, delivering the first eyewitness account of the invasion, the scoop that would mark the beginning of World War II.

Meanwhile, in England, Doreen sat by her radio on 3 September, hearing the words no one wanted to hear. As Neville Chamberlain's voice echoed through the airwaves, the dreadful confirmation of what had been feared arrived:

> *This country is at war with Germany. The state of war in which we find ourselves was brought about by the actions of the German Government. I have to tell you that we have been informed that the German Government has refused to respond to our final offer and has, in fact, initiated hostilities. We are now engaged in a state of war, and I have to ask that we now face the future with courage and determination.*

The announcement struck with the impact of a war drum, reverberating through the homes of millions. As the world scrambled to prepare for conflict, Robert Stopford had one final task left from his time in Prague. He was finishing typing his official report, to be submitted to the British Government, specifically about the impact of the BCRC:

The Refugee Institute estimate the number of refugees who emigrated between 15 October, 1938 and 13 May, 1939 was 7,500 (3,550 families), but this figure of course, does not include those who had emigrated illegally, which we estimate as a further 6,200, giving a total of 13,700.

Along with the additional numbers saved from the middle of May to the end of August, it took the total to 15,000 people saved by a group of remarkable women.

Aftermath

Hitler's advance into Poland in September 1939 not only signalled the start of another World War tragically soon after the end of the previous one, but also the slaughter of millions around Europe. It is estimated that 350,000 people were killed in Czechoslovakia before the Nazi surrender in 1945.

On top of the 15,000 evacuated by Doreen Warriner, Martha Sharp and their team were nearly 700 children, who left as part of one of the most celebrated rescue operations in recent times. The renowned architect of this was **Nicholas Winton**, who became known around the world following his appearance on Esther Rantzen's *That's Life!*. From that point, his life changed dramatically, as he was given multiple honours for what he achieved, including the freedom of Prague, the Order of Tomáš Masaryk and a knighthood before he died at the age of 106 in 2015.

Trevor Chadwick, who remained in Prague until 2 June, 1939, when he escorted a train with 123 children back to London, received no such plaudits. This was despite Nicholas Winton's attempts to get him recognised. 'Trevor dealt with all the considerable problems at the Prague end,' he wrote in 1999. 'This work he continued to carry on even when it became more difficult and dangerous when the Germans arrived. He deserves all praise.' However, he got none through his lifetime. He joined the Royal Navy and then Royal Air Force during the war, before skipping between various careers, including as a landlord, a driver and working in gambling. He died aged seventy-two from medical complications after a stroke in 1972.

Robert Stopford was flown to America after war was declared with Hitler, taking up a post as Financial Counsellor at the British Embassy in Washington until 1943. At this point he returned to London and joined the War Office as Directorate of Civil Affairs, a post he held until the end of the war. After the war, he was again thrown into deep negotiations as a member of the Council of Foreign Ministers Boundary Commission, tasked with negotiating the Italian-Yugoslavian territorial disputes. In later life, Stopford enjoyed his time as a semi-historian, taking a particular interest in Ypres and served as Chairman of the Board of Trustees for the Imperial War Museum, where his rich archives remain. He died aged eighty-three in 1978.

Walter Runciman, for whom Robert Stopford worked in 1938, was appointed as the President of the Royal Institute of International Affairs and was a member of the House of Lords. After the war, he continued his work in international relations, as well as in academia and publishing, until his death in 1953. His involvement in the Munich Agreement remained a contentious point in his career, something for which many people, including political leaders, never forgave him

One in particular was **Edvard Beneš** who became the President of Czechoslovakia in exile. Leading the government-in-exile from London, he worked closely with the Allies to ensure the country's post-war sovereignty. After the war, he was re-elected as President of Czechoslovakia, overseeing the reconstruction and rebuilding efforts. However, following the communist coup, he was forced to resign again on 7 February, 1948 and went into exile, dying shortly afterwards, aged sixty-four.

Beneš's first Prime Minister and Doreen's former lover, **Milan Hodža,** fled to France following the advance of the Nazis toward Czechoslovakia. After publishing his memoirs, in which he spoke briefly of Doreen, he died from pneumonia in Paris at the end of 1944, aged sixty-six.

Doreen's other serious love interest in Prague, ***Wenzel Jaksch***, continued to fight for the rights of Sudeten Germans while in London. He also began a long running feud with Beneš, who, after the war was able to persuade the British Government not to allow Wenzel back into his country, saying he 'demanded a strict separation of Czech and German regions and even proposed a transfer of national minorities.' This ban was only lifted in 1949, when he became the second President of the Federation of Expellees in Germany. Jaksch was killed in a road accident in 1966 aged seventy, a fate he had only narrowly avoided in 1938 before his first meetings with Doreen and the two Labour politicians.

Prior to his death, Wenzel had presented ***David Grenfell*** with a thanksgiving painting by Czech artist Ernst Neuschel, one of the men who the BCRC had helped to escape Prague, in recognition of his efforts. During the war, Grenfell acted as Chairman of the Welsh Parliamentary Labour Party and joined Churchill's coalition government as Secretary for Mines at the Board of Trade. In 1953 he controversially became the Father of the House, despite Winston Churchill having served longer than him. But the rule was that the title was for someone 'who has continuously served longer in the House of Commons than any other MP'. Churchill had broken his time as a MP in 1922 when he lost his seat. Grenfell died at his home in Swansea aged eighty-seven in 1968.

Labour Party MP ***William Gillies*** had a less celebrated career in politics. Although he served twenty-five years as International Secretary of the Labour Party, he was dismissed in 1944 in part because of his ardent support of the theory of Vansittartism, 'the assertion that Nazism was a product of specifically German tradition and culture'. He died aged seventy-three in 1958.

His colleague in the Houses of Parliament, ***Eleanor***

Rathbone remained an independent MP until her death one year after the end of the war in 1946 aged seventy-three. Despite dying before many of the other politicians involved in this story, she was still able to see the Family Allowance Act pass into law in 1945. She is credited for pioneering this act, which was the first ever child benefit law in Britain.

Konrad Henlein, Wenzel's arch nemesis, continued to collaborate with Hitler throughout the war as Reich Lieutenant of the Sudetenland. After the Allies declared victory over the Third Reich in 1945, he was arrested by American soldiers and imprisoned in Czechoslovakia. He died that year, by smashing his spectacles in his prison cell and using the glass to puncture the arteries in his wrist in May 1945.

He worked closely before his death with ***Konstantin von Neurath***, who remained as the Reich Protector of Bohemia and Moravia, overseeing the Nazi occupation of Czechoslovakia. After the war, he was arrested by the Allies and tried at the Nuremberg Trials, where he was convicted of war crimes. He was sentenced to fifteen years in prison but was released in 1954, in part because of his poor health which followed a heart attack. After that, he lived in Germany and died in 1956 aged eighty-three.

Von Neurath's deputy ***Karl Hermann Frank*** continued to play a central role in the repression of the Czech population, overseeing the infamous reprisals by the Nazis, including the destruction of the village of Lidice after Reinhard Heydrich's assassination in 1942. After the war, Frank was arrested by Czech authorities. He was tried for war crimes and crimes against humanity and was sentenced to death. Frank was executed by hanging on May 22, 1946, in Prague at the age of forty-four.

Working under Frank after the occupation of Czechoslovakia, Gestapo leader ***Karl Bömelburg*** was sent to France in 1940 following the Nazi invasion. He lived in a large commune, west of Paris called Neuilly-sur-Seine in a house which became known as Villa Bömelburg. He was deliberate in his cruelty there, following his dismissal for being too lenient in Prague. Under his command in Paris, he had hundreds of French Resistance suspects killed, ensured the regular use of torture in interrogations and helped the German collaborator Philippe Pétain escape to Switzerland after the Allied invasion in 1944. After the war, Bömelburg reinvented himself as Sergeant Bergman, a German soldier who had died shortly before the Nazi surrender. He moved to Munich where he found work as a gardener and librarian. A year later in 1946, he slipped on an icy pavement, fell and died of a head injury aged sixty-one. Although he never paid for his crimes, he was posthumously sentenced to death by French courts for war crimes. He has yet to be convicted of any crimes in Czechoslovakia.

His replacement in Prague, ***Adolf Eichmann*** initially fled to Argentina in 1950, where he lived under an assumed name. In 1960, Israeli agents tracked him down and captured him in a covert operation. He was transported to Israel, where he was put on trial for his role in the Holocaust. Eichmann was found guilty of war crimes, crimes against humanity, and other offenses, notable for his involvement in the Nazi Final Solution. He was sentenced to death and executed by hanging on June 1, 1962, at the age of fifty-six.

German Foreign Ministry representative, ***Dr Karl Ritter*** – who worked closely with Bömelburg and Eichmann – was arrested and tried for war crimes after the war, and sentenced to life imprisonment. He died in 1967, at the age of seventy. His assistant, ***Dr Karl Mitis*** remained in Prague until the end of the war, at which point he was arrested. At the time of writing, no details relating to what became of him were available.

Their opposite number in the British Legation, ambassador ***Sir Basil Newton*** remained in Prague after the invasion until

October 1939. He enjoyed a long career in the diplomatic service until his retirement, and then death in 1973.

A member of Newton's staff in Prague, **Harold 'Gibby' Gibson**, was known as the Passport Control Officer, but in reality was a British intelligence officer, helped ten Czech intelligence officers to fly to London to escape the Nazis in Prague, including František Moravec, who went on to plan *Operation Anthropoid*, the plot to assassinate Reinhard Heydrich. For this, Gibby was placed on a special 'wanted list' by the SS, who were to prioritise his arrest if Britain was successfully invaded. After the war he carried out diplomatic duties around Europe. He was found shot dead in 1960, two years after his retirement, in his flat in Rome. Originally suspected to be suicide, the exact cause of his death is still not known. The plot is further thickened by the fact that Gibson was posthumously suspected of being a Russian mole within MI5.

Father ***Jozef Tiso***, the Slovakian Prime Minister who collaborated with Hitler was sentenced to death in a Czech court in 1947. Tiso's Hlinka Guard, who Jaksch had nearly bumped into while escaping, were responsible for the deaths of thousands of Jews. Slovakia suffered terribly from the Holocaust because of the collaboration with Hitler, with 113,000 Jewish people being killed in the country alone, leaving a population of just 24,000 Jews in 1945.

Chairman of the BCRC ***Ewart Culpin*** served as the Labour Party Alderman for London County Council for Battersea North from 1925 until 1946, when he died aged sixty-nine.

The man who had appointed Culpin and himself been selected to establish the BCRC, ***Sir Walter Layton***, was drafted into government after war was declared. He held positions within the Ministry of Supply and the Ministry of Production from 1940 until 1942, when he was made Head of Joint Production Staff. Despite the respect he held in the British political circles, he was a hopelessly unsuccessful politician, losing all three of his attempts to stand for Parliament as a Liberal candidate. He did, however, influence a lot of the population with liberal ideas through his time as Chairman of *The Economist* and Editor of the *News Chronicle*. He died aged eighty-one in 1966.

His daughter, **Margaret Layton**, who remained secretary of the BCRC from London throughout, married to Reuters journalist Alfred Geiringer on 20 December, 1939. The couple moved back to his home country of Austria after the war, where she had four children. She died on 5 July, 1962 at the age fifty-one.

Her peer from the time she spent running operations in London with the Quakers, **Bertha Bracey,** had started off managing eighteen refugee cases. By the time war was declared against Germany by Britain, her operation was looking after more than 40,000 cases across the whole continent. She continued to toil valiantly in the Kindertransport movement. At the end of the war – after she arranged for the RAF to fly 300 orphans from the liberated Theresienstadt concentration camp in Czechoslovakia – she worked around Europe supporting refugees. She died aged ninety-five in 1989.

The first Quaker to set up operations in Prague in 1938, **Mary Penman**, returned to Hertfordshire, England, where she remained during the war with her South African husband, Frank. She died in 1952, aged sixty-eight and was survived by her two children and two stepchildren. Her brother, **Philip Noel-Baker** continued to be a leading figure in advocating for disarmament and international peace, for which he was awarded the Nobel Peace Prize in 1959. He died in 1982, at the age of ninety-two.

Jean Rowntree left her career as a teacher to join the BBC in 1940. She created and led the further education unit, where she produced series on science, the arts, current affairs, the environment and education itself. After a successful career, she retired to Kent in 1966, where she remained until her death in 2003 aged ninety-eight.

Her cousin, ***Tessa Rowntree***, continued working with the Quakers' relief effort upon her return to England from Prague, co-founding the women's section of the Friends Ambulance Unit. She married American Quaker John Cadbury in 1942, and after the war the couple relocated to New Jersey in the United States. She worked as a librarian at the Moorestown Free Library for twenty years, along with taking many courses at Burlington County College right into her late seventies. She died aged ninety in 1999.

Her colleague, **Hilde Patz** travelled to reunite with her husband in England, after fleeing Prague during the occupation. No records remain about her whereabouts upon her arrival. In a similar fashion, nothing is known about ***Christine Maxwell***, following her brief time in Prague. She had travelled there with ***Miss Margaret Dougan***, who then went on to Poland where she remained until the invasion started, at which point she left in a convoy with British consular staff while German bombs were falling all around them. She returned to Oxford, where she remained with no family until her death in 1949, aged fifty-one.

While fleeing Poland, she lent a skint ***Clare Hollingworth*** £10 to help her escape. During the war, Clare continued her fearless reporting from the front lines across Europe and North Africa, covering key events such as the Blitz and the liberation of Paris, gaining a reputation for her bravery and skill in war zones. After the war, she continued her journalism career, reporting on international conflicts, including the Algerian War and the Vietnam War. She died 2017, at the remarkable age of 105.

Following her arrest in March 1939, ***Marie Schmolka*** was extraordinarily released – following pressure from the British

Government – and fled to Paris at the end of the year. Her health never recovered following her time incarcerated, and she died from a heart attack 1940, at the age of forty-six. She had worked closely throughout 1938 and the start of 1939 with *Alice Masaryk* who had in turn fled to the United States. She returned to Czechoslovakia after the war, but following the Communist takeover in 1948, went back into exile. She died in 1966, at the age of eighty-seven. After ceasing operations during the occupation, her beloved Red Cross resumed its humanitarian work, focusing on post-war recovery, medical care, and aid to displaced persons, still working closely with Czechoslovakian Women's National Council. The organisation's founder, *Františka Plamínková*, who had gallantly returned to the country in 1939 was arrested as part of the mass round ups of 5,000 people by the Gestapo and sent to a camp at Milovice, twenty-five miles from the capital. From there, they were sent to concentration camps in Germany, before being released. She was re-arrested after the assassination of Reinhard Heydrich and taken to Theresienstadt concentration camp, where she was killed by firing squad on 30 June, 1942.

The Czech Commissioner for Refugees *Jaroslav Podhajsky*, who had fallen madly in love with Doreen, was listed for execution at the same time. However, his lawyer managed to get him exonerated on the grounds that a factory he ran was engaged in war production, exporting machinery to Germany. After the war, this was deemed to collaboration with the enemy, so Jaroslav was not allowed to return to his beloved homeland. He moved to Brazil with his family in 1950, where he lived until his death in 1973, aged eighty-nine.

Beatrice Wellington travelled around Europe throughout the war, before basing herself in Poland after the Nazi defeat to provide relief work for the next three years. Ill health forced her to return to America where she spent time in a mental hospital.

She unsuccessfully tried to join the U.N. before settling for a teaching role in an Alberta and British Columbia school. In the winter of 1970, she cut her foot on a piece of glass, which quickly became septic and eventually resulted in it being amputated. The surgery proved too much for her body to stand and a year later she died aged sixty-four, having slipped into a coma from which she never awoke.

Sudeten Jew **Lisl Xall**, who had worked so nobly with Martha, was rounded up in Prague along with her husband in 1941. They were sent to Theresienstadt concentration camp, followed by Auschwitz, where they were murdered.

The secretary to the Sharps, **Virginia Waistcoat**, went to Paris in late March 1939, before travelling back to America with her employers. From there, little is known about her onward endeavours.

After arriving back in America with Virgina and Martha in 1939, **Waitstill Sharp** continued his humanitarian work for the Unitarian Service Committee, where he organised the rescue of refugees from Nazi-occupied Europe. The strain of their travel eventually caused the breakdown of his marriage to Martha, and the couple divorced in 1947. Waitstill went on to work in various social justice causes – most notably the civil rights movement – before he died in 1984 at the age of ninety-one.

Martha Sharp continued with her humanitarian work after returning to America. She was sent with Waitstill to Lisbon in May 1940 to set up a new Unitarian operation. They carried out various initiatives including helping intellectuals escape Vichy France, distributed milk to poor children and at the end of the year, Martha escorted twenty-seven children and ten adults to America.

After the war ended, Martha decided to enter of politics, running unsuccessfully for Congress against future Republican

Speaker of the House Joe Martin. In 1950, Martha was appointed to the National Security Resources Board – set up to prepare for possible war following the detonation by the Soviet Union of its first atomic bomb in August 1949 – working in the White House under President Franklin D. Roosevelt. The Executive Office needed to find 'a woman who has overseas relief experience, knows the U.S. and especially women's organisations, who can speak effectively to audiences of any size and can write'. Martha ticked all the boxes and remained in post until 1952, when she joined Adlai Stevenson's unsuccessful Democratic presidential campaign.

Following her divorce to Waitstill, she remarried Eugene Cogan, a New York City businessman and philanthropist in 1951. After her time in politics, the couple continued to support refugee relief and humanitarian causes for the remainder of their lives. She died of natural causes aged ninety-four on 6 December, 1999. Along with Waitstill, in 2005 she was named by the historical remembrance organization Yad Vashem as Righteous Among the Nations 'In light of the risks taken [in her] meritorious assistance to Jewish fugitives of Nazi terror'. A medal and certificate of honour was presented on 13 June, 2006, to their daughter Martha Sharp Joukowsky – who was just three years-old when her parents travelled to Prague – in a ceremony with an audience which including members of the Sharp family, and Eva Esther Feigl, one of the Jews rescued by the Sharps.

Doreen Warriner spent the start of the war in London working for the war effort within the Ministry of Economic Welfare and the Political Warfare Executive. Thanks to Robert Stopford's recommendation, she was honoured with an OBE in 1941. He wrote, 'A large number of refugees owed their lives to her unremitting devotion to their cause ... regardless of the risks she herself ran.'

In 1943, Doreen left Britain, heading for the Middle East, where there was more relief work to be carried out. In her capacity as Chief of the United Nations Relief and Rehabilitation Administration food mission in Yugoslavia for the next two years, she helped save countless further lives. Returning to Britain in 1946, she joined the University College London (UCL) as a lecturer in the School of Slavonic and East European Studies.

For the next thirteen years she lectured in the world's leading research centre on Russia, the Baltics, and Central, Eastern and South-East Europe. In this time, she published many papers, including a diary of her time in Prague from 1938 to 1939. In 1965, Doreen was promoted to the role of professor with the UCL, a job she filled for seven years. She died of a stroke aged sixty-eight, in 1972.

Doreen had remained friends with Wenzel up until his death, although their romantic relationship ended. He never took for granted what Doreen, Martha and any others around them did. In what would turn out to be his final publication, he wrote: 'To these women our deepest gratitude is due.'

Doreen Warriner

Martha Sharp

Wenzel Jaksch

Milan Hodža

List of Acronyms

Amrelczech – American Committee for Relief in Czechoslovakia

BBC – British Broadcasting Corporation

BCRC – British Committee for Refugees from Czechoslovakia

DSAP – German Social Democratic Workers Party

IOU – I Owe You

KLM – Koninklijke Luchtvaart Maatschappij

LSE – London School of Economics

MP – Member of Parliament

RAF – Royal Air Force

SdP – Sudeten German Party

SIS – Secret Intelligence Service

UCL – University College London

UN – United Nations

YWCA – Young Women's Christian Association

Select Bibliography

Archives

British Newspaper Archive

Holocaust Memorial Centre, London

Imperial War Museum Archives, London

Library of the Society of Friends, London

Lowit Family Archive

National Archives, Kew

Nicholas Winton Private Archives

The Papers of Baron Noel-Baker, Cambridge University

The Rowntree Society

United States Holocaust Memorial Museum

Printed Sources

Abel Smith, Edward, *Active Goodness. The True Story of How Trevor Chadwick, Doreen Warriner & Nicolas Winton Rescued Thousands From The Nazis,* Kwill Books, 2017, London

Abel Smith, Edward, *The British Oskar Schindler, The Life and Work of Nicholas Winton,* Pen & Sword History, 2023, London

Alberight, Madeleine, *Prague Winter, A Personal Story of Remembrance and War, 1937-1948,* HarperPerennial, 2013, New York

Bachstein, Martin, *Wenzel Jaksch und die Sudentendeutsche Sozialdemokratie*, R. Oldenbourg, 1974

Bader, Marie, *Life and Love in Nazi Prague: Letters from an Occupied City*, Bloomsbury Academic, 2019, London

Bailey, Brenda, *A Quaker couple in Nazi Germany: Leonhard Friedrich survives Buchenwald,* Sessions, 1994, London

Bailey, Brenda, *The Integrity of German Friends During the Twelve Years of Nazi Rule,* https://quaker.org/legacy/minnfm/peace/integrity_of_german_friends_duri.htm

Balint, Benjamin, *Kafka's Last Trial, The Strange Case of a Literary Legacy,* Picador, 2018, London

Brade, Laura E, Holmes, Rose, *Troublesome Sainthood: Nicholas Winton and the Contested History of Child Rescue in Prague, 1938-1940,* from *History & Memory, Volume 29, Number 1, Spring/Summer 2017, pp.3-40,* Indiana University Press, 2017, Bloomington

Brown, Martin D, *A Munich Winter or a Prague Spring? The evolution of British policy towards the Sudeten Germans from October 1938 to September 1939,* http://www.academia.edu

Bryant, Chad, *Prague in Black: Nazi Rule and Czech Nationalism,* Harvard University Press, 2007, Massachusetts

Cesarani, David & Levine, Paul A., *Bystanders to the Holocaust: A Re-evaluation,* Taylor & Francis, 2014, London

Chadwick, William, *The Rescue of the Prague Refugees,* Troubador Publishing, 2010

Cohan, Susan, *A British Woman's Mission Abroad: Doreen Warriner and the British Committee for Refugees from Czechoslovakia,* University of Southampton, from: https://www.yumpu.com/en/document/read/12047578/pdf-a-british-womans-mission-abroad-united-academics

Cohan, Susan, *Rescue the Perishing. Eleanor Rathbone and the Refugees,* Vallentine Mitchell, 2010

Cohan, Susan, *Voluntary Refugee Work in Britain, 1933–39. An Overview,* https://publishup.uni-potsdam.de/opus4-ubp/frontdoor/deliver/index/docId/5929/file/pardes18_s21_34.pdf

Cornwall, Mark, *The Devil's Wall: The Nationalist Youth Mission of Heinz Rutha,* Harvard University Press, 2012. Cambridge, MA.

Crowhurst, Patrick. *Hitler and Czechoslovakia in World War II: Domination and Retaliation*. I.B. Tauris, 2013. London

Demetz, Peter, *Prague in Danger: The Years of German Occupation, 1939-45: Memories and History, Terror and Resistance, Theater and Jazz, Film and Poetry, Politics and War,* Farrar, Straus and Giroux, 2009, New York

Eisen, Norman, *The Last Palace, Europe's Turbulent Century in Five Lives and One Legendary House,* Crown Publishing Group, 2018, New York

Elelman, Marek, *The Ghetto Fights, Warsaw 1943-45,* Bookmarks, 1990, London

Emanuel, Muriel & Gissing, Vera, *Nicholas Winton and the Rescued Generation*, Vallentine Mitchell, 2002

Faber, David, *Munich, 1938: Appeasement and World War II,* Simon & Schuster, 2008, New York

Fast, Vera K., *Children's Exodus, A History of The Kindertransport,* I.B. Tauuris & Co Ltd, 2011, London

Frommer, Benjamin, *National Cleansing: Retribution against Nazi Collaborators in Postwar Czechoslovakia*. Cambridge University Press, 2005. Cambridge

Garrett, Patrick, *Of Fortunes and War. Clare Hollingworth, first of the female war correspondents,* Thistle Publishing, 2016, London

Gershon, Karen, *We Came As Children. A collective Autobiography of Refugees*, Victor Gollancz Ltd, 1966

Glassheim, Eagle, *Noble Nationalists: The Transformation of the Bohemian Aristocracy*. Harvard University Press, 2005. Cambridge, MA

Goeschel, Christian, *Mussolini and Hitler: The Forging of the Fascist Alliance*, Yale University Press, 2018, New Haven

Harbottle, Michael, *Philip Noel-Baker: A Tribute, International Affairs, Volume 59, Issue 1, Winter 1982, pp. 87–88,* https://doi.org/10.1093/ia/59.1.87

Hastings, Max, *The Secret War. Spies, Codes and Guerrillas 1939-45*, HarperCollins, 2015

Hauner, Milan L., *Edvard Beneš' Undoing of Munich: A Message to a Czech Politician in Prague*, Journal of Contemporary History, Vol. 38, No. 4, Sage Publications, 2003, London

Henig, Ruth, *The Origins of the Second World War 1933-1939*, Taylor & Francis, 2006, London

Hodza, Milan, *Federation in Central Europe. Reflections and Reminiscences*, Jarrold Publishers, 1942, London

Hollingworth, Clare, *Front Line*, Jonathan Cape, 1990, London

Holmes, Rose, *A Moral Business: British Quaker work with Refugees from Fascism, 1933-39*, Thesis submitted for the degree of Doctor of Philosophy, University of Sussex, 2013

Hubback, David, *No Ordinary Press Baron: A Life of Walter Layton*, Weidenfeld & Nicolson, 1985, London

Jaksch, Wenzel, *Farewell to Bohemia*, www.radio.cz, 2011

Jaksch, Wenzel, Kolarz, Walter, *England and The Last Free Germans, The Story of a Rescue*, Lincolns-Prager, 1941, London

Joukowsky, Artemis, *Defying the Nazis, The Sharps' War*, Beacon Press, 2016, Boston

Kennedy, Paul, *A Time to Appease*, The National Interest, No. 108, 2010, London

King, Jeremy. *Budweisers into Czechs and Germans: A Local History of Bohemian Politics, 1848–1948*. Princeton University Press, 2002, Princeton

Kovály, Heda Margolius, *Under a Cruel Star: A Life in Prague 1941–1968*, Holmes & Meier, 1997. New York

Láníček, Jan, *Czechs, Slovaks and the Jews, 1938–48: Beyond Idealisation and Condemnation*, Palgrave Macmillan, 2013, Basingstoke

Layton, Walter, Germany: the Last Four Years; An Independent Examination of the Results of National Socialism, Eyre & Spottiswoode, 1937, London

Lerski, Jerzy Jan, *Historical Dictionary of Poland, 966-1945*, Greenwood Publishing Group, 1996

Leverton, Bertha & Lowensohn, Shmuel, *I Came Alone: The Stories of the Kindertransports*, Book Guild Publishing, 2005, London

Lukes, Igor, *Czechoslovakia Between Stalin and Hitler: The Diplomacy of Edvard Benes in the 1930s*, Oxford University Press, 1996, Oxford

MacDonald, Callum & Kaplan, Jan, *Prague, In the Shadow of the Swastika, A History of the German Occupation 1939-1945*, Quaret Books Ltd, 1995

Martin, Nikolaus, *Prague Winter*, Peter Halban Publishers Ltd, 1990, London

McDonough, Frank, *Neville Chamberlain, Appeasement and the British Road to War*, Manchester University Press, 1998, Manchester

McDonough, Frank, *The Gestapo, The Myth and Reality of Hitler's Secret Police*, Coronet, 2015

Mináč, Matej, *Nicholas Winton's Lottery of Life*, American Friends of the Czech Republic, 2007

Moos, Merilyn, *Breaking the Silence: Voices Of The British Children Of Refugees From Nazism*, Rowman & Littlefield International, London

Neiberg, Michael S., *The World War I Reader*, New York University Press, 2007, New York

Nettlefold, Charles, *The Chamberlain Legacy*, Imprint Academic, London, 2017

Oldfield, Sybil, *"It Is Usually She": The Role of British Women in the Rescue and Care of the Kindertransport Kinder*, Vol. 23, No. 1, Special Issue: Kindertransport 1938/39—Rescue and Integration (Autumn 2004), pp. 57-70

Oldfield, Sybil, *Women Humanitarians. A Biographical Dictionary of British Women Active between 1900 and 1950*, Bloomsbury, 2001, New York

Oppenheimer, Deborah, *Into the Arms of Strangers: Stories of the Kindertransport*, Bloomsbury, 2017, London

Orzoff, Andrea, *Battle for the Castle: The Myth of Czechoslovakia in Europe, 1914–1948*, Oxford University Press, 2009, Oxford

Paldiel, Mordecai, *Saving One's Own: Jewish Rescuers During the Holocaust*, University of Nebraska Nebraska Press, 2017, Lincoln

Pedersen, Susan, *Eleanor Rathbone and the Politics of Conscience*, Yale University Press, 2004, New Haven

Prager, Dennis & Telushkin, Joseph, *Why the Jews? The Reason for Antisemitism*, Touchstone, 2003, London

Pynsent, Robert B. (Ed.), *The Literature of Nationalism: Essays on East European Identity*, Palgrave Macmillan, 1996, London

Raška, Francis D., *The Emigration Of Sudeten German Social Democrats To Canada In 1939*, Acta Universitatis Carolinae, 2003

Reed, Douglas, *Disgrace Abounding*, Jonathan Cape, 1939, London

Robbins, Keith G., *Konrad Henlein, the Sudeten Question and British Foreign Policy*, The Historical Journal Vol. 12, No. 4, 1969, Cambridge

Sayer, Derek, and Agnew, Hugh, *The Coasts of Bohemia: A Czech History*, Princeton University Press, 1998. Princeton

Seymour, Miranda, *Noble Endeavours: The Life of Two Countries, England and Germany, In Many Stories*, Simon & Schuster, 2013, London

Sharp Cogan, Martha, *Church Mouse In The White House*, Journey to Freedom LLC, 2016, New York

Sharp, Waitstill, *The Liberation of The Human Spirit*, Journey to Freedom LLC, 2016, New York

Shepherd, Naomi, *A Refuge from Darkness: Wilfrid Israel and the Rescue of the Jews*, Pantheon Books, 1984, Germany

Shepherd, Naomi, *Wilfrid Israel: German Jewry's Secret Ambassador*, Littlehampton Book Services, 1984, London

Sherman, Ari, *Island Refuge. Britain and Refugees from the Third Reich 1933-1939*, Frank Cass & Co Ltd, 1973, London

Siegel, Jesse E., *A Coercive Courtship: German Awareness of and Responses to the Sudeten Germans, 1929-1934*, Gettysburg College Student Publications, 2016, Pennsylvania

Smetana, Vít, *In the Shadow of Munich. British Policy towards Czechoslovakia from 1938 to 1942*, Karolinum Press, 2008, Prague

Smith, Lyn, *Heroes of The Holocaust. Ordinary Britons Who Risked Their Lives to Make a Difference*, Ebury Press

Sniegon, Tomas, *Vanished History: The Holocaust in Czech and Slovak Historical Culture,* Berghahn Books, 2014, New York

Steiner, Zara, *The Triumph of the Dark, European International History 1933-1939*, OUP Oxford, 2011, Oxford

Stocks, Mary D., *Eleanor Rathbone. A Biography,* Victor Gollancz Ltd, 1949, London

Strange, Joan, *Despatches From the Home Front: The War Diaries of Joan Strange 1939-1945,* PublishNation, 2013

Subak, Susan Elisabeth, *Rescue and Flight: American Relief Workers Who Defied the Nazis*, University of Nebraska Press, 2010, Nebraska

Teich, Mikuláš (Ed.), *Bohemia in History*, Cambridge University Press, 1998, Cambridge

Tombs, Isabelle, *The Victory of Socialist 'Vansittartism': Labour and the German Question, 1941–5*, from 20 Century British History volume 7 (issue 3) 1996

Turner, Barry, *And the Policeman Smiled: 10, 000 Children Escape from Nazi Europe*, Bloomsbury, 1990, London

Velecká, Hana, British aid to refugees from Czechoslovakia from the occupation to the outbreak of war in 1939, Contemporary History 2001 (vol.8) 4: 659-691

Vyšný, Paul, *The Runciman Mission to Czechoslovakia, 1938: Prelude to Munich,* Palgrave Macmillan, Basingstoke, 2003, pp. 128–33.

Warriner, Doreen, *Winter in Prague*, SEER, Vol 62, No 2, 1984

Warriner, Henry, *Doreen Warriner's War,* The Book Guild Ltd, 2019, London

Weisskopf, Kurt, *The Agony of Czechoslovakia '38/'39*, Elek Books Limited, 1958, London

Whittaker, David J., *Fighter for Peace. Philip Noel-Baker, 1889-1982,* W. Sessions, 1989, London

Williams, Bill, *Serious Concern: Manchester Quakers and Refugees, 1938-40*, University Press Scholarship Online, http://www.kindertransport.info/concern.html

Wingfield, Nancy M., *Flag Wars and Stone Saints: How the Bohemian Lands Became Czech,* Harvard University Press, 2007. Cambridge

Winton, Barbara, *If It's Not Impossible ... The Life of Sir Nicholas Winton*, Troubador Publishing Ltd, 2014, London

Winton, Barbara, *One Life*, Robinson, 2024, London

Notes & Sources

Introduction

'**We have got her**': Imperial War Museum Archives, Personal Papers of Robert Stopford, *Prague 1938-1939*, p.68.

PART ONE: LIBERTY

Chapter One – The Czech Affair

'**Hodža at 11**': Warriner, Henry, *Doreen Warriner's War*, The Book Guild Ltd, 2019, London, p.10.

'**In the morning**': Ibid., p.19.

'**Mil to be PM**': Ibid., p.18.

'**received a cordial reception**': *The Scotsman*, 05.11.1935.

These included 'Volks-Sport' which: details about Volks-Sport can be found in Siegel, Jesse E., A Coercive Courtship: German Awareness of and Responses to the Sudeten Germans, 1929-1934, Gettysburg College Student Publications, 2016, Pennsylvania, p.462.

'**had made the destruction**': *Neath Guardian*, 09.09.1938.

'**In the end, we want**': Robbins, Keith G., Konrad Henlein, *The Sudeten Question and British Foreign Policy*, The Historical Journal Vol. 12, No. 4 (Dec., 1969), p.674.

'**We must always demand**': Henig, Ruth, *The Origins of the Second World War 1933-1939*, Taylor & Francis, 2006, London, p.33.

'**a crawling beast**': Warriner, Henry, *Doreen Warriner's War*, The Book Guild Ltd, 2019, London, p.18.

'**had a tendency to**': Imperial War Museum Archives, Personal Papers of Robert Stopford, *letter from Robert Stopford sent 30.08.1938*.

'**Lord R arrived at 5pm**': Ibid.

'**antagonistic**': Ibid.

'**very tired in**': Warriner, Henry, *Doreen Warriner's War*, The Book Guild Ltd, 2019, London, p.22.

'**I would like to ascertain**': Imperial War Museum Archives, Personal Papers of Robert Stopford, *letter from Doreen Warriner to Robert Stopford sent 19.08.1938*.

'I have come to': Runciman, Walter, *Report on the Mission of Lord Runciman to Czechoslovakia,* His Majesty's Stationery Office, London, 21.09.1938.

'God did not create': Adolf Hitler's Speech 12.09.1938, from Bulletin of International News, Vol. 15, No. 19 (Sep. 24, 1938), p.8.

The next day, buoyed: Robbins, Keith G., *Konrad Henlein, The Sudeten Question and British Foreign Policy*, The Historical Journal Vol. 12, No. 4, 1969, p.676.

'remained positive that a': Runciman, Walter, *Report on the Mission of Lord Runciman to Czechoslovakia,* His Majesty's Stationery Office, London, 21.09.1938.

Chamberlain later remarked: Kennedy, Paul, *A Time to Appease*, The National Interest, No. 108, 2010, London, p.7.

'WE ARE NOT AUSTRIA': Weisskopf, Kurt, *The Agony of Czechoslovakia '38/'39*, Elek Books Limited, 1958, London, p.113.

'President Liberator, we shall': Ibid., pp.116-7.

'How horrible, fantastic, incredible': Steiner, Zara, *The Triumph of the Dark, European International History 1933-1939*, OUP Oxford, 2011, Oxford, p.631.

'I have now been informed': Weisskopf, Kurt, *The Agony of Czechoslovakia '38/'39*, Elek Books Limited, 1958, London, p.137.

'peace for our time': McDonough, Frank, *Neville Chamberlain, Appeasement and the British Road to War*, Manchester University Press, 1998, Manchester, p.3.

'You were given the': Prager, Dennis & Telushkin, Joseph, *Why the Jews? The Reason for Antisemitism*, Touchstone, 2003, London, p.8.

'Munich will not save': Hauner, Milan L., *Edvard Beneš Undoing of Munich: A Message to a Czech Politician in Prague*, Journal of Contemporary History, Vol. 38, No. 4, Sage Publications, 2003, London, p. 563.

'The Munich Agreement left us': Warriner, Doreen, *Winter in Prague*, SEER, Vol 62, No 2, 1984, p.212.

'Doreen Warriner took up': Hodza, Milan, *Federation in Central Europe. Reflections and Reminiscences*, Jarrold Publishers, 1942, London, p.167.

'We had driven as far': Lowit Family Archive, *Herbert Lowit personal account*, 2005, p.1

'Through the open window': Ibid.

'With these words the': Ibid.

'SdP banners and quite': Ibid.

'there were about sixty-four': The National Archives, HO 294/56, *Notes From a Report On Conditions In the District of Kaaden, 22.09.1938.*

'The last days of September': Mykura UK Family Archive, *When I Was Living In A Small Czech Village* by Franziska Mykura (1905-1966) https://www.mykura.co.uk/key-documents/when-i-was-living-in-a-small-czech-village.

'So that was goodbye': Ibid.

'unwillingness of the Government': Imperial War Museum Archives, Personal Papers of Robert Stopford, *letter from Robert Stopford sent 12.09.1938.*

'Working in co-operation': *The Scotsman*, 17.10.1938.

'from friends and': Warriner, Doreen, *Winter in Prague*, SEER, Vol 62, No 2, 1984, p.210.

'The Save the Children': *Nottingham Evening Post*, 15.10.1938.

'Cash for Czechs': *Daily Mirror*, 13.10.1938.

'were arrested on': Imperial War Museum Archives, Personal Papers of Robert Stopford, *Prague 1938-1939*, p.9.

'serve as an excuse': Imperial War Museum Archives, Personal Papers of Robert Stopford, *letter from Robert Stopford sent 12.09.1938.*

'the Chancellor of the': Cohan, Susan, *Rescue the Perishing. Eleanor Rathbone and the Refugees*, Vallentine Mitchell, 2010, p.108.

Chapter Two – Society of Friends

'Let us not be persuaded': Jaksch, Wenzel, *Farewell to Bohemia*, published on www.radio.cz, 2011.

'The forms of an honourable': Ibid.

'In London Herr Jaksch': *Belfast Telegraph*, 08.04.1938.

'Why must your government': *North Devon Journal*, 04.09.1938.

'understand that any attempt': *Reynolds's Newspaper*, 10.04.1938.

'This was the beginning': Imperial War Museum Archives, Personal Papers of Robert Stopford, *Prague 1938-1939*, p.10

'the greatest authority': John Bull, 13.08.1927.

'I have seen lots': Imperial War Museum Archives, Personal Papers of Robert Stopford, *Letter from Philip Noel-Baker to Robert Stopford, 14.09.1938.*

'Is disarmament so difficult': Lecture by Philip Noel-Baker, *Peace and the Arms Race*, 11.12.1959
https://www.nobelprize.org/prizes/peace/1959/noel-

baker/lecture/#:~:text=In%20the%20age%20when%20the,of%20the%20future%20of%20mankind.

'I doubt if any other': Harbottle, Michael, *Philip Noel-Baker: A Tribute*, *International Affairs*, Volume 59, Issue 1, Winter 1982, pp. 87–88.

'The fact that U.S.A.': *Dundee Evening Telegraph*, 25.07.1924.

'Have the armed forces': MacDonald, Callum & Kaplan, Jan, *Prague, In the Shadow of the Swastika, A History of the German Occupation 1939-1945*, Quaret Books Ltd, 1995, p.19.

'The Czechs may squeal': Ibid.

'They wanted some help': Imperial War Museum Archives, *Tessa Rowntree Interview with Lyn Smith*, 07.05.1994

'I went out to the countryside': Ibid.

'would have to emigrate': Imperial War Museum Archives, Personal Papers of Robert Stopford, *Prague 1938-1939*, p.12

'Tessa sent for me': Imperial War Museum Archives, *Jean Rowntree Interview with Lyn Smith*, 15.02.1995

'I think I went partly': Ibid.

'I have to tell you': Imperial War Museum Archives, *Tessa Rowntree Interview with Lyn Smith*, 07.05.1994

'We were much closer': Ibid.

'I went to see Mrs Penman': Warriner, Doreen, *Winter in Prague*, SEER, Vol 62, No 2, 1984, p.210.

Chapter Three – Labour of Love

'allegedly acting for': Hastings, Max, *The Secret War. Spies, Codes and Guerrillas 1939-45*, HarperCollins, 2015, p.2.

His hideout was not perfect: Robert Stopford's original notebooks are kept at the Imperial War Museum Archives, Personal Papers of Robert Stopford.

'horribly rude and very': Warriner, Doreen, *Winter in Prague*, SEER, Vol 62, No 2, 1984, p.211.

'a small, slight figure': Hastings, Max, *The Secret War. Spies, Codes and Guerrillas 1939-45*, HarperCollins, 2015, p.40.

'that Mr Gibson was': Warriner, Doreen, *Winter in Prague*, SEER, Vol 62, No 2, 1984, p.211.

'There are too many': Ibid.

'Book them': Ibid.

'We had to wait': Ibid.

'We sat in the sun': Ibid.

'Frozen and tired': Ibid., p.212.

'He pushed me on': Ibid.

'She looks like a': Ibid.

'Accompanied by Miss Tessa Rowntree': Lowit Family Archive, Herbert Lowit personal account, 2005, p.2.

'My British passport was': Imperial War Museum Archives, *Tessa Rowntree Interview with Lyn Smith, 07.05.1994*.

'Name': Ibid.

'Tessa Rowntree': Ibid.

'She was always and': Tessa Rowntree, 1909-1999: *Caring Humanitarian and 'Tough Girl'*, https://www.rowntreesociety.org.uk/tessa-rowntree-1909-1999-caring-humanitarian-and-tough-girl.

'The only time she': Ibid.

'It was touch and': Imperial War Museum Archives, *Tessa Rowntree Interview with Lyn Smith, 07.05.1994*.

'It was a fine effort': Imperial War Museum Archives, Personal Papers of Robert Stopford, *Prague 1938-1939*, p.8.

Chapter Four – Dire Conditions

'The men were running': Warriner, Doreen, *Winter in Prague*, SEER, Vol 62, No 2, 1984, p.213.

'The winter cold had': Ibid., pp.213-214.

'It was in a filthy': Ibid., p.214.

'The walls were covered': Ibid.

'We will make no': Ibid.

'We have lost our': Ibid.

'We will find a way': Ibid.

'I went with him': Imperial War Museum Archives, Personal Papers of Robert Stopford, *Prague 1938-1939*, p.10.

'Mrs Penman, with funds': Warriner, Doreen, *Winter in Prague*, SEER, Vol 62, No 2, 1984, p.214.

'After the Great War': *Alice Masaryková's Charity Heritage Remembered*, https://english.radio.cz/alice-masarykovas-charity-heritage-remembered-8207413.

'The peace of the': Ibid.

'After the war': *Františka Plamínková: the feminist suffragette who* *ensured Czechoslovakia's Constitution of 1920 lived up to the principle of equality,* https://english.radio.cz/Františka-Plamínková-feminist-suffragette-who-ensured-czechoslovakias-8106811.

'As an honest democrat': *Františka Plamínková, Teacher and Feminist,* https://praguepeacetrail.org/Františka-Plamínková-teacher-and-feminist#:~:text=In%201938%20she%20wrote%20an,%2C%20Edvard%20Bene%C5%A1%2C%20had%20lied.

'I've just purchased': *Tessa Rowntree, 1909-1999: Caring Humanitarian and 'Tough Girl',* from The Rowntree Society, 16.11.2023.

'concerned not with individual': Cazalet, Victor, Grenfell, David, Salter, Arthur & Rathbone, Eleanor, *The Birmingham Daily Post,* 04.01.1939.

'MP for refugees': Cohan, Susan, *Rescue the Perishing. Eleanor Rathbone and the Refugees,* Vallentine Mitchell, 2010, p.104.

'He detested her': Pedersen, Susan, *Eleanor Rathbone, Brief life of a Crusading M.P. 1872-1946,* https://www.harvardmagazine.com/2003/03/eleanor-rathbone-html.

'He and his colleagues': Cohan, Susan, *Rescue the Perishing. Eleanor Rathbone and the Refugees,* Vallentine Mitchell, 2010, p.102.

'Neither he nor anybody': Stocks, Mary D., *Eleanor Rathbone. A Biography,* Victor Gollancz Ltd, 1949, London, p. 250.

'Which would you rather': Imperial War Museum Archives, Personal Papers of Robert Stopford, *Prague 1938-1939,* p.16.

'She never dressed': Winton, Barbara, *If It's Not Impossible...The Life of Sir Nicholas Winton,* Troubador Publishing Ltd, 2014, p.23.

The response was incredibly: funds received by the News Chronicle appeal were reported in the News Chronicle, 31.10.1938.

'the meagreness of British': Stocks, Mary D., *Eleanor Rathbone. A Biography,* Victor Gollancz Ltd, 1949, London, p.250.

'use the funds collected': Brown, Martin D, *A Munich Winter or a Prague Spring? The evolution of British policy towards the Sudeten Germans from October 1938 to September 1939,* http://www.academia.edu.

'acquired a detailed': Hubback, David, *No Ordinary Press Baron: A Life of Walter Layton,* Weidenfeld & Nicolson, 1985, London, p.156.

'her return coincided': Edinburgh Evening News, 20.12.1939.

'long silences in conversation': Hubback, David, *No Ordinary Press Baron: A Life of Walter Layton,* Weidenfeld & Nicolson, 1985, London, p.150.

'standing round the fire': Ibid., p.32

'You do not need': Ibid., p.61.

'You will always': Ibid.

'Margaret was beginning': Ibid., p.150.

'there were many young': Ibid.

'Sir Walter Layton came': Warriner, Doreen, *Winter in Prague*, SEER, Vol 62, No 2, 1984, p.216.

'Sir Walter asked me': Ibid.

'Bertha, who worked hard': Woodford, Jane, *Bertha Bracey – Helping Children to a Safe Home*, Journeys in the Spirit, Quaker Life, 2011 p.57.

'He did me the honour': Warriner, Doreen, *Winter in Prague*, SEER, Vol 62, No 2, 1984, p.216.

'*Dear Miss Rathborne*': Cohan, Susan, *Rescue the Perishing. Eleanor Rathbone and the Refugees*, Vallentine Mitchell, 2010, p.109.

Chapter Five – Too Steady

'The train should leave': Essberger, Richard, *All Shall Be Well*, Radius Publishing Ltd, York, 2023, p.99.

'I believe two carriages': Lowit Family Archive, *Herbert Lowit personal account*, 2005, p.3.

'By God, it was bitter': Essberger, Richard, *All Shall Be Well*, Radius Publishing Ltd, York, 2023, p.103.

'As the train steamed': Lowit Family Archive, *Herbert Lowit personal account*, 2005, p.3.

'Behave calmly and quietly': Essberger, Richard, *All Shall Be Well*, Radius Publishing Ltd, York, 2023, p.100.

'Ignore them! We are': Ibid.

'We were safe': Ibid.

'Soon we'll arrive in': Ibid., p.101.

'Let's keep ourselves to': Ibid.

'You are now in': Ibid.

'They are friends of': Ibid., p.102.

'Gentlemen, ladies, do not': Ibid., p.103.

'I've already made this': Ibid.

'You are all asking': Ibid., p.107.

'I have some answers': Ibid.

'You will travel on': Ibid., p.108.

'Then by train to Denmark's': Ibid.

'We were waving': Lowit Family Archive, Lowit, Karl, *An English Journal*, 17.02.1940, p.5.

'Imagine it, being addressed': Essberger, Richard, *All Shall Be Well*, Radius Publishing Ltd, York, 2023, p.108.

'You ask what Prague': Ibid., p.89.

'*Sir – I want to call the*': *Daily Telegraph* – 14.12.1938.

LETTER IN DAILY TELEGRAPH: The National Archives, HO 294/53, *Telegram from Ewart Culpin to Doreen Warriner*, 14.12.1938.

'Your letter did put': The National Archives, HO 294/53, *Letter from Margaret Layton to Doreen Warriner*, 17.12.1938.

'Evening ticked off by': Warriner, Henry, *Doreen Warriner's War*, The Book Guild Ltd, 2019, London, p.40.

'Winton is doing splendid': The National Archives, HO 294/53, *Letter from Doreen Warriner to Margaret Layton*, 12.01.1939.

'a prominent position among': Shepherd, Naomi, *Wilfrid Israel, German Jewry's Secret Ambassador*, Littlehampton Book Services, 1984, London, p.1.

'facilitated entry for all children': Oldfield, Sybil, *It Is Usually She: The Role of British Women in the Rescue and Care of the Kindertransport Kinder*, Vol. 23, No. 1, Special Issue: Kindertransport 1938/39—Rescue and Integration, 2004, p.60.

'consider very substantially increasing': Cohan, Susan, *Rescue the Perishing. Eleanor Rathbone and the Refugees*, Vallentine Mitchell, 2010, p.111.

'I believe that we': *House of Commons Debate*, 21.11.1938, Hansard vol. 341 cc1428-814286.

'agreed to take over German': The National Archives, HO 294/53, *Letter from Margaret Layton to Doreen Warriner*, 17.12.1938.

'The refugees ceased to be': Warriner, Doreen, *Winter in Prague*, SEER, Vol 62, No 2, 1984, p.219.

'to cover the cost': Ibid.

'We would have a': Warriner, Henry, *Doreen Warriner's War*, The Book Guild Ltd, 2019, London, p.71.

'with that splendid energy': Warriner, Doreen, *Winter in Prague*, SEER, Vol 62, No 2, 1984, p.220.

'Miss Warriner is extremely': Stocks, Mary D., *Eleanor Rathbone. A Biography*, Victor Gollancz Ltd, 1949, London, p.261.

'She is though very overtired': Ibid.

'Unlike so many who came': Warriner, Doreen, Winter in Prague, SEER, Vol 62, No 2, 1984, p.220.

He was given specific: details of Eleanor Rathbone's visit to Bucharest taken from Cohan, Susan, *Rescue the Perishing, Eleanor Rathbone and the Refugees*, Vallentine Mitchell, 2010, p.116.

'It is a living grave': Cohan, Susan, *Rescue the Perishing, Eleanor Rathbone and the Refugees*, Vallentine Mitchell, 2010, p.115.

Remember what we owe: Ibid., p.113.

'A large move-out': Warriner, Doreen, *Winter in Prague*, SEER, Vol 62, No 2, 1984, p.221.

'In Prague we lived': Ibid., p.222.

'But London were detached': Ibid.

'a general sense of greater': Stocks, Mary D., Eleanor Rathbone. *A Biography*, Victor Gollancz Ltd, 1949, London, p.255.

'In spite of Miss Warriner's': Imperial War Museum Archives, Personal Papers of Robert Stopford, *Prague 1938-1939*, p.26.

'I decided that I': Warriner, Doreen, *Winter in Prague*, SEER, Vol 62, No 2, 1984, p.222.

RETURNING SUNDAY STOP: The National Archives, HO 294/53, *Telegram from Doreen Warriner to Margaret Layton*, 27.01.1939.

'how little of the true': Warriner, Doreen, *Winter in Prague*, SEER, Vol 62, No 2, 1984, p.222.

'No one I saw': Cohan, Susan, Rescue the Perishing. Eleanor Rathbone and the Refugees, Vallentine Mitchell, 2010, p.119.

'She argued valiantly to': Imperial War Museum Archives, Personal Papers of Robert Stopford, *Prague 1938-1939*, p.8

'Now let's start': Warriner, Doreen, *Winter in Prague*, SEER, Vol 62, No 2, 1984, p.222.

'February was wonderful': Ibid.

'Doreen Warriner has laboured': Imperial War Museum Archives, Personal Papers of Robert Stopford, *Prague 1938-1939*, p.8.

Chapter Six – American Contingent

'The foreign situation is less': McDonough, Frank, *Neville Chamberlain, Appeasement and the British Road to War*, Manchester University Press, 1998, Manchester, p.78.

'The air was full of': Joukowsky, Artemis, *Defying the Nazis, The Sharps' War*, Beacon Press, 2016, Boston, p16.

'The situation in Czechoslovakia': Ibid., p5.

'A quarter-million refugees': Ibid.

'We had deliberated at length': Ibid., p7.

'Do I understand from you': Ibid.

'Yes': Ibid.

'Why did they turn': Ibid.

'They didn't want to': Ibid.

'Refugees in the Sudetenland': Ibid., p5.

'I was torn between': Ibid., p8.

'A lot of people thought': Ibid., p9.

'Brother Sharp, Mrs': Ibid., p17.

'You've come to': Ibid.

'Thank you,' replied: Ibid.

'They were Social Democrats': Ibid.

'Where are they going?': Ibid.

'London, if they can': Ibid.

'woefully inadequate single': Sharp Cogan, Martha, *Church Mouse In The White House*, Journey to Freedom LLC, 2016, New York, Chapter 4.

'The situation is worsening': Imperial War Museum Archives, Personal Papers of Robert Stopford, *Prague 1938-1939*, p.25.

'We were surprised by': Sharp Cogan, Martha, *Church Mouse In The White House*, Journey to Freedom LLC, 2016, New York, Chapter 4.

'The surroundings intensified': Ibid.

'I tried [to] picture': Ibid.

'Tired? Homesick?': Joukowsky, Artemis, *Defying the Nazis, The Sharps' War*, Beacon Press, 2016, Boston, p18.

'I miss the children': Sharp Cogan, Martha, *Church Mouse In The White House*, Journey to Freedom LLC, 2016, New York, Chapter 4.

'That's natural': Ibid.

'What was the makeup': Imperial War Museum Archives, Personal Papers of Robert Stopford, *Prague 1938-1939*, p.9.

'Most of the German': Ibid.

'Who was the most': Ibid.

'The Jews in Czechoslovakia': Ibid.

'How many Jews are': Ibid.

'The census figure for': Ibid.

'hoped to be able': Sharp Cogan, Martha, *Church Mouse In The White House*, Journey to Freedom LLC, 2016, New York, Chapter 4.

'This was the end': Sharp, Waitstill, *The Liberation of The Human Spirit*, Journey to Freedom LLC, 2016, New York, Chapter 2.

'People would have to': Sharp Cogan, Martha, *Church Mouse In The White House*, Journey to Freedom LLC, 2016, New York, Chapter 4.

'She was a self-effacing': Joukowsky, Artemis, *Defying the Nazis, The Sharps' War*, Beacon Press, 2016, Boston, p.23.

'Do you know how': Ibid., p.14.

'No': Ibid.

'Would you like a': Ibid.

The situation is serious: Ibid., p.28.

'I'm in a strange hotel': Imperial War Museum Archives, *Tessa Rowntree Interview with Lyn Smith, 07.05.1994*.

'My impression of Bratislava': The National Archives, HO 294/53, *Tessa Rowntree Personal Account*, undated.

'The few happy folk': Ibid.

Chapter Seven – Invasion

'Situation very uncertain': Warriner, Doreen, *Winter in Prague*, SEER, Vol 62, No 2, 1984, p.224.

'tense and sultry, like': Imperial War Museum Archives, Personal Papers of Robert Stopford, *Prague 1938-1939*, p.26.

'It may be impossible': Warriner, Doreen, *Winter in Prague*, SEER, Vol 62, No 2, 1984, p.225.

'Put all the women': Ibid.

'No, tomorrow!': Ibid.

'The strain of waiting': Ibid.

'The children were all': Gershon, Karen, *We Came As Children. A collective Autobiography of Refugees*, Victor Gollancz Ltd, 1966, p.22.

'Chadwick secretly pointed out': Sharp Cogan, Martha, *Church Mouse In The White House*, Journey to Freedom LLC, 2016, New York, Chapter 8.

'All day the phones rang': Warriner, Doreen, *Winter in Prague*, SEER, Vol 62, No 2, 1984, p.225.

'We are going to be united': Gershon, Karen, *We Came As Children. A collective Autobiography of Refugees*, Victor Gollancz Ltd, 1966, p.29.

'Prague's Orchestra's rendition': MacDonald, Callum & Kaplan, Jan, *Prague, In the Shadow of the Swastika, A History of the German Occupation 1939-1945*, Quaret Books Ltd, 1995, p.41.

'The Passport Control Officer': Warriner, Doreen, *Winter in Prague*, SEER, Vol 62, No 2, 1984, p.225.

'He has put his seal': Ibid.

'My office [had] been': Jaksch, Wenzel, *Farewell to Bohemia*, www.radio.cz, 2011.

'and seized all the': Warriner, Doreen, *Winter in Prague*, SEER, Vol 62, No 2, 1984, p.226.

'Return the passports!': Ibid.

'About two hundred had': Ibid.

'The odds are that': Ibid.

'It seems better to send': Ibid.

'A peaceful occupation would': MacDonald, Callum & Kaplan, Jan, *Prague, In the Shadow of the Swastika, A History of the German Occupation 1939-1945*, Quaret Books Ltd, 1995, p.19.

The conviction was unanimously: Ibid., p.20.

'Guns were mounted in': Warriner, Doreen, *Winter in Prague*, SEER, Vol 62, No 2, 1984, p.226.

'The soldier looked like': Balint, Benjamin, *Kafka's Last Trial, The Strange Case of a Literary Legacy*, Picador, 2018, London, p.142.

'Truth be told, he was': Ibid.

'You'll never guess': Warriner, Doreen, *Winter in Prague*, SEER, Vol 62, No 2, 1984, p.226.

'How well he carried': Imperial War Museum Archives, Personal Papers of Robert Stopford, *Prague 1938-1939*, p.27.

German Army infantry and: MacDonald, Callum & Kaplan, Jan, *Prague, In the Shadow of the Swastika, A History of the German Occupation 1939-1945*, Quaret Books Ltd, 1995, p.19.

'All well': Warriner, Doreen, *Winter in Prague*, SEER, Vol 62, No 2, 1984, p.226.

'As a result of a': Hollingworth, Clare, *Front Line*, Jonathan Cape, 1990, London, p.8.

'I gather I am about': Ibid.

'The refugees had to': Garrett, Patrick, *Of Fortunes and War. Clare Hollingworth, First of the Female War Correspondents*, Thistle Publishing, 2016, London, p.38.

'I was given a list': Hollingworth, Clare, *Front Line*, Jonathan Cape, 1990, London, p.8.

PART TWO: OCCUPATION
Chapter Eight – Panic Stations

'What does a person': Sharp Cogan, Martha, *Church Mouse In The White House*, Journey to Freedom LLC, 2016, New York, Chapter 9.

'First, he cannot believe': Ibid.

'There is a heaviness': Joukowsky, Artemis, *Defying the Nazis, The Sharps' War*, Beacon Press, 2016, Boston, p.36.

'Are you afraid?': Ibid.

'I'd like to stay if': Ibid.

'Good, I want to': Ibid.

'What office do you': Ibid., p.41

'American Relief for': Ibid.

'You must wait your': Ibid.

'But that is our': Ibid.

'Who are you?': Ibid.

'Sharp!': Ibid.

'Please': Sharp Cogan, Martha, *Church Mouse In The White House*, Journey to Freedom LLC, 2016, New York, Chapter 9.

'this is American territory': Ibid.

'saw the beginning of': Imperial War Museum Archives, Personal Papers of Robert Stopford, *Prague 1938-1939*, p.26.

'Quiet!': Sharp Cogan, Martha, *Church Mouse In The White House*, Journey to Freedom LLC, 2016, New York, Chapter 9.

'The American Relief for': Ibid.

'I came for help, so': Ibid.

'Here are my wife': Ibid.

'Come alone with me': Ibid.

'If you force me': Ibid.

'Cigarette?': Ibid.

'They had vowed to': Ibid.

'This emergency demands': Ibid.

'All these people want': Ibid.

'We've got to do': Ibid.

'Might this be the': Ibid.

'My God, I hope': Ibid.

'all desperate': Warriner, Doreen, *Winter in Prague*, SEER, Vol 62, No 2, 1984, p.226.

'You must get away!': Ibid., p.227.

As the driver asked: Recollections from the first day of the Nazi occupation of Czechoslovakia were reported in MacDonald, Callum & Kaplan, Jan, *Prague, In the Shadow of the Swastika, A History of the German Occupation 1939-1945*, Quaret Books Ltd, 1995, p.23.

***Call to the people!*:** Ibid.

'the Government are acting': Stocks, Mary D., Eleanor Rathbone. *A Biography*, Victor Gollancz Ltd, 1949, London, p.259.

'Why not come home?': Warriner, Doreen, *Winter in Prague*, SEER, Vol 62, No 2, 1984, p.227.

'There is still too': Ibid.

'We spent about a day': Imperial War Museum Archives, *Tessa Rowntree Interview with Lyn Smith*, 07.05.1994.

'As if drawn by': Sharp Cogan, Martha, *Church Mouse In The White House*, Journey to Freedom LLC, 2016, New York, Chapter 9.

'I realised for the first': Ibid.

'I flattened myself': Ibid.

'I am here to pick': Ibid.

'A moment': Ibid.

'Mr X could be': Ibid.

Martha barely had: The identity of Wenzel Jaksch as 'Mr X' was revealed in his book Jaksch, Wenzel, Kolarz, Walter, *England and The Last Free Germans, The Story of a Rescue*, Lincolns-Prager, 1941, London.

'I am Mr X': Sharp Cogan, Martha, *Church Mouse In The White House*, Journey to Freedom LLC, 2016, New York, Chapter 9.

'We'd better walk': Ibid.

'Americans ... on our': Ibid.

'Identity cards': Ibid.

'I don't speak': Ibid.

'Go!': Ibid.

'Are we to fail': Ibid.

'We would never': Ibid.

'Will you please tell': Ibid.

'Oh, I am not the': Ibid.

'We have been chilled': Ibid.

'There was no time': Imperial War Museum Archives, *Tessa Rowntree Interview with Lyn Smith*, 07.05.1994.

'We have barely enough': Sharp Cogan, Martha, *Church Mouse In The White House*, Journey to Freedom LLC, 2016, New York, Chapter 9.

Chapter Nine – Trapped

At their request I: The National Archives, FO371/22897. *Foreign Office to Basil Newton* 15 March 1939.

'We must go back': Warriner, Doreen, *Winter in Prague*, SEER, Vol 62, No 2, 1984, p.227.

'Even if we got to': Ibid.

'I know exactly how': Ibid.

'Patz cannot stay': Ibid., p.228.

Persons mentioned may: The National Archives, FO371/22897. *Foreign Office to Basil Newton* 15 March 1939.

'But she has stayed': Warriner, Doreen, *Winter in Prague*, SEER, Vol 62, No 2, 1984, p.228.

'We must go at': Ibid.

'I panted up the': Ibid.

'You wouldn't mind': Imperial War Museum Archives, *Tessa Rowntree Interview with Lyn Smith*, 07.05.1994.

'Of course!': Ibid.

'We walked up': Warriner, Doreen, *Winter in Prague*, SEER, Vol 62, No 2, 1984, p.228.

'It was getting': Ibid.

'Achtung, Achtung, anyone': Sharp Cogan, Martha, *Church Mouse In The White House*, Journey to Freedom LLC, 2016, New York, Chapter 9.

'We wish to be': Ibid.

'The food somehow': Ibid.

'I now proclaim this state': History Place (n.d.) The Triumph of Adolf Hitler: Czechoslovakia Ceases to Exist. Available at: https://www.historyplace.com/worldwar2/triumph/tr-czech.htm.

'He was so old he': Sharp Cogan, Martha, *Church Mouse In The White House*, Journey to Freedom LLC, 2016, New York, Chapter 9.

'how unbearable life': Garrett, Patrick, *Of Fortunes and War. Clare Hollingworth, First of the Female War Correspondents*, Thistle Publishing, 2016, London, p.20.

'I don't know how': Imperial War Museum Archives, *Jean Rowntree Interview with Lyn Smith*, 15.02.1995.

MARGARET DOUGAN AND: The National Archives, HO 294/53, *Telegram from Margaret Layton to Doreen Warriner*, 14.03.1939.

'Come, we get need': Joukowsky, Artemis, *Defying the Nazis, The Sharps' War*, Beacon Press, 2016, Boston, p.59.

'I am so happy to be': Ibid.

Chapter Ten – Defiance

'the deafening buzz': Sharp Cogan, Martha, *Church Mouse In The White House*, Journey to Freedom LLC, 2016, New York, Chapter 9.

'I have also heard': Joukowsky, Artemis, *Defying the Nazis, The Sharps' War*, Beacon Press, 2016, Boston, p.57.

'Wishful thought': Ibid.

By the end of the: Mary Penman's radio technique is explained in Robert Stopfords records, Imperial War Museum Archives, Personal Papers of Robert Stopford, *Prague 1938-1939*, p.42.

'So far she has': Sharp Cogan, Martha, Church Mouse In The White House, Journey to Freedom LLC, 2016, New York, Chapter 12.

'There is a machine': Joukowsky, Artemis, *Defying the Nazis, The Sharps' War*, Beacon Press, 2016, Boston, p.57.

'You are a brave': Imperial War Museum Archives, *Tessa Rowntree Interview with Lyn Smith*, 07.05.1994.

Dear Miss Allen: The National Archives, HO 294/56, *Letter from Clare Hollingworth to Acland Allen*, 14.07.1939.

'It was pointed': Imperial War Museum Archives, Personal Papers of Robert Stopford, *Prague 1938-1939*, p.42.

'one of the worst': MacDonald, Callum & Kaplan, Jan, *Prague, In the Shadow of the Swastika, A History of the German Occupation 1939-1945*, Quaret Books Ltd, 1995, p.31.

'grumblers, carpers and fault-finders': Ibid., p.95.

'I found myself so': Joukowsky, Artemis, *Defying the Nazis, The Sharps' War*, Beacon Press, 2016, Boston, p.57.

'I am encouraged to': MacDonald, Callum & Kaplan, Jan, *Prague, In the Shadow of the Swastika, A History of the German Occupation 1939-1945*, Quaret Books Ltd, 1995, p.37.

'Nobody can do': Sharp Cogan, Martha, *Church Mouse In The White House*, Journey to Freedom LLC, 2016, New York, Chapter 10.

'Saving endangered people': Ibid.

'Why do you want': Ibid.

'We only want to': Ibid.

'I am afraid that': Ibid.

'I am afraid that': Ibid.

'My mother needs': Ibid.

'by someone in the': Imperial War Museum Archives, *Tessa Rowntree Interview with Lyn Smith*, 07.05.1994.

'Some of your group': Sharp Cogan, Martha, *Church Mouse In The White House*, Journey to Freedom LLC, 2016, New York, Chapter 10.

'They're yours!': Ibid.

'Their parents were a': Ibid.

'Where are you': Ibid.

'To London': Ibid.

'Don't forget us poor': Ibid.

'Lovely valleys, streams': Lowit Family Archive, *Lowit, Karl, An English Journal*, 17.02.1940, p.4

'Mrs Sharp! Mrs': Sharp Cogan, Martha, *Church Mouse In The White House*, Journey to Freedom LLC, 2016, New York, Chapter 10.

'What is the meaning': Ibid.

'No but we must': Ibid.

'Does anybody here': Ibid.

'Very well, I shall': Ibid.

'I will call my': Ibid.

'Yes, you may have': Ibid.

'They may go': Ibid.

'Mrs Sharp! Mrs': Ibid.

'What is it now?': Ibid.

'They say our names': Ibid.

'These two men are': Ibid.

'I am sure the names': Ibid.

'Thank you': Ibid.

'Is Mrs Sharp here?': Ibid.

'Here I am': Ibid.

'Come into my': Ibid.

'Now, I'll go': Ibid.

'We haven't any': Ibid.

'But your people': Ibid.

'And this will be': Ibid.

'Nearly all of us': The National Archives, HO 294/56, *unknown refugee account*

'It was probably not': Subak, Susan Elisabeth, *Rescue and Flight: American Relief Workers Who Defied the Nazis*, University of Nebraska Press, 2010, Lincoln, p.xxvii.

'Thank you': Sharp Cogan, Martha, *Church Mouse In The White House*, Journey to Freedom LLC, 2016, New York, Chapter 10

'My dear, your face': Ibid.

Dear Mrs Sharp: Joukowsky, Artemis, *Defying the Nazis, The Sharps' War*, Beacon Press, 2016, Boston, p.57.

'We admired all the': The National Archives, HO 294/56, *unknown refugee account*

'In some respects': Stocks, Mary D., Eleanor Rathbone. A Biography, Victor Gollancz Ltd, 1949, London, p.263.

Chapter Eleven – The Great Escape

'get him dead or': Daily Herald, 16.03.1939.

'Hitler had been my': Jaksch, Wenzel, Kolarz, Walter, *England and The Last Free Germans, The Story of a Rescue*, Lincolns-Prager, 1941, London, p.54.

'because he knew': Jaksch, Wenzel, *Farewell to Bohemia*, www.radio.cz, 2011.

'the uninvited guest': Ibid.

'You must give me': Warriner, Henry, *Doreen Warriner's War*, The Book Guild Ltd, 2019, London, p.69.

'he looked like a': Warriner, Doreen, *Winter in Prague*, SEER, Vol 62, No 2, 1984, p.232.

'throwing up his': Ibid.

'It was chaos': Lowit Family Archive, How My Aunt Escaped Nazi-Occupied Prague, 2005.

'for a consideration been': Jaksch, Wenzel, *Farewell to Bohemia*, www.radio.cz, 2011.

'steered straight to': Ibid.

'from our backpacks': Ibid.

'they took me for': Ibid.

'to laugh, which': Ibid.

'I felt particularly': Imperial War Museum Archives, Personal Papers of Robert Stopford, *Prague 1938-1939*, p.34.

'I will shoot myself': Ibid.

'My main preoccupation': Ibid., p.32.

'No one will be': Imperial War Museum Archives, Personal Papers of Robert Stopford, *Prague 1938-1939*, p.32.

'His only Nazi-ish remark': Gershon, Karen, We Came As Children. A collective Autobiography of Refugees, Victor Gollancz Ltd, 1966, p.22.

'Finally, Herr Jaksch': Imperial War Museum Archives, Personal Papers of Robert Stopford, *Prague 1938-1939*, p.32.

'not practiced winter': Jaksch, Wenzel, *Farewell to Bohemia*, www.radio.cz, 2011.

'the colourful composition': Ibid.

'the tiredness [of] the': Ibid.

'Sacher's pleading voice': Ibid.

'For eight hours we': Warriner, Henry, *Doreen Warriner's War*, The Book Guild Ltd, 2019, London, p.216.

'here is Poland': Jaksch, Wenzel, Kolarz, Walter, *England and The Last Free Germans, The Story of a Rescue*, Lincolns-Prager, 1941, London, p.55.

'We then came down': Warriner, Henry, *Doreen Warriner's War*, The Book Guild Ltd, 2019, London, p.216.

'We should either have': Ibid.

'Monday in Bohumín': Warriner, Doreen, *Winter in Prague*, SEER, Vol 62, No 2, 1984, p.231.

'I motored to Ostrava': The National Archives, HO 294/56, *Letter from Clare Hollingworth to Margaret Layton*, 24.03.1939.

'As I walked out of the station': Warriner, Doreen, *Winter in Prague*, SEER, Vol 62, No 2, 1984, p.231.

Dear Miss Layton: The National Archives, HO 294/56, *Letter from Clare Hollingworth to Margaret Layton*, 27.03.1939.

'Apart from Mr Jaksch': Imperial War Museum Archives, Personal Papers of Robert Stopford, *Letter 13.04.1939*.

'Mr Jaksch has disappeared': Ibid.

'Disappeared? How?': Ibid.

'Just disappeared': Ibid.
'This alters the whole': Ibid.
'The Legation is not': Ibid.
'The Gestapo will': Ibid.

Chapter Twelve – Enter the Gestapo

'the right to name': Sharp Cogan, Martha, Church Mouse In The White House, Journey to Freedom LLC, 2016, New York, Chapter 10.

'What It Would': Ibid.

The next thing she knew: Martha's ordeal on the Orient Express were written in her memoir Church Mouse In The White House and further details provided in interviews with Artemis Joukowsky and written in *Defying the Nazis, The Sharps' War*.

'I'm just tired': Sharp Cogan, Martha, Church Mouse In The White House, Journey to Freedom LLC, 2016, New York, Chapter 10.

'For a short time': Imperial War Museum Archives, Personal Papers of Robert Stopford, *Prague 1938-1939*, p.35.

'From their black uniforms': Martin, Nikolaus, *Prague Winter*, Peter Halban Publishers Ltd, 1990, London, p.28.

'One saw them lurking': Imperial War Museum Archives, Personal Papers of Robert Stopford, *Prague 1938-1939*, p.42.

'elderly, smiling gentleman': Gershon, Karen, *We Came as Children. A collective Autobiography of Refugees*, Victor Gollancz Ltd, 1966, p.24.

Emmi had a reputation: Warriner, Doreen, *Winter in Prague*, SEER, Vol 62, No 2, 1984, p.232.

'We sat in the lounge': Ibid.

'It is high time': Ibid.

'When?': Ibid.

Doreen replied excitedly: Ibid.

'Who are you?': Ibid., p.233.

'Secret State Police': Ibid.

'This woman has': Ibid.

'And she has an': Ibid.

'Why can't she': Ibid.

'The Gestapo gives': Ibid.

'the lying and traitorous': Ibid.

'Communist muck': Ibid.

***A Viennese film producer*:** Martin, Nikolaus, *Prague Winter*, Peter Halban Publishers Ltd, 1990, London, p.xiv.

'Her determined cheerfulness': Warriner, Doreen, *Winter in Prague*, SEER, Vol 62, No 2, 1984, p.233.

'The Gestapo': Ibid.

'It was obviously too': Ibid.

'Best wishes, Ilse': Ibid., p.232

'In appearance we were': Ibid., p.237.

'Any movement or attempt': MacDonald, Callum & Kaplan, Jan, *Prague, In the Shadow of the Swastika, A History of the German Occupation 1939-1945*, Quaret Books Ltd, 1995, p.101.

'Where is the British': Warriner, Doreen, *Winter in Prague*, SEER, Vol 62, No 2, 1984, p.237.

'Look in the telephone': Ibid.

'Everything that you do': Ibid.

'Every day I wondered': Sharp Cogan, Martha, *Church Mouse In The White House*, Journey to Freedom LLC, 2016, New York, Chapter 12.

'She was not released': Imperial War Museum Archives, Personal Papers of Robert Stopford, *Prague 1938-1939*, p.39.

'I will take you': Ibid.

'I am exhausted': Ibid.

'They have probably caught': Ibid.

***ARRANGEMENTS IN GDYNIA*:** National Archives, HO 294/58, *Telegram from Doreen Warriner to Margaret Layton*, 04.04.1939.

'Come at once': Sharp Cogan, Martha, *Church Mouse In The White House*, Journey to Freedom LLC, 2016, New York, Chapter 12.

'The reason I asked you': Ibid.

'put one or two': Imperial War Museum Archives, Personal Papers of Robert Stopford, *Prague 1938-1939*, p.35.

'Our old Atlantic has': Sharp Cogan, Martha, *Church Mouse In The White House*, Journey to Freedom LLC, 2016, New York, Chapter 11.

'Densely over-crowded': Oldfield, Sybil, *It Is Usually She: The Role of British Women in the Rescue and Care of the Kindertransport Kinder*, Vol. 23, No. 1, Special Issue: Kindertransport 1938/39—Rescue and Integration, 2004, p.59.

'I am afraid that such': Nettlefold, Charles, *The Chamberlain Legacy*, Imprint Academic, London, 2017, p. 81.

Chapter Thirteen – Doreen's Farewell to Prague

'It sent shivers down': Imperial War Museum Archives, Personal Papers of Robert Stopford, *Prague 1938-1939*, p.38

'What is his room': Ibid.

'I do not know': Ibid.

'If you do not know': Ibid.

'I have an appointment': Ibid.

'Robert Stopford': Ibid.

'You are Herr Stopford': Ibid.

'Yes': Ibid.

'I apologise. I had': Ibid.

'They can leave by': Ibid.

'I want to tell them': Ibid.

'I will give them': Ibid.

'I will put it to': Warriner, Doreen, *Winter in Prague*, SEER, Vol 62, No 2, 1984, p.239.

'I quickly learnt the': Imperial War Museum Archives, Personal Papers of Robert Stopford, *Prague 1938-1939*, p.37

'It would be': Warriner, Doreen, *Winter in Prague*, SEER, Vol 62, No 2, 1984, p.239.

'The Kriminalrat was': Imperial War Museum Archives, Personal Papers of Robert Stopford, *Prague 1938-1939*, p.64

When no one answered: details about Marie Greiss's suicide are taken from Doreen Warriner's memoir *Winter in Prague* and Robert Stopford's personal papers

'It was misery to': Warriner, Doreen, *Winter in Prague*, SEER, Vol 62, No 2, 1984, p.239.

But in a black saloon: details of the events surrounding the Jewish tailor were recorded in Robert Stopford's personal papers, specifically *Prague 1938-1939*, Martha Sharp's memoir *Church Mouse In The White House*, Tessa Rowntree's interview with Lyn Smith and Cesarani, David & Levine, Paul A., *Bystanders to the Holocaust: A Re-evaluation*, Taylor & Francis, 2014, London

'I had got to': Warriner, Doreen, *Winter in Prague*, SEER, Vol 62, No 2, 1984, p.239.

'You are traitors to': Ibid., p.240.

'Mr Stopford is on': Ibid.

Chapter Fourteen – Keeping Going

'during all this [shouting]': Imperial War Museum Archives, Personal Papers of Robert Stopford, *Prague 1938-1939*, p.38.

'We work with Beatrice': United States Holocaust Memorial Museum, Martha and Waitstill Sharp Collection, RG-67.017, *Waitstill Sharp to Robert Dexter*, 20.05.1939.

'I doubt the motives': Imperial War Museum Archives, Personal Papers of Robert Stopford, *Beatrice Wellington Report*, p.4.

'Whatever might have been': Ibid.

'The obstacles created': Stocks, Mary D., Eleanor Rathbone. *A Biography*, Victor Gollancz Ltd, 1949, London, p.123.

'Absolutely no word of': Joukowsky, Artemis, *Defying the Nazis, The Sharps' War*, Beacon Press, 2016, Boston, p.86.

'We must prevent her': Ibid., p.90.

'Don't you remember': Ibid., p.91.

'Why are you': Ibid.

'Just to collect an': Ibid.

'What is her': Ibid.

'Františka Plamínková': Ibid.

'That's a funny': Ibid.

'Shall I stay in comfort': Ibid.

'What happened to': Ibid.

'We blew them': Ibid.

'There are some hundreds': The National Archives, HO 294/56, *Letter from Clare Hollingworth to Margaret Layton*, 26.07.1939.

'His evil face and': Sharp Cogan, Martha, Church Mouse In The White House, Journey to Freedom LLC, 2016, New York, Chapter 13.

'Oh, excuse me': Ibid.

'I have heard that': Ibid.

'Who is this?': Ibid.

'If you leave tomorrow': Ibid.

'You have helped': Ibid.

This country is at: Chamberlain, N. (1939). *This country is at war speech.* [Speech] 3 September 1939. Available at: https://www.british-history.ac.uk.

The Refugee Institute estimate: Imperial War Museum Archives, Personal Papers of Robert Stopford, *Prague 1938-1939*, p.57.

Aftermath

'Trevor dealt with': Winton, Nicholas, *What Makes a Hero? A letter from Nicholas Winton,* Holocaust Education Trust 28.03.1999.

'demanded a strict separation': Hahn, Fred, *Slavic Review,* 27.01.2017.

'who has continuously': Hartlepool Northern Daily Mail, 02.08.1957.

'the assertion that': Tombs, Isabelle, *The Victory of Socialist 'Vansittartism': Labour and the German Question, 1941–5,* from 20 Century British History volume 7 (issue 3) 1996 p.287.

'a woman who has': Sharp, Martha, The Outline and Partial Narrative of Martha Sharp Cogan's Work for the Years 1941-1952, from Church Mouse In The White House, Journey to Freedom LLC, 2016, New York.

'In light of the': Waitstill and Martha Sharp, https://www.yadvashem.org/righteous/stories/sharp.html.

'A large number of': Chadwick, William, *The Rescue of the Prague Refugees,* Troubador Publishing, 2010, p.36.

'To these women': Jaksch, Wenzel, Kolarz, Walter, *England and The Last Free Germans, The Story of a Rescue,* Lincolns-Prager, 1941, London, p.54.

Index

Page numbers in **bold** refer to illustrations

A Zet, *158*
Alcron Hotel, 76, 85, 97, 111, 115, 140, 178, 196, 206
Algerian War, 228
American Relief, 74, 79, 104-5, 135, 140, 186, 187, 212-3, 217
Amrelczech, 74
Antwerp Olympics, 26
Archbishop of Canterbury, 61
Associated Press, 148
Attlee, Clement, 25
Austria-Hungary, 7, 8, 23
Austria, 8, 23, 30, 52, 65, 74, 81, 227

Bad Godesberg, 15
Baker, Everett, 74
Barnard College, 186
Bauernfeind, Wanda, 179-183
Belfast Telegraph, 24, 246
Belgium, 27
Beneš, Edvard, 10, 12, 14-7, 52, 222-3
Berlin, 15, 21, 28, 47, 54, 65, 81, 85, 91, 94, 98, 129-130, 177, 208
Birmingham, 54
Blake, Martin, 64
Blaskowitz, General Johannes
Bohemia, 7, 23, 112, 132, 224
Bohumín, 170-1
Bömelburg, Herr Kriminalrat Karl von
    appointment as Gestapo leader, 177-8
    meeting Robert Stopford, 192-7
    reaction to Doreen Warriner's escape, 206
    leaving Prague, 208-9
    later life, 224-5
    death, 225

Bowater, Sir Frank Henry, 63
Bracey, Bertha, 54-5, 65, 133, 157, 227
Bratislava, 83-4, 86, 111
Brazil, 166, 229
Britain, 4, 15-6, 19-21, 24, 27, 32, 38, 41-2, 44, 49, 51-2, 56, 62, 65-7, 69-70, 86, 89, 99, 112, 115, 127, 134, 139, 143, 148, 156, 161-2, 171-2, 191, 198, 224, 226-7, 232
British Committee for Refugees from Czechoslovakia (BCRC)
    establishment, 52, 54-7, 79, 219, 223, 226-7
    interactions with Doreen Warriner, 61, 63-6, 87-89, 171
    transports, 68-9, 96, 98
    tasks in Prague, 69-73
    interactions with Czech officials, 77, 203, 214
    working with American Relief, 79-81, 107, 156, 217
    invasion of Prague, 91, 109-110, 113
    Nazis raiding offices, 123-4
    appointment of Clare Hollingworth, 133, 135
    removing Tessa Rowntree, 156-7
    interactions with the Gestapo, 182, 186-9, 203, 208-211
    arrival of Beatrice Wellington, 186-7
    success, 219
British Passport Control Office, 35, 92, 157, 226
Berchtesgaden, Germany, 14
Buckingham Palace, 16
British Unitarian Women, 156

Brod, Elsa, 96
Buchenwald Concentration Camp, 3, 148
Buschova, Lydia, 147
British Government, 14, 21, 34, 65-6, 87, 219, 223, 226

Cadbury, Emma, 29-30
Cadbury, John, 228
Cambridge Union Society, 27
Cambridge, 3, 27
Canada, 2, 4, 34, 186, 198
Carpathian Ruthenia, 7
Carr, Wilbur, 151
Cazalet, Victor, 49
Central Committee on Refugees, 50
Chadwick, Trevor, 66, 89, 190, 199, 221
Chamberlain, Neville, 12, 14-6, 21, 24-5, 37, 50, 68-9, 73, 139, 191, 219
Chancellor of the Exchequer, 21
Charles Bridge, 144, 119
Churchill, Sir Winston, 16, 159, 223
Chvalkovský, František, 91
Cogan, Eugene, 231
Commission for Service in Czechoslovakia of the American Unitarian Association, 74
Committee for Development of Refugee Industries, 50
Congress, 230
Copenhagen, 60
Corniche Hotel, 59-60
Council on Aliens, 50
Culpin, Ewart Gladstone, 56, 63-4, 226
Czech Criminal Investigation Department, 146
Czech Refugee Fund, 20
Czech Social Democratic Workers' Party, 120
Czechoslovakia, 1, 3, 4, 7-12, 14-5, 17-21, 23, 33-4, 38-42, 44, 47-8, 50-2, 56-8, 61, 63-5, 67, 70-1, 73-4, 78, 80, 82-3, 86-7, 89, 94, 96, 98-9, 104-5, 118, 126, 132, 134-5, 139, 142-3, 145, 154, 157-8, 166, 173-4, 177-8, 183, 203, 209, 212-7, 221-2, 224-5, 227, 229
Czechoslovakian Legation, London, 50
Czechoslovakian Women's National Council, 47, 229

Daily Herald, 158
Daily Mail, 20
Daily Telegraph, 61, 63, 219
Dalton, Hugh, 25
Danzig (see also Gdansk), 59
Dejvice District, Prague, 105
Denison House, 107
Derby, 25
Dexter, Robert, 74-5
Döllin, Emmi, 178-9, 185
Döllin, Rudolf, 178
Dolná Krupá, 19, 45, 67, 68
Dougan, Margaret, 135, 137, 173, 178, 180, 182, 184-5, 189, 197-8, 205, 228
Downe House, 31
Downing Street, 51, 73
Dundee Evening Telegraph, 27
Dvořák, 91

East Prussia, 59
Eichmann, Adolf, 208-12, 225
Europe, 3-4, 7, 12, 16-8, 25-6, 29-30, 32, 36, 43, 48, 50, 54, 65, 69-70, 73, 77, 83, 95, 134, 152, 155, 186, 208, 214, 221, 226-8, 230, 232

Feigl, Eva Esther, 231
France, 174, 177, 222, 224, 230
Frank, Karl Hermann, 142, 144, 176, 224
Friendly Aliens Protection Committee, 50

Garrigue, Charlotte, 8
Gdansk (see also Danzig), 59
Gdynia, 39, 41-2, 59, 98-9, 133, 189
Geneva, 145, 212, 214
German Invasion of Czechoslovakia, 85-99
German Social Democratic Workers Party (DSAP), 11, 18, 23-5, 92, 115, 167
Germany, 3, 8, 11, 14-7, 25, 30, 51, 57, 59, 61, 65, 74, 129, 133, 145, 148, 150, 153-4, 166, 216, 218-9, 223-4, 227, 229
Gestapo, 1-4, 33, 81, 89, 111, 116, 123, 157-8, 165, 172-7, 182, 185-196, 200-6, 208-9, 211-2, 216, 224, 229
Gestapo Headquarters (see also Petschek Palace), 2, 176, 186-8, 192, 200, 203
Gibson, Harold, 35, 38, 85, 87-8, 90, 92, 226
Gillies, William, 34-5, 37-8, 88, 223
Goebbels, Joseph, 32
Goerlich, Emma, 179, 189, 197
Göring, Hermann, 95, 130, 148
Gower, 34
Greiss, Marie, 179, 189, 198
Grenfell, David
    arrival in Prague, 34-5
    organising first transport, 37-9, 55
    acting as courier, 39-42
    joining committees, 49
    later life, 223,
    death, 223

Hácha, Emil, 17, 90-1, 94-5, 130
Halifax, Lord, 37-8
Henlein, Konrad, 11-4, 18, 23-4, 46, 224
Herman Hertz, Chief Rabbi Dr. Joseph, 61
Heydrich, Reinhard, 130, 224, 226, 229

Highbury, 27
Hitler, Adolf, 3, 11, 13-6, 18, 23-5, 28, 30, 32-3, 41, 46, 48, 50, 68, 85-6, 90, 93-5, 120, 128, 130-2, 134, 142-4, 152, 158, 196, 221, 24, 226
Hlinka Guard, 165, 226
Hoare, Samuel, 65
Hodža, Emília, 9
Hodža, Milan
    appearance, 8-9, **234**
    relationship with Doreen Warriner, 10-7, 32
    appointment as Prime Minister, 10
    negotiations with the SdP, 12-3
    resignation as Prime Minister, 15
    later life and death, 222
Hollingworth, Clare
    early life, 98
    joining the BCRC, 98-9
    work for the BCRC, 110, 133, 228
    making up a code, 141-2
    reporting World War II, 218-9
    later life, 228
    death, 228
Holocaust, 225-6
Hook of Holland, 145, 150
Hostel Elf, 1, 187
Hotel Atlantic, 76, 121, 140, 190
Hotel Pariz, 191, 217
House of Commons, 16, 52, 223
Hradcany Castle, 14
Hubback, David, 53
Hull, Cordell, 79

Ingram, John, 96, 98
Israel, 225

Jaksch, Wenzel
    Appearance, 33, **234**
    early life, 23-4
    pleading with the British, 25-6
    meeting Doreen Warriner, 32-6

relationship with Doreen
Warriner, 55, 64, 66, 77, 121, 129, 223
meeting Walter Layton, 54
visiting camps, 45-6, 68
invasion of Czechoslovakia, 92-3
being smuggled across the city, 118-122, 190, 196
staying at the British Legation, 123, 125, 128-130
escaping Czechoslovakia, 158-172
later life, 223
death, 223
Jewish persecution, 18, 21, 24, 31, 36, 41, 65, 66, 78, 84, 133, 135, 137-8, 148, 200-4, 209, 216, 231
Joyce, James, 134

Kaaden, 18
Karlín District, 1
Kavarna Artia, 136, 138
Kent, 228
Kiel Canal, 59
Kindertransport, 65, 227
King George VI, 16
KLM, 69
Kminek, Mr, 160-1, 163-4, 168-9, 171
Kocourek, Franta, 97
Krakow, 39, 41-2
Krejčí, František Václav, 120, 122

Labour Party, 24-5, 34-5, 53, 55-6, 223, 226
Lang, Most Reverend and Right Honourable Cosmo, 61
Langstrobnitz, 23
Layton, Margaret
  early life, 53-4
  visiting Prague, 52
  role with the BCRC, 55, 60, 73, 82-3, 98, 133-5, 156, 171-2, 189, 211, 216, 219
  correspondence with Doreen Warriner, 64-7, 69-71, 112, 140-1
  later life, 227
  death, 227
Layton, Sir Walter, 51-5, 60, 211-2, 226
League of Nations Committee for Refugees, 36
League of Nations, 25, 36, 59, 134
Leysin, 53
Liberal Party, 51
Lidice Massacre, 224
London County Council, 56, 226
London School of Economics (LSE), 30
London, 14, 16, 22, 24, 27, 29-30, 34, 37-9, 44, 50-1, 54-7, 60, 63-4, 66-73, 76, 80, 82-3, 86-9, 96, 98, 112-3, 122, 126, 133, 135, 141, 146-7, 149, 151, 156-7, 160, 171-2, 174, 191, 193, 211-2, 214, 217, 219, 221-7, 231-2
Lord Mayor's Fund, 20, 56, 61
Lowit, Herbert, 17-8, 57
Lowit, Karl, 42
Luftwaffe, 140
Luxtorpeda Train, 41

Mala Strana, 158
Malmar, Folke, 201-4
Malypetr, Jan, 10
Martin, Joe, 231
Martin, Nikolaus, 176
Masaryk, Alice, 47, 56, 81, 91, 144, 174, 229
Masaryk, Tomáš, 7, 10, 15, 130, 221
Maxwell, Christine, 135, 137, 178, 188, 197, 228
MI6 (see also Secret Intelligence Service), 35, 85
Middlesex, 27
Milovice, 229
Ministry of Foreign Affairs, Paris, 174
Moravec, František, 226
Moravia, 7, 132, 162, 164, 225

Munich Agreement, 17-8, 24, 37, 50, 52, 74, 85, 170, 222
Munich, 16, 68, 225
Mykura, Franziska, 19
Secret Intelligence Service (see also MI6), 35, 85

Na Porici Street, 76
National Czech Church, 81
Nazi Party, 1-4, 19, 21, 24, 28, 35, 37, 81, 83, 86, 106, 110-1, 125, 133-5, 138-139, 142-3, 146, 158, 160-4, 166-7, 174, 176, 183, 189, 190, 194, 202-6, 218, 222-4, 226
Nerudova Street, 139
Neuschel, Ernst, 223
New York, 60, 186, 231
Newbury, 31
News Chronicle, 52, 55-6, 98, 109, 227
Newton, Sir Basil, 14-5, 115, 122, 125-6, 261
Nížkov, 19, 45-6
Noel-Baker, Philip, 25-6, 34, 227
Nottingham Evening Post, 20
Nowi Targ, 42
Nuremberg Trials, 224
Nuremburg, 224

Occupation of Czechoslovakia, 3, 85-90, 92-4, 97-8, 103
Old Town Square, Prague, 114
Opel Blitz Truck, 176
Operation Anthropoid, 226
Operation Fence, 177
Opletalova Street, 111
Orava Castle, 40
Oravský Podzámok, 40
Orient Express, 73, 174, 190, 218
Ostrava, 57-8, 94-5, 127, 171
Oxford, 4, 9, 31, 228

Pankrac Prison, 144

Panzer Tank, 111, 176
Paris, 174, 177, 212, 218, 222, 225, 228, 229-230
Parliamentary Committee on Refugees, 49-51
Patz, Hilde, 55, 88, 94, 122, 125-6, 135, 228
Penman, Frank Garfield, 27
Penman, Mary, 31-2, 38, 47, 55, 139, 227
Pétain, Philippe, 225
Petschek Palace (see also Gestapo Headquarters), 2, 176, 186-8, 192, 200, 203
Plamínková, Františka, 48, 56, 144, 214-5, 229
Podhajsky, Jaroslav, 77, 93, 123-5, 127-8, 205, 229
Poland, 8, 38-40, 42-3, 57-9, 83, 85-7, 99, 110, 127, 132-4, 141, 145, 162, 167-8, 170-1, 173, 185, 189, 216, 218, 221, 228-9
Polish Legation, Prague, 38, 87, 92-4
Polsudski Liner, 60
Prague, 1, 3, 4, 7, 10, 12, 15-6, 18-22, 25-6, 28-31, 34, 36, 38-9, 40-2, 45-8, 52-8, 60-1, 63-4, 66-7, 69-70, 73-4, 76-9, 81-3, 85-97, 99, 110-111, 113, 116, 118, 121, 125-8, 130-1, 134-5, 138-140, 142-3, 145-7, 151, 153, 156, 158, 160-1, 163-4, 166, 171-2, 174, 176-7, 180, 183, 189, 191-2, 197-200, 202-3, 205, 208-9, 211, 214, 218-9, 221, 223-8, 230-2

Quakers (see also Society of Friends), 23, 25, 27, 29-32, 48, 54-5, 59, 65, 227-8

RAF, 227
Rantzen, Esther, 221
Rathbone, Eleanor, 49, 51, 65, 112, 191, 211, 224

Ravensbrück Concentration Camp, 197
Red Cross, 47-8, 81, 229
Reich Chancellery, Berlin, 94
Reine in Westphalia, 150
Ritter, Dr Karl, 166-7, 172, 225
River Vltava, 119, 198
Riviera Hotel, 60
Rojko, Stefan, 183
Roosevelt, President Franklin D., 231
Rowntree and Co, 30
Rowntree, Alison, 43
Rowntree, Jean, 31-2, 40, 54-5, 71, 89, 126, 135, 227
Rowntree, Tessa
  early life, 29-32
  organising transports, 40, 54-4, 71
  selected as courier, 42-3, 135
  visiting camps, 49
  leading transports, 57-60, 73-4, 76, 145-8, 160
  being considered to replace Doreen Warriner, 63-4
  visiting Slovakia, 83, 86
  invasion of Czechoslovakia, 89, 111-5, 120-1, 125-8
  hiding refugees, 131
  watching Hitler's speech, 132
  leaving the BCRC, 157
  later life, 228
  death, 228
Roztoky
Runciman, Viscountess, 12
Rusalka, 131
Ruzyne Airport, 28
Runciman, Walter, 12, 14
Runciman Mission, 12-3, 21, 25, 50

Sacher, Mr, 161, 163, 168-170
Salten, Felix, 30
Salter, Arthur, 49
Save the Children Fund, 20
Schaffarsch, Mr., 109-110
Schmolka, Marie, 36-7, 93, 116, 228
Schnabel, Frau, 197
Sharp, Martha, 4
  Appearance, **233**
  arrival in Prague, 4, 74-6
  children, 74-5
  staying at Hotel Atlantic, 76, 128-9
  first day in Prague, 74-80
  office, 79
  meeting Doreen Warriner, 80-1
  being followed, 80-2, 89
  relationship with Alice Masaryk, 81, 144
  invasion of Czechoslovakia, 85-91, 113-5, 135, 143
  carrying on working, 103-9
  held at gunpoint, 106-9, 204
  collecting Mr X, 115-121, 158
  watching Hitler's parade, 132-3
  meeting Clare Hollingworth, 133
  reacting to the attack on Lisl Xal, 137-8
  secret meetings with Doreen Warriner, 139-141
  acting as courier, 145-157
  increase in arrests, 166
  attack on the Orient Express, 174-6, 190
  interactions with the Gestapo, 178, 185. 190, 207
  meeting Beatrice Wellington, 186
  reacting to Beatrice Wellington's arrest, 188-190
  moving to Hotel Pariz, 191
  lasts days in Prague, 210-8
  trying to prevent Františka Plamínková from returning, 214-6
  life after Prague, 230-1
  divorce and remarriage, 230-1
  death, 231
Sharp, Waitstill

arrival in Prague, 74-6
children, 74-5
staying at Hotel Atlantic, 76, 128-9
first day in Prague, 74-80
office, 79
letter from Cordell Hull, 79
solution for refugees, 79-80
visiting Alice Masaryk, 81
invasion of Czechoslovakia, 91, 103-108, 113-4, 121, 128-9
bugging, 139-40
travelling to Geneva, 145, 147
collecting Martha from the Orient Express, 176
money exchange system, 212-4
life after Prague, 230-1
divorce, 230-1
death, 230
Simon, Sir John, 51
Slovakia, 40, 85, 87, 164-5, 167, 226
Smetana, 91
Society of Friends (see also Quakers), 23, 25, 27, 29-32, 48, 54-5, 59, 65, 227-8
Sokolovská Street, 1
Somerville College, 31
Spanish Civil War, 186
St Hugh's College, 9
St Wenceslas Square, 15, 111
Stevenson, Adlai, 231
Stockholm Olympics, 26
Stopford, Robert
   background, 12
   Runciman Mission, 13, 21
   appointment in Prague, 21-2, 25-6
   meeting Doreen Warriner, 13, 21
   reporting on the refugee crisis, 30-1, 44, 78
   introducing Doreen Warriner to Wenzel Jaksch, 34
   witnessing devastation, 46
   meetings in London, 51

   views about the BCRC, 70
   refugee transports, 71, 94, 96
   invasion of Czechoslovakia, 86-8, 104, 138, 142, 176-7
   British Legation, 112, 115, 125-6
   relationship with Wenzel Jaksch, 165-7, 172-3
   meetings with the Gestapo, 165-7, 172-3, 179, 188, 190-8, 206, 208-212
   forcing Doreen Warriner to leave Prague, 190-8
   Swedish Legation incident, 203
   leaving Prague, 214
   later life, 219, 221-222
   recommending OBE, 231
   death, 222
Suchá Hora, 40
Sudeten German Party (SdP), 11-3, 18
Sudetenland, 8, 10-2, 14-9, 21, 26, 28, 31, 33, 46, 48, 58, 66, 75-6, 79, 85, 98, 106, 123, 130, 166, 194, 224
Světlá Castle, 19, 40, 45-6
Swastikas, 3, 83, 128
Swedish Legation, Prague, 201, 203
Switzerland, 49, 53, 225

Taub, Siegfried, 115, 128, 167
The Economist, 51, 227
The Mount School, 30
The New Statesman and Nation, 191
The Scotsman, 10, 20
The Times, 65
Thunovská Street, 119, 128, 159, 160, 197
Thwaites, John, 134
Tiso, Jozef Gašpar, 85, 226
Trafalgar Square, 50
Treaty of Versailles, 8, 26

Unitarian Church, 74, 105, 156, 230
United Press, 148

United States Legation, Prague, 151
United States, 151, 228
Úvoz Street, 200, 202

Van Gogh, 147
Vansittartism, 223
Vienna, 29, 30, 32, 54, 84
Vietnam War, 228
Vinohrady, 96, 123
Vlissingen, 154
Volks-Sport, 11
von Neurath, Baron Konstantin, 132, 142, 224
Voriliska Street, 55

Waistcoat, Virginia, 76, 79, 104, 230
Wales, 34
Warriner, Doreen
    appearence, 4, **233**
    arrival in Prague, 4-9
    staying at the Alcron Hotel, 76
    relationship with Milan Hodža, 9-10, 12-3, 17, 222
    views on the Munich Agreement, 17
    initial aid work, 20-2
    first meeting with Robert Stopford, 13
    introduction to the Society of Friends, 32
    meeting Wenzel Jaksch, 33-4
    first meeting with David Grenfell and William Gilles, 34-5
    deciding on the first list of evacuees, 35-7
    first transports, 38-40, 57-60
    acting as courier, 40-2
    arguing with David Grenfell, 42-4
    visiting refugee camps, 45-7, 54
    planning transports, 49
    appointed as Prague representative at the BCRC, 54-5
    recruiting her team, 55
    arguing with BCRC in London, 60-3, 211-2
    letter to the *Daily Telegraph*, 61-2
    initiating the Children's Section, 64-6
    opinion of Nicholas Winton, 64-5
    relationship with Wenzel Jaksch, 66, 121, 129, 223
    meeting Eleanor Rathbone, 66-7
    beginning larger transports, 69-72, 145-6, 148, 186
    visiting London, 70-2
    relationship with Jaroslav Podhajsky, 77, 205-6, 229
    meeting Martha Sharp, 79-81, 82
    learning about the situation in Slovakia, 84
    invasion of Czechoslovakia, 85-90, 92-4, 97-8, 103
    panic after the occupation, 109-13
    looking for Marie Schmolka, 113-6
    collecting papers from her office, 122-5
    bidding farewell to Hilde Patz, 126-9
    asking Tessa Rowntree to borrow her passport, 128
    trapped refugee women and children, 130-3
    new team arriving, 135
    thoughts about Neville Chamberlain, 139
    being followed, 140-1
    trying to persuade Františka Plamínková to leave, 144
    asking Martha Sharp to act as courier, 145-6, 152-3
    organising Wenzel Jaksch's escape, 159-162, 164, 171
    transporting Wenzel Jaksch's passport, 171-2
    interaction with the Gestapo, 178, 180-3, 208-10

working with Emmi Döllin, 178-9
witnessing arrests, 180-183
collecting escaped refugees, 185-6
Beatrice Wellington arrest, 2-3, 187-9
working conditions, 191
forced to leave Prague, 195-200
Gestapo arrest warrant, 196, 206-7
arrest of colleagues, 197
finding Marie Greiss, 198-9
Swedish Legation incident, 200-4
departing Prague, 205-6
meeting transports in London, 217
hearing the outbreak of war, 219
life after Prague, 231-2
death, 232
Warsaw, 41, 98
Wedgwood Benn, William, 25
Wellington, Beatrice
  arrest, 1-4, 186-9, 192
  arrival in Prague, 186
  taking over from Doreen Warriner, 198-9
  refusing to leave, 210-2, 216
  leaving Prague, 217
  later life, 229
  death, 229
Wenceslas Square, 15, 105, 111, 131
Westminster, 25, 37, 112
Wilson Station, 39-40, 71, 76, 90, 94, 130, 132, 161-3, 176, 180, 184-5, 188, 196, 204, 206
Wilson, President Woodrow, 185
Winton, Nicholas, 64-8, 89, 200, 221
World War I, 12, 15,
World War II, 219

Xall, David, 136-8
Xall, Lisl, 109, 135-9, 143, 230

York, 30-1
Young Women's Christian Association (YWCA), 56, 64, 185, 199, 214
Youth Relief and Refugee Council, 50
Yugoslavia, 222, 232

Zagreb University, 133
Žilina, 42